Why We Are At War

Members of the Oxford Faculty of Modern History

Table of Contents

Why We Are At War

Members of the Oxford Faculty of Modern History

WHY WE ARE AT WAR

GREAT BRITAIN'S CASE

Why We Are At War

With an Appendix of Original Documents including the Authorized English Translation of the White Book issued by the German Government

Second Edition Revised (fourth impression) containing the Russian Orange Book

BY

MEMBERS OF THE OXFORD FACULTY OF MODERN HISTORY

1914

PREFACE.

We are not politicians, and we belong to different schools of political thought. We have written this book to set forth the causes of the present war, and the principles which we believe to be at stake. We have some experience in the handling of historic evidence, and we have endeavoured to treat this subject historically. Our fifth chapter, which to many readers will be the most interesting, is founded upon first–hand evidence—the documents contained in the British White Book (Parliamentary Paper, Cd. 7467; hereafter cited as *Correspondence respecting the European Crisis*), and the German White Book, which is an official apology, supplemented by documents. The German White Book, as being difficult of access, we have printed *in extenso*. It exists in two versions, a German and an English, both published for the German Government. We have reproduced the English version without correcting the solecisms of spelling and expression. From the English White Book we have reprinted, in the second appendix, a small selection of the more significant documents; many more are quoted in the body of our work.

Our thanks are due to Sir H. Erle Richards, Chichele Professor of International Law and Diplomacy; and to Mr. W.G.S. Adams, Gladstone Professor of Political Theory and Institutions, for valuable suggestions and assistance.

The sole responsibility for the book rests, however, with those who sign this Preface.

Any profits arising from the sale of this work will be sent to the Belgian Relief Fund, as a mark of sympathy and respect for the Belgian nation, and especially for the University of

Louvain.

E. BARKER
H. W. C. DAVIS
C. R. L. FLETCHER
ARTHUR HASSALL
L. G. WICKHAM LEGG
F. MORGAN

Preface to Second Edition.

By the courtesy of His Excellency the Russian Ambassador we are now able to print in an appendix (No. VI) those documents contained in the Russian Orange Book which have not been already published in the German and the British White Books. In the light of the evidence afforded by the Russian Orange Book, we have modified one or two sentences in this edition.

21 September, 1914.

CHIEF DATES

1648 Jan. The Treaty of Munster.
    Oct. The Treaty of Westphalia.
1713 April. The Treaty of Utrecht.
1772 First Partition of Poland.
1783 William of Nassau becomes Grand Duke of Luxemburg.
1788 July. The Triple Alliance of England, Holland, and Prussia.
1789 The French Revolution begins.
1792 Nov. 6. Battle of Jemappes. French Conquest of the Austrian Netherlands and Liege.
    Nov. 19. French decree offering 'freedom to all nations'.
    Dec. 15. Compulsory freedom declared.
1793 Jan. Second Partition of Poland.

Feb. 1. Declaration of War by France against England and Holland.

1795 Third Partition of Poland.

1801 Feb. 9. The Treaty of Luneville. France guarantees the independence of Holland (then called 'Batavian Republic').

1802 Mar. 27. The Treaty of Amiens.

1803 Mar. 13. Napoleon's famous interview with Lord Whitworth.

May 12. Declaration of War by England against France.

1814 Mar. 1. The Treaty of Chaumont.

May 30. The First Peace of Paris.

Sept. 29. Opening of the Congress of Vienna.

1815 Mar–June. The Hundred Days.

May 31. Belgium and Luxemburg placed under the Prince of Orange as King of the United Netherlands.

Nov. 20. The Second Peace of Paris.

1830 Revolutions in France (July) and in Belgium (Aug.).

1830–1878 Servia autonomous.

1831 Nov. 15. Independence and Neutrality of Belgium guaranteed by England, Austria, France, Prussia, and Russia.

1839 April 19. Final recognition of the Independence and Neutrality of Belgium by the above–named Powers.

1867 May 11. European guarantee of the Neutrality of Luxemburg. Declaration by Lord Stanley and Lord Clarendon.

1870 Aug. 9. Independence and Neutrality of Belgium again guaranteed by Germany and France.

1871 May 10. The Treaty of Frankfort.

1872 The *Dreikaiserbund*; Alliance of Russia, Germany, and Austria.

1875 Threatened attack on France by Germany prevented by Russia and England.

1878 The Treaty of Berlin.

Proclamation of Servian Independence under King Milan.

1879 Secret Treaty between Germany and Austria.

1883 Triple Alliance between Germany, Austria, and Italy.

1885 Formation of United Bulgaria.

War between Bulgaria and Servia.

1886 Peace between Bulgaria and Servia.

Why We Are At War

1890 Fall of Bismarck. Cession of Heligoland to Germany.

1891 Beginning of an understanding between Russia and France.

1893 Caprivi's Army Act.

1896 Germany begins to show aggressive tendencies in the field
of Colonial Expansion.

Treaty between England and France regarding their interests
in Indo–China.

Definite Alliance between Russia and France.

1898 Reconquest of the Sudan.

Tsar's rescript for an International Peace Conference.

1899 Anglo–French Agreement respecting Tripoli.

June. First Peace Conference at the Hague.

New German Army Act.

1902 Anglo–Japanese Alliance.

The Peace of Vereeniging closes the South African War.

1903 Revolution in Belgrade.

1904 April. The Treaty of London between England and France
with regard to North Africa.

1905 Mar. Visit of the German Emperor to Tangier.

June. Germany demands the dismissal of M. Delcasse.

Aug. The Treaty of Portsmouth between Russia and Japan.

Renewal of the Anglo–Japanese Alliance.

German Army Act.

Sept. France agrees to the holding of the Algeeiras
Conference.

1907 Agreement between Russia and England concerning Persia,
Afghanistan, and Tibet.

June–Oct. Second Peace Conference at the Hague.

1908 Young Turk Revolution in Constantinople.

Oct. Annexation of Bosnia and Herzegovina by Austria.

German Navy Law.

1909 Mar. Servia declares she will no longer protest against the
annexation of Bosnia by Austria.

1909 Mr. Asquith's speech on necessity for increasing the Navy.

1910 The Potsdam interview between the Tsar and the Kaiser.

1911 European Crisis over the question of Morocco, followed by a closer Anglo–French *entente*.

German Army Act.

1912 Sensational German Army Bill.

War in the Balkans.

Nov. 26. German Navy construction estimates L11,416,700.

Dec. 29. Peace Conference of Balkan States with Turkey broken off.

1913 Jan. 17. M. Poincare elected French President.

Jan. 23. The Young Turkish Party overthrow the Government at Constantinople.

May 26. Peace made between Turkey and the Balkan States.

May 28. The New German Army Bill passes the Budget Committee of the Reichstag.

June 20. Universal military service in Belgium.

June 26. Conference between the French President, the French Foreign Minister, and Sir Edward Grey.

June 30. Bulgaria is attacked by Servia and Greece.

New German Army Bill.

July. Roumania attacks Bulgaria.

The Turks re–occupy Adrianople.

New Russian Army Bill.

French Army Bill.

Aug. 6. The Treaty of Peace between Bulgaria, Servia, Greece, and Roumania.

Sept. 22. The Treaty of Peace between Bulgaria and Turkey.

Oct. 20. Servia at Austria's demand abandons Albania.

Austrian War Fund increased.

1914 Attacks by the German Press upon France and Russia.

CHAPTER I. THE NEUTRALITY OF BELGIUM AND LUXEMBURG

I

The kingdom of Belgium is a comparatively new creation, but the idea of a Belgian nation is older than the kingdom. Historically and geographically the kingdom has no doubt an artificial character; its boundaries have been determined by the Great Powers and cut across the ancient provinces of the Netherlands. And it must be added that its population is heterogeneous both in race and language. These facts, however, in no sense diminish the legal rights of Belgium as a nation. She is a sovereign state by the same charter as Italy or Greece; and for the convenience of Europe she has been solemnly declared a neutral state, endowed with special privileges but burdened with corresponding obligations. While those privileges were maintained—and they have been rigidly maintained for more than eighty years—the Belgian people punctually fulfilled their obligations; and, because they have declined to betray Europe by becoming the dependant of a powerful neighbour, or by participating in the violation of European public law, their country is a wilderness of smoking ruins.

In the tremendous and all but crushing ordeal of August, 1914, Belgium has proved that she possesses other titles to existence and respect than those afforded by treaties, by the mutual jealousies of neighbours, or by the doctrines of international law. She has more than satisfied the tests which distinguish the true from the fictitious nationality. Those who have hitherto known Belgium only as a hive of manufacturing and mining industry, or as a land of historic memories and monuments, are now recognizing, with some shame for their past blindness, the moral and spiritual qualities which her people have developed under the aegis of a European guarantee. It is now beyond dispute that, if Belgium were obliterated from the map of Europe, the world would be the poorer and Europe put to shame. The proofs which Belgium has given of her nationality will never be forgotten while liberty has any value or patriotism any meaning among men. We cannot do less than echo the general sentiment of admiration for a constancy to national ideals which has left Belgium at the mercy of Huns less forgivable than those of Attila. But the case against her oppressor is not to be founded solely or mainly on her peculiar merits. In a special sense it rests upon the legal rights and duties with which she has been invested for the convenience of her neighbours and for the welfare of the European state system. It was in their interest, rather than her own, that the Great Powers made her a sovereign independent state. As such she is entitled, equally with England or with Germany, to immunity from unprovoked attack. But the Powers which made her a sovereign state, also, and for the same reasons of convenience, made her a neutral state. She was therefore debarred from consulting her own safety by making alliances upon what terms she would. She could not lawfully join either of the two armed camps into which Europe has fallen since the year 1907. And, if she had been as contemptible as she is actually the reverse, she would still be entitled to expect from England and from every other of her guarantors the utmost assistance it is in their power to give. In fighting for Belgium we fight for the law of nations; that is, ultimately, for the peace of all nations and for the right of the weaker to exist.

* * * * *

The provinces which now constitute the kingdom of Belgium—with the exception of the bishopric of Liege, which was until 1795 an ecclesiastical principality—were known in the seventeenth century as the Spanish, in the eighteenth as the Austrian, Netherlands. They received the first of these names when they returned to the allegiance of Philip II, after a short participation in the revolt to which Holland owes her national existence. When the independence of Holland was finally recognized by Spain (1648), the Spanish Netherlands were subjected to the first of the artificial restrictions which Europe has seen fit to impose upon them. The Dutch monopoly of navigation in the Scheldt was admitted by the Treaty of Muenster (1648), and Antwerp was thus precluded from developing into a rival of Amsterdam. In the age of Louis XIV the Spanish Netherlands were constantly attacked by France, who acquired at one time or another the chief towns of Artois and Hainault, including some which have lately come into prominence in the great war, such as Lille, Valenciennes, Cambray, and Maubeuge. The bulk, however, of the Spanish Netherlands passed at the Treaty of Utrecht to Austria, then the chief rival of France on the Continent. They passed with the reservation that certain fortresses on their southern border were to be garrisoned jointly by the Dutch and the Austrians as a barrier against French aggression. This arrangement was overthrown at the French Revolution. The French annexed the Austrian Netherlands and Liege in November, 1792; and immediately afterwards threw down a gauntlet to England by opening to all nations the navigation of the Scheldt. This, and the threatened French attack on Holland, her ally, drew England into conflict with the Revolution; for, first, Antwerp in French hands and as an open port would be a dangerous menace; and secondly, the French had announced a new and anarchic doctrine hostile to all standing treaties: 'Our reasons are that the river takes its rise in France and that a nation which has obtained its liberty cannot recognize a system of feudalism, much less adhere to it'.[1] The answer of William Pitt, which in effect declared war upon the Revolution, contains a memorable statement of the attitude towards public law which England held then, as she holds it to–day: 'With regard to the Scheldt France can have no right to annul existing stipulations, unless she also have the right to set aside equally the other treaties between all Powers of Europe and all the other rights of England and her allies.... England will never consent that France shall arrogate the power of annulling at her pleasure and under the pretence of a pretended natural right, of which she makes herself the only judge, the political system of Europe, established by solemn treaties and guaranteed by the consent of all the Powers'.[2]

This was not our attitude in the case of Belgium only. It was an attitude which we adopted with regard to all the minor Powers of Western Europe when they were threatened by Napoleon. On precisely the same grounds England defended in 1803 the independence of Holland, a commercial rival if an old political ally, and of Switzerland, where she had no immediate interests to protect. By the Treaty of Luneville (February, 1801) France and Austria had mutually guaranteed the independence of the Batavian Republic and the right of the Dutch to adopt whatever form of government seemed good to them. In defiance of these stipulations Napoleon maintained a garrison in Holland, and forced upon her a new Constitution which had been prepared in Paris (November, 1801). Identical stipulations had been made for the Helvetian Republic and had been similarly violated. Early in 1803 England demanded that the French should evacuate Holland and Switzerland: to which Napoleon replied that 'Switzerland and Holland are mere trifles'. His interview with the English Ambassador on March 13, 1803, has many points of resemblance with the now famous interview of August 4, 1914, between Sir Edward Goschen and Dr. von Bethmann–Hollweg. The First Consul then, like the Imperial Chancellor to–day, was unable, or professed himself unable, to understand why Great Britain should insist upon the observance of treaties.

To return to Belgium. It became apparent in the Napoleonic Wars that Belgium and Holland were individually too weak to protect themselves or the German people against an aggressive French Government. The allies therefore, in the year 1813, handed over to Holland the Austrian Netherlands and the bishopric of Liege in order 'to put Holland in a position to resist attack until the Powers could come to its aid'. This arrangement was ratified at the Treaty of Chaumont (1814). As there was no government or visible unity in

9

the Belgian provinces after the retirement of the French, the union with Holland, originally suggested by Lord Castlereagh, seemed reasonable enough. It gave the Belgians the great privilege of freely navigating the Scheldt. It was confirmed at the Congress of Vienna, and the new kingdom of the United Netherlands was declared neutral by the common consent of the Powers.

But the events of the years 1815–1830 proved conclusively that this union was unsatisfactory to the Belgian population. The Belgians complained that they were not allowed their just share of influence and representation in the legislature or executive. They resented the attempt to impose the Dutch language and Dutch Liberalism upon them. They rose in revolt, expelled the Dutch officials and garrisons, and drew up for themselves a monarchical and parliamentary constitution. Their aspirations aroused much sympathy both in England and in France. These two countries induced the other Great Powers (Austria, Prussia, Russia) to recognize the new kingdom as an independent neutral state. This recognition was embodied in the Treaty of the Twenty–Four Articles signed at London in October, 1831; and it was not too generous to the aspirations of Belgian nationality. Since the Belgians had been defeated in the field by Holland and had only been rescued by a French army, they were obliged to surrender their claims upon Maestricht, parts of Luxemburg, and parts of Limburg. Some time elapsed before this settlement was recognized by Holland. But at length this last guarantee was obtained; and the Treaty of London, 1839, finally established the international status of Belgium. Under this treaty both her independence and her neutrality were definitely guaranteed by England, France, Austria, Prussia, and Russia.

We have recently been told by the Imperial Chancellor that the Treaty of 1839 is nothing but 'a scrap of paper'. It is therefore desirable to point out that Bismarck made full use of it in 1870 to prevent England from supporting the cause of France. It was with this object that he published the proposal alleged to have been made to him by the French representative, Benedetti, in 1866, that Prussia should help France to acquire Belgium as a solace for Prussian annexations in Northern Germany. Then, as now, England insisted upon the Treaty of 1839. The result was that, on the instance of Lord Granville, Germany and France entered into an identic treaty with Great Britain (Aug. 1870) to the effect that, if either belligerent violated Belgian territory, Great Britain would co–operate with the other for the defence of it. The treaty was most strictly construed. After the battle of Sedan (Sept. 1870) the German Government applied to Belgium for leave to transport the German wounded across Belgian territory. France protested that this would be a breach of neutrality and Belgium refused.

Such is the history of the process by which Belgium has acquired her special status. As an independent state she is bound by the elementary principle of the law of nations, that a neutral state is bound to refuse to grant a right of passage to a belligerent. This is a well–established rule, and was formally affirmed by the Great Powers at the Hague Peace Conference of 1907. The fifth Article of the Convention [3] then drawn up respecting the Rights and Duties of Neutral Powers and Persons in War on Land runs as follows:—

'A neutral power ought not to allow on its territory any of
the acts referred to in Articles 2 to 4'.

Of the Articles thus specified the most important is No. 2:—

'Belligerents are forbidden to move across the territory of
a neutral power troops or convoys, either of munitions of war
or supplies'.

By the Treaty of London the existence of Belgium is contingent upon her perpetual neutrality:—

'ARTICLE VII. Belgium within the limits specified in
Articles I, II, and IV shall form an independent and perpetually
neutral state. It shall be bound to observe such
neutrality towards all other states'.[4]

It is unnecessary to elaborate further the point of law. That, it seems, has been admitted by the Imperial Chancellor before the German Reichstag. What is necessary to remember is that, in regard to Belgium, Germany has assumed the position which the Government of the French Revolution adopted towards the question of the Scheldt, and which Napoleon adopted towards the guaranteed neutrality of Switzerland and Holland. Now, as then, England has special interests at stake. The consequences of the oppression or the extinction of the smaller nationalities are bound to excite peculiar alarm in England. In particular she cannot forget how she would be menaced by the establishment of a militarist state in Belgium. But since in England's case the dangers and uncertainties of a state of things in which Might is treated as Right are particularly apparent, it is only to be expected that she should insist with special emphasis upon the sanctity of treaties, a sanctity which in the long run is as necessary to the strongest nation as to the weakest. If treaties count for nothing, no nation is secure so long as any imaginable combination of Powers can meet it in battle or diplomacy on equal terms; and the stronger nations must perforce fight one another to the death for the privilege of enslaving civilization. Whether the progress of such a competition would be a trifling evil, whether the success of any one among such competitors would conduce to the higher interests of humanity, impartial onlookers may debate if they please. England has answered both these questions with an unhesitating negative.

II

Under existing treaty law the Grand Duchy of Luxemburg stands for all practical purposes in the same legal position as its northern neighbour; and the ruler of Luxemburg has protested against the German invasion[5] of her territory no less emphatically than King Albert, though with less power of giving expression in action to her just resentment. If the defence of Belgium has appealed more forcibly to the ordinary Englishman, it is because he is more familiar with the past history of Belgium and sees more clearly in her case the ultimate issues that are involved in the German violation of her rights. As the following narrative will show, the neutrality of Luxemburg was guaranteed in the interests and at the instance of the Prussian state, as a protection against French aggression. The legal case could not be clearer, and it might perhaps be asked why the attack on Luxemburg, which preceded that on Belgium, was not treated by this country as a *casus belli*. England's attitude towards Luxemburg is that which she has consistently adopted towards those smaller states of Europe which lie outside the reach of naval power. It is an attitude which she has maintained in the case of Servia even more clearly than in that of Luxemburg. England holds herself bound to exert her influence in procuring for the smaller states of Europe equitable treatment from their more powerful neighbours. But the duty of insisting upon equitable treatment falls first upon those Powers whose situation enables them to support a protest by effective action. Just as Servia is the special concern of Russia, so Luxemburg must look to France in the first instance for protection against Germany, to Germany if she is assailed from the French side. In either case we should hold ourselves bound to exercise our influence, but not as principals. Any other course would be impossibly quixotic, and would only have the effect of destroying our power to help the states within our reach.

Why We Are At War

The Grand Duchy of Luxemburg was a revival of an ancient state which had lost its existence during the French Revolution. Although it was placed under the rule of the King of the Netherlands, a descendant of its former sovereign, it was not incorporated in his kingdom, but retained its own identity and gave to its ruler the secondary title of Grand Duke of Luxemburg. The position it occupied after 1815 was in some ways anomalous; for lying as it did between the Meuse and the Rhine, and possessing in the town of Luxemburg a fortress whose natural strength some competent critics reckoned as second only to that of Gibraltar among the fortresses of Europe, it was considered to be an indispensable link in the chain of defences of Germany against French aggression. Not being able to trust the Dutch to hold this great fortress against the French, the Congress of Vienna laid down as a principle that all land between the Meuse and the Rhine must be held by Prussian troops on behalf of the newly formed Germanic Confederation. Thus Luxemburg was held by Prussian troops on behalf of this foreign confederation, and over this garrison the only right allowed to the Grand Duke, the sovereign of the country, was that of nominating the governor.

This strange state of affairs was not modified by the Belgian Revolution of 1830; for though more than half the Grand Duchy threw in its lot with Belgium to form the modern province of Belgian Luxemburg, the Grand Duchy, confined to its modern limits, still contained the great fortress with its garrison of Prussian troops. It is not surprising that, under these circumstances, the Grand Duchy joined the Prussian *Zollverein*, and so drew nearer to Germany, in spite of the independent character of its inhabitants, who have strenuously resisted any attempt at absorption into Germany. France naturally continued to cast envious eyes upon the small state with the powerful citadel, but no opportunity presented itself for reopening the question until 1866.

In that year Napoleon III had anticipated that the war between Prussia and Italy on one side and Austria and the small German states on the other would be long and exhausting, and would end in France imposing peace on the weary combatants with considerable territorial advantage to herself. His anticipation was entirely falsified; the war lasted only seven weeks and Prussia emerged victorious and immensely strengthened by the absorption of several German states and by the formation of the North German Confederation under her leadership. This, the first shattering blow which the French Emperor's diplomatic schemes had received, led him to demand compensation for the growth of Prussian power, and one of his proposals was the cession of Luxemburg to France.

This suggestion had some legal plausibility quite apart from the question of the balance of power. For the Prussian garrison held Luxemburg in the name of the German Confederation, which had been destroyed by the war of 1866; and, the authority to which the garrison owed its existence being gone, it was only logical that the garrison should go too. After much demur Count Bismarck acknowledged the justice of the argument (April, 1867), but it did not by any means follow that the French should therefore take the place vacated by the Prussians. At the same time the fortress could not be left in the hands of a weak Power as a temptation for powerful and unscrupulous neighbours. The question of Luxemburg was therefore the subject discussed at a Congress held in London in the following May.

Here the Prussians showed themselves extremely politic and reasonable. Realizing that, with the advance of artillery, the great rock–fortress no longer had the military value of earlier days, they not only raised no objections to the evacuation of Luxemburg by their troops, but in the Congress it was they who proposed that the territory of the Grand Duchy should be neutralized 'under the collective guarantee of the Powers'.[6] A treaty was therefore drawn up on May 11, 1867, of which the second article ran as follows:—

'The Grand Duchy of Luxemburg, within the Limits determined by the Act annexed to the Treaties of the 19th April, 1839, under the Guarantee of the Courts of Great Britain, Austria, France, Prussia, and Russia, shall henceforth form a perpetually Neutral State.

'It shall be bound to observe the same Neutrality towards all other States.

'The High Contracting Parties engage to respect the principle of Neutrality stipulated by the present Article.

'That principle is and remains placed under the sanction of the collective Guarantee of the Powers signing as Parties to the present Treaty, with the exception of Belgium, which is itself a Neutral State'.[7]

The third article provided for the demolition of the fortifications of Luxemburg and its conversion into an open town, the fourth for its evacuation by the Prussian garrison, and the fifth forbade the restoration of the fortifications.

Such then was the treaty guaranteeing the neutrality of Luxemburg, which was proposed, it may be observed, by Prussia herself; but, until the treaty was broken by the very Power which had proposed the neutrality, only one incident need be noted in the history of the country, namely, the part it played in the war of 1870–1. On December 3, 1870, Count Bismarck issued from Versailles a circular to the Prussian Ambassadors, calling attention to the fact that both the French and the Luxemburgers had violated the neutrality of the Grand Duchy, mainly by giving facilities for French soldiers to return to France. Precautions were taken by the Prussian Government on the frontier to prevent such abuses occurring in the future, and as no violation of the neutrality of Luxemburg was committed by the Prussians, the neutral co–guarantors were satisfied with the Prussian attitude, and the subject dropped. At the end of the war, M. Thiers vainly attempted to obtain Luxemburg as compensation for the loss of Metz.

In accordance with the Family Compact of 1783, the Grand Duchy passed on the death of the late King of Holland to Prince William of Nassau, on whose death the present Grand Duchess succeeded to her father's throne.

There is one point in the Treaty of 1867 which calls for special comment. The neutrality of the Grand Duchy is 'placed under the collective guarantee of the Powers signing'. The phrase originally proposed by Count Bismarck was 'the formal and individual guarantee of the Powers,' and it was altered at the instance of the English Foreign Minister, Lord Stanley. The phrase actually adopted was suggested by the Russian diplomat, Baron Brunnow, and was accepted both by England and by Prussia. Lord Stanley's objection had been based upon the fear that England might incur an unlimited liability to assist Luxemburg single–handed if all other Powers failed to meet their obligations. In other words, Luxemburg might have been used as the infallible means of dragging us into every and any war which might arise between Germany and France. From that danger we were protected by Lord Stanley's objection; as the case stands the treaty gives us, in his own words, 'a right to make war, but would not necessarily impose the obligation,' should Luxemburg be attacked. To this doctrine a reference will be found in the British White Paper (No. 148), where Sir Edward Grey informs M. Cambon of 'the doctrine' concerning Luxemburg, 'laid down by Lord Derby and Lord Clarendon in 1867'. It may also be observed that two of the co–guarantors of the Treaty of 1867, namely Italy and Holland, have also not thought it necessary to make the violation of Luxemburg a *casus belli*.

III

It is evident to all who study closely the map of France that her eastern frontier falls into two sharply contrasted divisions, the north–eastern which reaches from the sea to the valley of the Sambre, and the south–eastern which extends from that river to, and along the Swiss boundary. The former is flat country, easy for military operations; the latter is mountainous, intersected with many deep valleys. After the loss of Alsace–Lorraine, the French set to work to rectify artificially the strategical weakness of their frontier; and in a chain of fortresses behind the Vosges Mountains they erected a rampart which has the reputation of being impregnable. This is the line Belfort, Epinal, Toul, Verdun. A German attack launched upon this line without violating neutral territory would have to be frontal, for on the north the line is covered by the neutral states of Belgium and Luxemburg, while on the south, although the gap between the Vosges and the Swiss frontier apparently gives a chance of out–flanking the French defences, the fortress of Belfort, which was never reduced even in the war of 1870–1, was considered too formidable an obstacle against which to launch an invading army. A rapid advance on Paris was therefore deemed impossible if respect were to be paid to the neutrality of Belgium and Luxemburg, and it was for this purely military reason that Germany has to–day violated her promises to regard the neutrality of these states. This was frankly admitted by Herr von Jagow to Sir Edward Goschen: 'if they had gone by the more southern route they could not have hoped, in view of the paucity of roads and the strength of the fortresses, to have got through without formidable opposition entailing great loss of time'.[8]

In the case of Belgium a very easy road was afforded into French territory up the Valley of the Meuse, past Liege and thence into France past Namur and through what is known as the Gap of Namur. A German army could debouch into France through this gap the more easily inasmuch as the French, relying on the neutrality of these two states, had not strongly fortified the frontier from the sea to Maubeuge. Moreover, as the country to the west of the Sambre was very easy country for manoeuvring and furnished with good roads and railways, it was reckoned that the formidable French lines to the south could be turned in this manner, and the German army could march upon Paris from the north–east.

As to Luxemburg, plainly it could not in such a scheme remain neutral. It would lie between the two wings of the German army, and controlling as it did the roads to Brussels, Metz, and Aix—la—Chapelle, it could not be allowed to cause such inconvenience as to prevent easy communication between one portion of the German army and another.

That such a plan was contemplated by the Germans has been for some years past a matter of common knowledge in England; and it has been also a matter of common opinion that the attempt to execute this plan would involve the active resistance of the British forces, to whom the duty was supposed to have been assigned of acting on the left flank of the French opposing the entry of the Germans from Belgian territory. The plea therefore that has been put forward that the British have now dealt the Germans 'a felon's blow' can only be put forward by persons who are either ignorant or heedless of what has been a matter of casual conversation all over England these last three years; and Sir Edward Grey himself was so convinced that the German Government knew what the consequences of a violation of Belgian neutrality would be that he informed Sir Francis Bertie on July 31st that the 'German Government do not expect our neutrality'.[9] There has been no secret about it whatever. It is incredible that the excitement and surprise of the Imperial Chancellor on the receipt of the ultimatum of August 4th should have been genuine, seeing that it involves miscalculation or misinformation entirely incompatible with what we know of the thoroughness of German methods. At the time of the Agadir crisis the military situation was the same, and the German War Office knew quite well what our part would then have been. Surprise at such action on our part in 1914 is little else than comedy, and can only have been expressed in order to throw the blame of German aggression on to the shoulders of Great Britain.

This argument that Great Britain has taken the aggressive falls to the ground entirely when it is confronted with the hard facts of chronology. Far from attacking the Germans, we were so anxious to keep the peace that we were actually three days late in our mobilization to join the French on their left wing; and had it not been for the defence offered by Liege, our scruples would have gravely imperilled the common cause. For it was not until we were certain that Germany had committed what was tantamount to an act of war against us, by invading the neutral state of Belgium, that we delivered the ultimatum which led to the war.

Notes:

[Footnote 1: Cam. Mod. Hist. viii 301.]

[Footnote 2: Ibid. 304.]

[Footnote 3: Printed by A. Pearce Higgins, *The Hague Peace Conferences*, pp. 281–9.]

[Footnote 4: The entire treaty will be found in Hertslet, *Map of Europe by Treaty*, vol. ii, pp. 979–98.]

[Footnote 5: *Correspondence respecting the European Crisis*, (Cd. 7467), No. 147. Minister of State, Luxemburg, to Sir E. Grey, Aug. 2.]

[Footnote 6: Edward Hertslet, *The Map of Europe by Treaty*, vol. iii, p. 1806, no. 406. 'Proposal of *Prussia* of Collective Guarantee by Powers of Neutrality of *Luxemburg*, London, 7th May, 1867.']

[Footnote 7: Hertslet, *ut sup.*, vol. iii, p. 1803. The High Contracting Powers were Great Britain, Austria, France, Belgium, Italy, the Netherlands, Prussia, and Russia.]

[Footnote 8: *Dispatch from His Majesty's Ambassador at Berlin respecting the rupture of diplomatic relations with the German Government* (Cd. 7445), Miscellaneous, no. 8, 1914.]

[Footnote 9: *Correspondence respecting the European Crisis*, p. 62, no. 116. July 31, 1914. See also *infra* pp. 82 *et seqq.*]

CHAPTER II. THE GROWTH OF ALLIANCES AND THE RACE OF ARMAMENTS SINCE 1871

Even at the risk of being tedious it is essential that we should sketch in outline the events which have produced the present grouping of belligerent states, and the long–drawn–out preparations which have equipped them for conflict on this colossal scale. To understand why Austria–Hungary and Germany have thrown down the glove to France and Russia, why England has intervened not only as the protector of Belgium, but also as the friend of France, we must go back to the situation created by the Franco–German War. Starting from that point, we must notice in order the formation of the Triple Alliance between Germany, Austria–Hungary, and Italy, of the Dual Alliance between France and Russia, of the Anglo–French and the Anglo–Russian understandings. The Triple Alliance has been the grand cause of the present situation; not because such a grouping of the Central European Powers was objectionable, but because it has inspired over–confidence in the two leading allies; because they have traded upon the prestige of their league to press their claims East and West with an intolerable disregard for the law of nations. Above all it was the threatening attitude of Germany towards her Western neighbours that drove England forward step by step in a policy of precautions which, she hoped, would avert a European conflagration, and which her rivals have attempted to represent as stages in a Machiavellian design to ruin Germany's well–being. These precautions, so obviously necessary that they were continued and expanded by the most pacific Government which England has seen since Mr. Gladstone's retirement, have taken two forms: that of diplomatic understandings, and that of naval preparations. Whichever form they have taken, they have been adopted in response to definite provocations, and to threats which it was impossible to overlook. They have been strictly and jealously measured by the magnitude of the peril immediately in view. In her diplomacy England has given no blank cheques; in her armaments she has cut down expenditure to the minimum that, with reasonable good fortune, might enable her to defend this country and English sea–borne trade against any probable combination of hostile Powers.

Let us consider (1) the development of the diplomatic situation since 1870, (2) the so–called race of armaments since 1886.

The Treaty of Frankfort (May 10, 1871), in which France submitted to the demands of the new–born German Empire, opened a fresh era of European diplomacy and international competition. The German Empire became at once, and has ever since remained, the predominant Power in Western Europe. The public opinion of this new Germany has been captured to no small extent by the views of such aggressive patriots as Treitschke, who openly avowed that 'the greatness and good of the world is to be found in the predominance there of German culture, of the German mind, in a word of the German character'. The school of Treitschke looked for the establishment of a German world–empire, and held that the essential preliminary to this scheme would be the overthrow of France and England. But until 1890, that is to say so long as Prince Bismarck remained Chancellor, no such ambitious programme was adopted by the German Government. Bismarck was content to strengthen the position of the Empire and to sow disunion among her actual or suspected enemies. In 1872 he brought about a friendly understanding with Austria and Russia, the other two great Powers of Eastern Europe, the so–called *Dreikaiserbuendnis*, which was designed to perpetuate the *status quo*. But the friendship with Russia quickly cooled; it received a sharp set–back in 1875, when the Tsar Alexander II came forward rather ostentatiously to save France from the alleged hostile designs of Germany; it was certainly not improved when Bismarck in his turn mediated between Russia and her opponents at the Congress of Berlin (1878). On the other hand, a common interest in the Eastern Question drew closer the bonds between Germany and Austria. The latter felt herself directly menaced by the Balkan policy of Russia; the former was not prepared to see her southern neighbour despoiled of territory. Hence in 1879 was initiated that closer union between Germany and Austria which has been so largely responsible for the present situation. The Treaty of 1879, which was kept secret until 1887, was purely defensive in its character; but the terms showed that Russia was the enemy whom both the contracting Powers chiefly feared. Neither was bound to active measures unless the other should be attacked by Russia, or any Power which had Russian support. In 1882 the alliance of the two great German Powers was joined by Italy—a surprising development which can only be explained on the ground of Italy's feeling that she could not hope for security at home, or for colonial expansion in the Mediterranean, so long as she remained in isolation. The Triple Alliance so constituted had a frail appearance, and it was hardly to be expected that Italy would receive strong support from partners in comparison with whose resources her own were insignificant. But the Triple Alliance has endured to the present day, the most permanent feature of the diplomatic system of the last thirty–two years. Whether the results have been commensurate with the sacrifices of sentiment and ambition which Italy has made, it is for Italy to judge. On the whole she has been a sleeping partner in the Alliance; its prestige has served almost exclusively for the promotion of Austrian and German aims; and one of its results has been to make Austria a formidable rival of Italy in the Adriatic.

Meanwhile the remaining Great Powers of Europe had continued, as Prince Bismarck hoped, to pursue their separate paths, though England was on friendly terms with France and had, equally with Russia, laboured to avert a second Franco–German War in 1875. After 1882 the English occupation of Egypt constituted for some years a standing grievance in the eyes of France. The persistent advance of Russia in Asia had in like manner been a source of growing apprehension to England since 1868; and, for a long time after the Treaty of Berlin, English statesmen were on the watch to check the growth of Russian influence in the Balkans. But common interests of very different kinds were tending to unite these three Powers, not in any stable alliance, even for mutual defence, but in a string of compacts concluded for particular objects.

One of these interests was connected with a feeling that the policy of the principal partners in the Triple Alliance, particularly that of Germany, had become incalculable and was only consistent in periodic outbursts of self–assertiveness, behind which could be discerned a steady determination to accumulate armaments which should be strong enough to intimidate any possible competitor. The growth of this feeling dates from the dismissal of Prince Bismarck by the present Kaiser. Bismarck had sedulously courted the friendship of Russia, even after 1882. He entered in fact into a defensive agreement with Russia against Austria. While he increased the war strength of the army, he openly announced that Germany would always stand on the defensive; and he addressed a warning to the Reichstag against the 'offensive–defensive' policy which was even then in the air, though it was still far from its triumph:—

'If I were to say to you, "We are threatened by France and Russia;
it is better for us to fight at once; an offensive war is more
advantageous to us," and ask for a credit of a hundred millions, I
do not know whether you would grant it—I hope not.'[10]

But Bismarck's retirement (1890) left the conduct of German policy in less cautious hands. The defensive alliance with Russia was allowed to lapse; friction between the two Powers increased, and as the result Germany found herself confronted with the Dual Alliance of France and Russia, which gradually developed, during the years 1891–6, from a friendly understanding into a formal contract for mutual defence. There is no doubt that this alliance afforded France a protection against that unprovoked attack upon her eastern frontier which she has never ceased to dread since 1875; and it has yet to be proved that she ever abused the new strength which this alliance gave her.

It is only in the field of colonial expansion that she has shown aggressive tendencies since 1896; and even here the members of the Triple Alliance have never shown serious cause for a belief that France has invaded their lawful spheres of interest. Her advance in Morocco was permitted by Italy and Spain; her vast dominion in French West Africa has been recognized by treaties with Germany and England; in East Africa she has Madagascar, of which her possession has never been disputed by any European Power; her growing interests in Indo–China have impinged only upon an English sphere of interest and were peacefully defined by an Anglo–French Agreement of 1896. France has been the competitor, to some extent the successful competitor, of Germany in West Africa, where she partially envelops the Cameroons and Togoland. But the German Government has never ventured to state the French colonial methods as a *casus belli*. That the German people have viewed with jealousy the growth of French power in Africa is a notorious fact. Quite recently, on the eve of the present war, we were formally given to understand that Germany, in any war with France, might annex French colonies[11]; and it is easy to see how such an object would reconcile the divergent policies of the German military and naval experts.

Up to the eve of the present war Great Britain has consistently refused to believe that Germany would be mad enough or dishonest enough to enter on a war of aggression for the dismemberment of colonial empires. German diplomacy in the past few weeks has rudely shattered this conviction. But up to the year 1914 the worst which was generally anticipated was that she would pursue in the future on a great scale the policy, which she has hitherto pursued on a small scale, of claiming so–called 'compensations' when other Powers succeeded in developing their colonial spheres, and of invoking imaginary 'interests' as a reason why the efforts of explorers and diplomatists should not be allowed to yield to France their natural fruits of increased colonial trade. It is not our business to impugn or to defend the partition of Africa, or the methods by which it has been brought about. But it is vital to our subject that we should describe the methods by which Germany has endeavoured to intimidate France at various stages of the African question. The trouble arose out of a Moroccan Agreement between England and France, which was the first definite proof that these two Powers were drifting into relations closer than that of ordinary friendship.

In 1904 England and France settled their old quarrel about Egypt. France recognized the English occupation of Egypt; England, on her side, promised not to impede the extension of French influence in Morocco. It was agreed that neither in Egypt nor in Morocco should there be a political revolution; and that in both countries the customs tariff should make no distinction between one nation and another. This compact was accompanied by a settlement of the old disputes about French fishing rights in Newfoundland, and of more recent difficulties concerning the frontiers between French and English possessions in West Africa.[12] The whole group formed a step in a general policy, on both sides, of healing local controversies which had little meaning except as instruments of diplomatic warfare. The agreement regarding Egypt and Morocco is distinguished from that concerning West Africa and Newfoundland in so far as it recognizes the possibility of objections on the part of other Powers. It promised mutual support in the case of such objections; but not the support of armed force, only that of diplomatic influence.

At the moment of these agreements Count Buelow told the Reichstag that Germany had no objection, as her interests were in no way imperilled by them. Later, however, Germany chose to regard the Moroccan settlement as an injury or an insult or both. In the following year the Kaiser made a speech at Tangier (March, 1905) in which he asserted that he would uphold the important commercial and industrial interests of Germany in Morocco, and that he would never allow any other Power to step between him and the free sovereign of a free country. It was subsequently announced in the German Press that Germany had no objection to the Anglo–French Agreement in itself, but objected to not having been consulted before it was arranged. This complaint was met, on the part of France, by the retirement of M. Delcasse, her Minister of Foreign Affairs, and by her assent to an International Conference regarding Morocco. The Conference met at Algeciras, and German pretensions were satisfied by an international Agreement.[13] It is to be observed that in this Conference the original claims of Germany were opposed, not only by Russia, from whom she could hardly expect sympathy, but even by Italy, her own ally. When Germany had finally assented to the Agreement, her Chancellor, in flat contradiction with his previous utterance 'that German interests were in no way imperilled by it', announced that Germany had been compelled to intervene by her economic interests, by the prestige of German policy, and by the dignity of the German Empire.

The plain fact was that Germany, soon after the conclusion of the Anglo–French agreements, had found herself suddenly delivered from her preoccupations on the side of Russia, and had seized the opportunity to assert herself in the West while Russia was involved in the most critical stage of her struggle with Japan. But this war came to an end before the Convention of Algeciras had begun; and Russia, even in the hour of defeat and internal revolutions, was still too formidable to be overridden, when she ranged herself beside her Western ally.

Of the part which England played in the Moroccan dispute there are different versions. What is certain is that she gave France her diplomatic support. But the German Chancellor officially acknowledged, when all was over, that England's share in the Anglo–French Agreement had been perfectly correct, and that Germany bore England no ill—will for effecting a *rapprochement* with France. Still there remained a strong impression, not only in England and France, that there had been on Germany's part a deliberate intention to test the strength of the Anglo—French understanding and, if possible, to show France that England was a broken reed.

It is not surprising that under these circumstances England has taken, since 1906, the precaution of freeing herself from any embarrassments in which she had previously been involved with other Powers. In 1905 she had shown her goodwill to Russia by exercising her influence to moderate the terms of the settlement with Japan. This was a wise step, consonant alike with English treaty—obligations to Japan and with the interests of European civilization. It led naturally to an amicable agreement with Russia (1907) concerning Persia, Afghanistan, and Tibet, the three countries which touch the northern borders of our Indian Empire. It cannot be too strongly emphasized that this agreement was of a local character, exactly as was that with France; that our friendly understandings with France and with Russia were entirely separate; and that neither related to the prosecution of a common policy in Europe; unless indeed the name of a policy could be given to the precaution, which was from time to time adopted, of permitting consultations between the French and English military experts. It was understood that these consultations committed neither country to a policy of common action.[14] England was drifting from her old attitude of 'splendid isolation'; but she had as yet no desire to involve herself, even for defensive purposes, in such a formal and permanent alliance as that which had been contracted by Germany, Austria, and Italy.

But her hand was forced by Germany in 1911. Again the question of Morocco was made to supply a pretext for attacking our friendship with France. The German occupation of Agadir had, and could have, only one meaning. It was 'fastening a quarrel on France on a question that was the subject of a special agreement between France and us'.[15] The attack failed in its object. War was averted by the prompt action of the British Government. Mr. Asquith[16] announced that Great Britain, in discussing the Moroccan question, would have regard to British interests, which might be more directly involved than had hitherto been the case, and also to our treaty obligations with France. Somewhat later Mr. Asquith announced that if the negotiations between France and Germany did not reach a satisfactory settlement, Great Britain would become an active party to the discussion.[17] The nature of British interests were appropriately defined by Mr. Lloyd George in a Guildhall speech as consisting in the peace of the world, the maintenance of national honour, and the security of international trade.[18] The last phrase was a significant reference to the fact that Agadir, though valueless for commercial purposes, might be invaluable to any Power which desired to molest the South Atlantic trade routes. No one doubted then, or doubts to–day, that England stood in 1911 on the brink of a war which she had done nothing to provoke.

The situation was saved in 1911 by the solidarity of England and France. Two Powers, which in the past had been separated by a multitude of prejudices and conflicting ambitions, felt at last that both were exposed to a common danger of the most serious character. Hence a new phase in the Anglo–French *entente*, which was cemented, not by a treaty, but by the interchange of letters between the English Secretary for Foreign Affairs (Sir Edward Grey) and the French Ambassador in London (M. Paul Cambon). On November 22, 1912, Sir Edward Grey[19] reminded M. Cambon of a remark which the latter had made, 'that if either Government had grave reason to expect an unprovoked attack by a third Power, it might become essential to know whether it could in that event depend on the armed assistance of the other.' Sir Edward Grey continued:—'I agree that if either Government had grave reason to expect an unprovoked attack by a third Power, or something that threatened the general peace, it should immediately discuss with the other whether both Governments should act together to prevent aggression and to preserve peace, and, if so, what measures they would be prepared to take in common. If these measures involved action, the plans of the General Staffs would at once be taken into consideration, and the Governments would then decide what effect should be given to them.'

M. Cambon replied on the following day that he was authorized to accept the arrangement which Sir E. Grey had offered.[20]

The agreement, it will be seen, was of an elastic nature. Neither party was bound to co–operate, even diplomatically, with the other. The undertaking was to discuss any threatening situation, and to take common measures if both agreed to the necessity; there was an admission that the agreement might result in the conduct of a joint defensive war upon a common plan. Such an understanding between two sovereign states could be resented only by a Power which designed to attack one of them without clear provocation.

The date at which these notes were interchanged is certainly significant. In November, 1912, the Balkan Allies were advancing on Constantinople, and already the spoils of the

Balkan War were in dispute. Servia incurred the hostility of Austria–Hungary by demanding Albania and Adriatic ports; and the Dual Monarchy announced that it could never accept this arrangement. Behind Servia Austrian statesmen suspected the influence of Russia; it was, they said, a scheme for bringing Russia down to a sea which Austria regarded as her own preserve. Austria mobilized her army, and a war could hardly have been avoided but for the mediation of Germany and England. If England had entertained the malignant designs with which she is credited in some German circles, nothing would have been easier for her than to fan the flames, and to bring Russia down upon the Triple Alliance. The notes show how different from this were the aims of Sir Edward Grey. He evidently foresaw that a war between Austria and Russia would result in a German attack upon France. Not content with giving France assurance of support, he laboured to remove the root of the evil. A congress to settle the Balkan disputes was held at London in December, 1912; and it persuaded Servia to accept a reasonable compromise, by which she obtained commercial access to the Adriatic, but no port. This for the moment pacified Austria and averted the world–war. To whom the solution was due we know from the lips of German statesmen. The German Chancellor subsequently (April 7, 1913) told the Reichstag:—

> 'A state of tension had for months existed between Austria–Hungary
> and Russia which was only prevented from developing into war by the
> moderation of the Powers.... Europe will feel grateful to the
> English Minister of Foreign Affairs for the extraordinary ability
> and spirit of conciliation with which he conducted the discussion of
> the Ambassadors in London, and which constantly enabled him to
> bridge over differences.'

The Chancellor concluded by saying: 'We at any rate shall never stir up such a war'—a promise or a prophecy which has been singularly falsified.

It is no easy matter to understand the line of conduct which Germany has adopted towards the great Slavonic Power on her flank. Since Bismarck left the helm, she has sometimes steered in the direction of subservience, and sometimes has displayed the most audacious insolence. Periodically, it is to be supposed, her rulers have felt that in the long run the momentum of a Russian attack would be irresistible; at other times, particularly after the Russo–Japanese War, they have treated Russia, as the Elizabethans treated Spain, as 'a colossus stuffed with clouts.' But rightly or wrongly they appear to have assumed that sooner or later there must come a general Armageddon, in which the central feature would be a duel of the Teuton with the Slav; and in German military circles there was undoubtedly a conviction that the epic conflict had best come sooner and not later. How long this idea has influenced German policy we do not pretend to say. But it has certainly contributed to her unenviable prominence in the 'race of armaments' which all thinking men have condemned as an insupportable, tax upon Western civilization, and which has aggravated all the evils that it was intended to avert.

The beginning of the evil was perhaps due to France; but, if so, it was to a France which viewed with just alarm the enormous strides in population and wealth made by Germany since 1871. The 'Boulanger Law' of 1886 raised the peace footing of the French army above 500,000 men, at a time when that of Germany was 427,000, and that of Russia 550,000. Bismarck replied by the comparatively moderate measure of adding 41,000 to the German peace establishment for seven years; and it is significant of the difference between then and now that he only carried his Bill after a dissolution of one Reichstag and a forcible appeal to its successor.

France must soon have repented of the indiscretion to which she had been tempted by a military adventurer. With a population comparatively small and rapidly approaching the stationary phase it was impossible that she could long maintain such a race. In 1893 Count Caprivi's law, carried like that of Bismarck after a stiff struggle with the Reichstag, raised the peace establishment to 479,000 men. Count Caprivi at the same time reduced the period of compulsory service from three years to two; but while this reform lightened the burden on the individual conscript, it meant a great increase in the number of those who passed through military training, and an enormous increase of the war strength. The Franco–Russian *entente* of 1896 was a sign that France began to feel herself beaten in the race for supremacy and reduced to the defensive. In 1899 the German peace strength was raised to 495,000 for the next six years; in 1905 to 505,000. On the second of these occasions the German Government justified its policy by pointing out that the French war strength was still superior to that of Germany, and would become still stronger if France should change the period of service from three years to two. The German law was announced in 1904; it had the natural effect. The French Senate not only passed the new law early in 1905, but also swept away the changes which the Lower House had introduced to lighten the burden of annual training upon territorial reserves. France found her justification in the Moroccan episode of the previous year.

This was not unreasonable; but since that date France has been heavily punished for a step which might be taken to indicate that *Revanche* was still a feature of her foreign policy. Since 1886 her utmost efforts have only succeeded in raising her peace establishment to 545,000 (including a body of 28,000 colonial troops stationed in France), and her total war strength to 4,000,000. In the same period the peace establishment of Germany was raised to over 800,000, and her total war strength of fully trained men to something like 5,400,000. It is obvious from these figures that a policy of isolation has long ceased to be possible to France; and that an alliance with Russia has been her only possible method of counterbalancing the numerical superiority of the German army, which is certainly not less well equipped or organized than that of France.

This Russian alliance of France has been the only step in her continental policy which could be challenged as tending to overthrow the European balance. Undoubtedly it is France's prime offence in German eyes; and her colonial policy has only been attacked as a pretext for picking a quarrel and forcing on a decisive trial of strength before the growth of Russian resources should have made her ally impregnable.

Let us now look at the German military preparations from a German point of view. The increases of the last twenty years in military expenditure and in fighting strength have been openly discussed in the Reichstag; and the debates have usually run on the same lines, because the Government up to 1912 pursued a consistent policy, framed for some years ahead and embodied in an Army Act. The underlying principle of these Army Acts (1893, 1899, 1905, 1911) was to maintain a fairly constant ratio between the peace strength and the population. But the war strength was disproportionately increased by the Caprivi Army Act of 1893, which reduced the period of compulsory service from three years to two. The hardly−veiled intention of the German War Staff was to increase its war resources as rapidly as was consistent with the long−sufferance of those who served and those who paid the bill. It was taken as axiomatic that an increasing population ought to be protected by an increasing army. National defence was of course alleged as the prime consideration; and if these preparations were really required by growing danger on the two main frontiers of Germany, no German could do otherwise than approve the policy, no foreign Power could feel itself legitimately aggrieved.

Unfortunately it has been a maxim of German policy in recent years that national independence means the power of taking the aggressive in any case where national interests or *amour−propre* may prompt it. The increase of the German army, either in numbers or in technical efficiency, seems to be regularly followed by masterful strokes of diplomacy in which the 'mailed fist' is plainly shown to other continental Powers. Thus in 1909, at the close of a quinquennium of military re-equipment, which had raised her annual army budget from L27,000,000 to L41,000,000, Germany countenanced the Austrian annexation of Bosnia and the Herzegovina, and plainly told the authorities at St. Petersburg that any military action against Austria would bring Russia into a state of war with Germany. It was a startling step; *radix malorum* we may call it, so far as the later development of the continental situation is concerned. Russia withdrew from the impending conflict in 1909, but it is improbable that she has ever forgiven the matter or the manner of the German ultimatum.

In 1911 followed the episode of Agadir, which was clearly an attempt to 'force a quarrel on France.' But in 1911 Germany realized that her military calculations had been insufficient, if she wished to continue these unamiable diplomatic manners. It was not a question of self-preservation; it was a question, as the German Chancellor told the Reichstag, of showing the world that 'Germany was firmly resolved not to be pushed aside.' Hence the sensational Army Bill of 1912, necessitated, as the Government told the Reichstag, by the events of 1911. The Russian peril could hardly be described as imminent. The Prussian Minister of War said publicly in 1911 that 'there was no Government which either desired or was seeking to bring about a war with Germany.' Russia had recently taken steps which, at Berlin, perhaps, were read as signs of weakness, but elsewhere were hailed as proofs of her desire for general peace. M. Isvolsky, the supposed champion of Balkan ideals, had retired from office; his successor, M. Sazonof, had accompanied the Czar to the Potsdam interview (1910); the outstanding disputes of Germany and Russia over their Persian interests had been settled by agreement in 1911.

But the German Army Bill of 1912 was followed by Russia's intervention in the Balkans to secure for Servia at least commercial access to the Adriatic. This compromise, ostensibly promoted and belauded by German statesmanship, only increased the determination of the German Government to 'hold the ring' in the Balkans, to claim for Austria the right of settling her own differences with Servia as she would, and to deny Russia any interest in the matter. In 1913 came the supreme effort of the German General Staff: an Army Act for raising the peace strength by instalments until it reached 870,000, and for the eventual provision of a war strength of 5,400,000 men. This enormous increase was recommended 'by the unanimous judgement of the military authorities' as being 'necessary to secure the future of Germany.' The Chancellor warned the Reichstag that, although relations were friendly with Russia, they had to face the possibilities involved in the Pan–Slavist movement; while in Russia itself they had to reckon with a marvellous economic development and an unprecedented reorganization of the army. There was also a reference to the new law for a return to three years' service which France was introducing to improve the efficiency of her peace establishment. But it was obvious that Russia was the main preoccupation. Germany had forced the pace both in the aggrandizement of her military strength and in the methods of her diplomatic intercourse. Suddenly she found herself on the brink of an abyss. She had gone too far; she had provoked into the competition of armaments a Power as far superior to Germany in her reserves of men as Germany thought herself superior to France. It was not too late for Germany to pause. On her future behaviour towards other Powers it depended whether the Bill of 1913 should be taken as an insurance against risks, or as a challenge to all possible opponents.

The other Powers shaped their policy in accordance with Germany's example. In France, on March 4, the Supreme Council of War, having learned the outline of the German programme, decided to increase the effective fighting force by a return to the rule of three years' service. Before the German Bill had passed (June 30), the French Prime Minister announced (May 15) that he would of his own authority keep with the colours those who were completing their second year's service in the autumn. The French Army Bill, when finally passed (July 16), lowered the age limit for commencing service from twenty–one to twenty, and brought the new rule into force at once. A few weeks earlier (June 20) Belgium introduced universal military service in place of her former lenient system. In Russia a secret session of the Duma was held (July 8) to pass a new Army Budget, and the term of service was raised from three to three and a quarter years. Austria alone provided for no great increase in the numerical strength of her army; but budgeted (October 30) for extraordinary naval and military expenditure, to the extent of L28,000,000, to be incurred in the first six months of 1914. Thus on all sides the alarm was raised, and special preparations were put in hand, long before the crisis of 1914 actually arrived. It was Germany that had sounded the tocsin; and it is difficult to believe that some startling *coup* was not even then being planned by the leaders of her military party.

We have been told that, whatever the appearance of things might be, it was Russia who drove Germany to the extraordinary preparations of 1913; that Germany was arming simply in self–defence against a Slavonic Crusade. What are the facts? Economically

Why We Are At War

Russia, as a state, is in a stronger position than the German Empire. In 1912 we were told that for the past five years the revenue of Russia had exceeded expenditure by an average sum of L20,000,000 per annum. The revenue of Russia in 1913 was over L324,000,000; she has budgeted for L78,000,000 of military expenditure in 1914, of which some L15,000,000 is emergency expenditure. The total revenue of the German Empire in 1913 was L184,000,000; she has budgeted for a military expenditure in 1914 of L60,000,000. To adopt the usual German tests of comparison, Russia has a population of 173 millions to be defended on three land–frontiers, while Germany has a population of 65 millions to be defended on only two. The military efforts of Russia, therefore, have been made on a scale relatively smaller than those of Germany.

We must, however, add some further considerations which have been urged by German military critics; the alleged facts we cannot test, but we state them for what they may be worth. The reorganization of the Russian army in recent years has resulted, so we are told, in the grouping of enormously increased forces upon the western frontier. The western fortresses also have been equipped on an unparalleled scale. New roads and railways have been constructed to accelerate the mobilization of the war strength; and, above all, strategic railways have been pushed towards the western frontier. Thus, it is argued, Russia has in effect gone behind the Potsdam Agreement of 1910, by which she withdrew her armies to a fixed distance behind the Russo–German frontier. We confess that, in all this, while there may have been cause for watchfulness on the part of Germany, we can see no valid cause for war, nothing that of necessity implies more than an intention, on the part of Russia, not to be brow–beaten in the future as she was in 1909 and 1912.

These military developments did not escape English notice. They excited endless speculation about the great war of the future, and the part which this country might be asked to bear in it. Few, however, seriously supposed that we should commit ourselves to a share in the fighting upon land. The problem most usually discussed in this connexion was that of preparation to resist a sudden invasion from abroad. Was it possible to avoid compulsory service? Was the Territorial Force large enough and efficient enough to defend the country if the Expeditionary Force had gone abroad? Great Britain was infinitely better equipped for land warfare in August, 1914, than she had ever been in the nineteenth century. But her Expeditionary Force was a recent creation, and had been planned for the defence of India and the Colonies. In practice the country had clung to the 'Blue Water' policy, of trusting the national fortunes entirely to the Navy. The orthodox theory was that so long as the Navy was kept at the 'Two Power' standard, no considerable invasion of the British Isles was possible.

But from 1898 the programmes of the German Navy Laws constituted a growing menace to the 'Two Power' standard, which had been laid down as our official principle in 1889, when France and Russia were our chief European rivals at sea. That France or Russia would combine with Germany to challenge our naval supremacy was improbable; but other states were beginning to build on a larger scale, and this multiplied the possible number of hostile combinations. That Germany should wish for a strong fleet was only natural. It was needed to defend her foreign trade, her colonial interests, and her own seaports. That Germany should lay down a definite programme for six years ahead, and that the programme should become more extensive at each revision, was no necessary proof of malice. But this country received a shock in 1900, when the programme of 1898 was unexpectedly and drastically revised, so that the German Navy was practically doubled. England was at that moment involved in the South African War, and it was hard to see against whom the new fleet could be used, if not against England. This was pointed out from time to time by the Socialist opposition in the Reichstag. The orthodox official reply was that Germany must be so strong at sea that the strongest naval Power should not be able to challenge her with any confidence. But the feeling of the semi–official Navy League was known to be violently hostile to England; and it was obvious that the German navy owed its popularity to the alarmist propaganda of that league.

It was impossible for English statesmen to avoid the suspicion that, on the sea as on land, the Germans meant by liberty the right to unlimited self–assertion. Common prudence dictated close attention to the German Navy Laws; especially as they proved capable of unexpected acceleration. The 'Two Power' standard, under the stress of German competition, became increasingly difficult to maintain, and English Liberals were inclined to denounce it as wasteful of money. But, when a Liberal Government tried the experiment of economizing on the Navy (1906–8), there was no corresponding reduction in the German programme. The German Naval Law of 1906 raised the amount of the naval estimates by one–third; and German ministers blandly waved aside as impracticable a proposal for a mutual limitation of armaments.

In 1909 this country discovered that in capital ships—which now began to be considered the decisive factor in naval warfare—Germany would actually be the superior by 1914 unless special measures were taken. The British Government was awakened to the new situation (it arose from the German Naval Law of 1908), and returned unwillingly to the path of increasing expenditure. The Prime Minister said that we regretted the race in naval expenditure and were not animated by anti—German feeling; but we could not afford to let our supremacy at sea be imperilled, since our national security depended on it (March 16, 1909). The 'Two Power' standard was dropped, and the Triple Alliance became the object of special attention at the Admiralty. The First Lord said on March 13, 1911, that we should make our navy superior to any foreign navy and to any *probable* combination which we might have to meet single—handed. In practice this meant a policy of developing, in the matter of Dreadnoughts, a superiority of sixty per cent, over the German navy; this, it was officially explained in 1912, had been for some years past the actual Admiralty standard of new construction (Mr. Winston Churchill, March 18, 1912).

But even this programme had to be stiffened when the year 1912 saw a new German Navy Bill which involved an increased expenditure of L1,000,000 annually for six years, and had the effect of putting nearly four—fifths of the German navy in a position of immediate readiness for war. Earlier in the year the British Government had announced that, if the German policy of construction were accelerated, we should add to our programme double the number which Germany put in hand; but if Germany relaxed her preparations we should make a fully proportionate reduction. The German Bill came as an answer to this declaration; and it was followed in this country by supplementary estimates on naval account, amounting to nearly a million pounds; and this was announced to be 'the first and smallest instalment of the extra expenditure entailed by the new German law.' The new British policy was maintained in 1913 and in 1914, though in 1913 the First Lord of the Admiralty made a public offer of a 'naval holiday,' a suspension of new construction by mutual consent. The Imperial Chancellor responded only by suggesting that the proposal was entirely unofficial, by asking for concrete proposals, and by saying that the idea constituted a great progress; and his naval estimates in 1913 were half a million higher than those of 1912.

From these facts, viewed in their chronological order, it is clear that on sea as on land Germany has set the pace. Thirty years ago the German navy did not enter into England's naval calculations. For the last six years, if not for a longer period, it has been the one navy which our Admiralty felt the necessity of watching from year to year, and indeed from month to month. It is the first time for more than a hundred years that we have had to face the problem of 'a powerful homogeneous navy under one government and concentrated within easy distance of our shores.'

Why We Are At War

On German principles we should long ago have adopted the 'offensive–defensive.' We have been at least as seriously menaced by Germany at sea as Germany has been menaced by Russia upon land. But we can confidently say that in the period of rivalry our fleet has never been used as a threat, or turned to the purposes of an aggressive colonial policy. Rightly or wrongly, we have refused to make possible intentions a case for an ultimatum. We have held by the position that only a breach of public law would justify us in abandoning our efforts for the peace of Europe.

NOTE

Abstract of Anglo–French Agreement on Morocco.

In April, 1904, England and France concluded an agreement for the delimitation of their interests on the Mediterranean littoral of North Africa. The agreement included five secret Articles which were not published until November, 1911. The purport of the Articles which were published at the time was as follows. By the first Article England stated that she had not the intention of changing the political state of Egypt; and France declared that she would not impede the action of England in Egypt by demanding that a term should be fixed for the British occupation or in any other way. By the second Article France declared that she had not the intention of changing the political state of Morocco; and England recognized that it appertained to France, as the Power conterminous with Morocco, to watch the tranquillity of this country and to assist it in all administrative, economic, financial, and military reforms which it required, France promised to respect the customary and treaty rights of England in Morocco; and by the third Article England made a corresponding promise to France in respect of Egypt. By the fourth Article the two Governments undertook to maintain 'the principle of commercial liberty' in Egypt and Morocco, by not lending themselves in either country to inequality in the establishment of Customs–duties or of other taxes or of railway rates. The sixth and seventh Articles were inserted to ensure the free passage of the Suez Canal and of the Straits of Gibraltar. The eighth declared that both Governments took into friendly consideration the interests of Spain in Morocco, and that France would make some arrangements with the Spanish Monarchy. The ninth Article declared that each Government would lend its diplomatic support to the other in executing the clauses relative to Egypt and Morocco.[21] Of the secret Articles two (Nos. 3 and 4) related to Spain, defining the territory which she was to receive 'whenever the Sultan ceases to exercise authority over it,' and providing that the Anglo–French agreement would hold good even if Spain declined this arrangement. Article 1 stipulated that, if either Government found itself constrained, by the force of circumstances, to modify its policy in respect to Egypt or Morocco, nevertheless the fourth, sixth, and seventh Articles of the public declaration would remain intact; that is, each would under all circumstances maintain the principle of 'commercial liberty,' and would permit the free passage of the Suez Canal and the Straits of Gibraltar. In Article 2 England, while disclaiming any intention to alter the system of Capitulations or the judicial organization of Egypt, reserved the right to reform the Egyptian legislative system on the model of other civilized countries; and France agreed on condition that she should not be impeded from making similar reforms in Morocco. The fifth Article related to the Egyptian national debt.

Notes:

[Footnote 10: Quoted from Headlam's *Bismarck*, p. 444.]

[Footnote 11: *Correspondence respecting the European Crisis* (Cd. 7467), No. 85. Sir E. Goschen to Sir E. Grey, July 29, 1914. See *infra*, Appendix II.]

[Footnote 12: For these agreements see *The Times*, April 12, 1904, and November 25, 1911. See note at end of this chapter.]

[Footnote 13: White Paper, Morocco No. 1 (1906).]

[Footnote 14: *Correspondence*, No. 105 (Enclosure 1). Sir E. Grey to M. Cambon, November 22, 1912. See Appendix II.]

[Footnote 15: *Correspondence*, No. 87. Sir E. Grey to Sir F. Bertie, July 29, 1914.]

[Footnote 16: *Times*, July 7, 1911.]

[Footnote 17: *Times*, July 27, 1911.]

[Footnote 18: *Times*, July 22, 1911.]

[Footnote 19: *Correspondence*, p. 57 (Enclosure 1 in No. 105). See Appendix II.]

[Footnote 20: *Ibid.* p. 57 (Enclosure 2 in No. 105).]

[Footnote 21: *Times*, April 12, 1904.]

CHAPTER III. THE DEVELOPMENT OF RUSSIAN POLICY

Until the year 1890 Russia and Germany had been in close touch. Dynastic connexions united the two imperial houses; and the common policy of repression of Polish nationality—the fatal legacy of the days of Frederic the Great and Catharine II—united the two empires. National sentiment in Russia was, however, always anti–German; and as early as 1885 Balkan affairs began to draw the Russian Government away from Germany. In 1890 Bismarck fell; and under William II German policy left the Russian connexion, and in close touch with Austria embarked on Balkan adventures which ran counter to Russian aims, while Russia on her side turned to new allies.

The new direction of Russian policy, which has brought the aims of the Russian Government into close accord with the desires of national Slav sentiment, was determined by Balkan conditions. Bismarck had cherished no Balkan ambitions: he had been content to play the part of an 'honest broker' at the Congress of Berlin, and he had spoken of the Bulgarian affair of 1885 as 'not worth the bones of a Pomeranian grenadier.' William II apparently thought otherwise. At any rate Germany seems to have conducted, for many years past, a policy of establishing her influence, along with that of Austria, through South–Eastern Europe. And it is this policy which is the *fons et origo* of the present struggle; for it is a policy which is not and cannot be tolerated by Russia, so long as Russia is true to her own Slav blood and to the traditions of centuries.

After Austria had finally lost Italy, as she did in 1866, she turned for compensation to the Balkans. If Venetia was lost, it seemed some recompense when in 1878 Austria occupied Bosnia and the Herzegovina. Hence she could expand southwards—ultimately perhaps to Salonica. Servia, which might have objected, was a vassal kingdom, the protege of Austria, under the dynasty of the Obrenovitch. As Austria might hope to follow the line to Salonica,[22] so Germany, before the end of the nineteenth century, seems to have conceived of a parallel line of penetration, which would carry her influence through Constantinople, through Konieh, to Bagdad. She has extended her political and economic influence among the small Slav states and in Turkey. In 1898 the King of Roumania (a

Hohenzollern by descent) conceded direct communication through his territories between Berlin and Constantinople: in 1899 a German company obtained a concession for the Bagdad railway from Konieh to the head of the Persian Gulf. In a word, Germany began to stand in the way of the Russian traditions of ousting the Turk and ruling in Constantinople: she began to buttress the Turk, to train his army, to exploit his country, and to seek to oust Russia generally from South–Eastern Europe.

In 1903 the progress of Austria and Germany received a check. A blood–stained revolution at Belgrade ousted the pro–Austrian Obrenovitch, and put in its place the rival family of the Karageorgevitch. Under the new dynasty Servia escaped from Austrian tutelage, and became an independent focus of Slav life in close touch with Russia. The change was illustrated in 1908, when Austria took advantage of the revolution in Turkey, led by the Young Turks, to annex formally the occupied territories of Bosnia and the Herzegovina. Servia, which had hoped to gain these territories, once a part of the old Servian kingdom, was mortally offended, and would have gone to war with Austria, if Russia, her champion under the new dynasty, could only have given her support. But Russia, still weak after the Japanese war, could not do so; Russia, on the contrary, had to suffer the humiliation of giving a pledge to the Austrian Ambassador at St. Petersburg that she would not support Servia. That humiliation Russia has not forgotten. She has saved money, she has reorganized her army, she has done everything in her power to gain security for the future. And now that Austria has sought utterly to humiliate Servia on the unproved charge (unproved, in the sense that no legal proof was offered)[23] of complicity in the murder of the Archduke Franz Ferdinand and his wife, Russia has risked war rather than surrender her protection of a Slav kingdom. Slav sentiment imperatively demanded action in favour of Servia: no government could refuse to listen to the demand. The stake for Russia is not merely the integrity of Servia: it is her prestige among the Slav peoples, of which she is head; and behind all lies the question whether South–Eastern Europe shall be under Teutonic control, and lost to Russian influence.

Germany has not only threatened Slav life in South–Eastern Europe: she has irritated Slav feeling on her own Eastern frontier. The vitality and the increase of the Slavs in Eastern Germany has excited deep German alarm. The German Government has therefore of late years pursued a policy of repression towards its own Slav subjects, the Poles, forbidding the use of the Polish language, and expropriating Polish landowners in order to plant a German garrison in the East. Teutonism is really alarmed at the superior birth–rate and physical vigour of the Slavs; but Russia has not loved Teutonic policy, and there has been an extensive boycott of German goods in Russian Poland. The promise made by the Tsar, since the beginning of the war, that he would re–create the old Poland, and give it autonomy, shows how far Russia has travelled from the days, not so far distant in point of time, when it was her policy to repress the Poles in conjunction with Germany; and it has made the breach between Germany and Russia final and irreparable.

It is thus obvious that Germany is vitally opposed to the great Slav Empire in South–Eastern Europe and on her own eastern borders. But why, it may be asked, should Russian policy be linked with English? Is there any bond of union except the negative bond of common opposition to Germany? There is. For one thing England and Russia have sought to pursue a common cause—that of international arbitration and of disarmament. If neither has succeeded, it has been something of a bond between the two that both have attempted to succeed. But there are other and more vital factors. England, which in 1854–6 opposed and fought Russia for the sake of the integrity of Turkey, has no wish to fight Russia for the sake of a Germanized Turkey. On the contrary, the interest of England in maintaining independence in the South–East of Europe now coincides with that of Russia. Above all, the new constitutional Russia of the Duma is Anglophil.

'The political ideals both of Cadets and Octobrists were learnt
chiefly from England, the study of whose constitutional history had
aroused in Russia an enthusiasm hardly intelligible to a present–day
Englishman. All three Dumas ... were remarkably friendly to England,
and England supplied the staple of the precedents and parallels for
quotation.'[24]

In a word, the beginnings of Russian constitutionalism not only coincided in time with the Anglo–Russian agreement of 1907, but owed much to the inspiration of England.

Notes:

[Footnote 22: Count Aehrenthal, foreign minister of Austria (1906–1912), started the scheme of the Novi Bazar railway to connect the railways of Bosnia with the (then) Turkish line to Salonica. See also *Correspondence*, No. 19, Sir R. Rodd to Sir E. Grey, July 25: 'There is reliable information that Austria intends to seize the Salonica railway.']

[Footnote 23: For a summary of so–called proofs, see Appendix IV, *infra*.]

[Footnote 24: *Camb. Mod. Hist.* xii. 379.]

CHAPTER IV. CHRONOLOGICAL SKETCH OF THE CRISIS

The following sketch of events from June 28 to August 4, 1914, is merely intended as an introduction to the analytical and far more detailed account of the negotiations and declarations of those days which the reader will find below (Chap. V). Here we confine the narrative to a plain statement of the successive stages in the crisis, neither discussing the motives of the several Powers involved, nor distinguishing the fine shades of difference in the various proposals which were made by would–be mediators.

The crisis of 1914 began with an unforeseen development in the old quarrel of Austria–Hungary and Russia over the Servian question. On June 28 the Archduke Franz Ferdinand, heir–apparent of the Austro–Hungarian monarchy, and his wife, the Duchess of Hohenberg, paid a visit of ceremony to the town of Serajevo, in Bosnia, the administrative centre of the Austrian provinces of Bosnia and the Herzegovina. In entering the town, the Archduke and the Duchess narrowly escaped being killed by a bomb which was thrown at their carriage. Later in the day they were shot by assassins armed with Browning pistols. The crime was apparently planned by political conspirators who resented the Austrian annexation of Bosnia and the Herzegovina (*supra*, p. 54), and who desired that these provinces should be united to Servia.

The Austrian Government, having instituted an inquiry, came to the conclusion that the bombs of the conspirators had been obtained from a Servian arsenal; that the crime had been planned in Belgrade, the Servian capital, with the help of a Servian staff–officer who provided the pistols; that the criminals and their weapons had been conveyed from Servia into Bosnia by officers of Servian frontier–posts and by Servian customs–officials. At the moment the Austrian Government published no proof of these conclusions,[25] but, on July 23, forwarded them to the Servian Government in a formal note containing certain demands which, it was intimated, must be satisfactorily answered by Servia within forty–eight hours.[26] This ultimatum included a form of apology to be published on a specified date by the Servian Government, and ten engagements which the Servian Government were to give the Austro–Hungarian Government. The extraordinary nature of some of these engagements is explained in the next chapter (pp. 103–7).

On July 24 this note was communicated by Austria–Hungary to the other Powers of Europe,[27] and on July 25 it was published in a German paper, the *Norddeutsche Allgemeine Zeitung*. It was therefore intended to be a public warning to Servia. On July 24 the German Government told the Powers that it approved the Austrian note, as being necessitated by the 'Great-Servian' propaganda, which aimed at the incorporation in the Servian monarchy of the southern Slav provinces belonging to Austria–Hungary; that Austria, if she wished to remain a Great Power, could not avoid pressing the demands contained in the note, even, if necessary, by military measures; and that the question was one which concerned no Powers except Austria–Hungary and Servia.[28]

Russia did not agree that the Austrian note was directed against Servia alone. On July 24 the Russian Minister of Foreign Affairs told the British Ambassador at St. Petersburg that Austria's conduct was provocative and immoral; that some of her demands were impossible of acceptance; that Austria would never have taken such action unless Germany had first been consulted; that if Austria began military measures against Servia, Russia would probably mobilize. The Russian Minister hoped that England would proclaim its solidarity with France and Russia on the subject of the Austrian note; doubtless Servia could accept some of the Austrian demands.[29] To the Austro–Hungarian Government the Russian Minister sent a message, on the same day, July 24, that the time-limit allowed to Servia for her reply was quite insufficient, if the Powers were to help in smoothing the situation; and he urged that Austria–Hungary should publish the proofs of the charges against Servia.[30] On July 25 Russia told England[31] that Servia would punish those proved to be guilty, but would not accept all the demands of Austria; that no independent state could do so. If Servia appealed to arbitration, as seemed possible, Russia was, she said, prepared to leave the arbitration in the hands of England, France, Germany, and Italy—the four Powers whom Sir Edward Grey had suggested as possible mediators.

On the day on which Russia made this suggestion, July 25, the Servian Government replied to the Austrian note, conceding part of the Austrian demands, and announcing its readiness to accept, on the other points, the arbitration of the Hague Tribunal or of the Great Powers. The Austrian Government found the Servian note unsatisfactory, and criticized its details in an official memorandum.[32] The Austro–Hungarian Minister left Belgrade on July 25; on July 26 a part of the Austro–Hungarian army was mobilized; and on July 28 Austria–Hungary declared war on Servia.

Why We Are At War

Sir Edward Grey had from the first declined to 'announce England's solidarity' with Russia and France on the Servian question. On and after July 26 he was taking active steps to bring about the mediation, between Austria–Hungary and Servia, of four Powers (Italy, Germany, France, England). To this mediation Russia had already agreed, July 25; and Italy and France were ready to co-operate with England.[33] Germany, however, made difficulties on the ground that anything like formal intervention would be impracticable, unless both Austria and Russia consented to it.[34] Russia had already (July 25) prepared the ukase ordering mobilization,[35] but had not yet issued it; on July 27 the Russian Foreign Minister announced his readiness to make the Servian question the subject of direct conversations with Vienna.[36] This offer was at first declined by the Austro–Hungarian Government, but subsequently accepted; and conversations were actually in progress between the representatives of the two Powers as late as August 1.[37]

No doubt the hesitation of Austria was due to the fact that, on July 28, the Russian Government warned Germany of the mobilization of the southern military districts of Russia, to be publicly proclaimed on July 29.[38] Austria replied to this intimation by offering assurances that she would respect the integrity and independence of Servia;[39] these assurances, considered inadequate by the Russian Government, seem to have been the subject of the last conversations between Russia and Austria–Hungary.

Russia persisted that Germany was the real obstacle to a friendly settlement; and this conviction was not affected by the appeals for peace which the Kaiser telegraphed to the Tsar on July 28, July 29, and July 31.[40] On July 29 Germany told England that the Russian mobilization was alarming, and that France was also making military preparations;[41] at the same time Germany threatened to proclaim 'imminent state of war' (*drohende Kriegsgefahr*) as a counter measure to the French preparations;[42] German military preparations, by July 30, had in fact gone far beyond the preliminary stage which she thus indicated.[43] Germany had already warned England, France, and Russia that, if Russia mobilized, this would mean German mobilization against both France and Russia.[44] But on July 27, Russia had explained that her mobilization would in no sense be directed against Germany, and would only take place if Austrian forces crossed the Servian frontier.[45] On July 29, the day on which Russia actually mobilized the southern districts, Russia once more asked Germany to participate in the 'quadruple conference' now proposed by England, for the purpose of mediating between Austria and Servia. This proposal was declined by the German Ambassador at St. Petersburg.[46]

Germany in fact believed, or professed to believe, that the Russian mobilization, though not proclaimed, was already far advanced.[47]

On July 30 Austria, although her conversations with Russia were still in progress, began the bombardment of Belgrade. The next day, July 31, Russia ordered general mobilization; on August 1 France and Germany each took the like step; Germany presented an ultimatum to Russia, demanding that Russian mobilization should cease, and another ultimatum to France asking what course she would take in the event of war between Germany and Russia.

Before these decisive steps of July 30–August 1, and while Sir Edward Grey was still engaged in efforts of mediation, Germany made overtures to England, with the object of securing England's neutrality in the event of a war between Germany and France. On July 29 Germany offered, as the price of English neutrality, to give assurances that, if victorious, she would make no territorial acquisitions at the expense of France; but refused to give a similar assurance respecting French colonies, or to promise to respect Belgian neutrality.[48] These proposals were refused by England on July 30.[49] On August 1 the German Ambassador unofficially asked England to remain neutral on condition that Germany would not violate Belgian neutrality. Sir Edward Grey replied that England's hands were still free, and that he could not promise neutrality on that condition alone.[50]

Meanwhile, on July 30, Sir Edward Grey was told by France that she would not remain neutral in a war between Germany and Russia.[51] On July 31 the English Cabinet, being asked by France to declare definitely on her side, replied that England could give no pledge at present.[52] On the same day England asked France and Germany to engage to respect Belgian neutrality. France assented, Germany evaded giving a reply.[53] But, on August 2, German forces entered the neutral state of Luxemburg; and England promised to defend the French coasts and shipping if attacked by the German fleet in the Channel, or through the North Sea.[54] On August 4 the King of the Belgians telegraphed to King George announcing that Germany had demanded passage for her troops through Belgian territory, and appealing to England for help.[55] On the same day, August 4, England sent an ultimatum to Germany asking for assurance, before midnight, that Germany would respect Belgian neutrality.[56] This demand was taken at Berlin as equivalent to a declaration of war by England against Germany.

42

Why We Are At War

DIARY OF THE EVENTS LEADING TO THE WAR

June 28. Assassination at Sarajevo of the Archduke Franz Ferdinand and the Duchess of Hohenberg.

July 6. The Kaiser leaves Kiel for a cruise in Northern waters.

July 9. Results of Austro–Hungarian investigation into the Servian crime laid before the Emperor.

July 13, 14. Serious disclosures about condition of French army.

July 13, 14, 15, 16. Heavy selling of Canadian Pacific Railway Shares, especially by Berlin operators.

July 16. Count Tisza, the Hungarian Premier, speaking in the Hungarian Chamber, describes war as a sad *ultima ratio*, 'but every state and nation must be able and willing to make war if it wishes to exist as a state and a nation.'

The *Times* leading article 'Austria–Hungary and Servia' is commented on in Berlin as an 'English warning to Servia.'

July 19. The King summons a conference to discuss the Home–Rule problem.

July 21. The *Frankfurter Zeitung* warns Austria–Hungary of the folly of its campaign against Servia.

July 23. Thursday. Austria presents her Note to Servia giving her 48 hours in which to accept.

July 24. Friday. Russian Cabinet Council held. The Austro–Hungarian demands considered as an indirect challenge to Russia.—Strike at St. Petersburg.

Failure of the conference on Home Rule.

July 25. Saturday. Servian reply; considered unsatisfactory by Austria–Hungary, whose Minister and Legation–staff leave Belgrade.

Russian Ambassador at Vienna instructed to request extension of time–limit allowed to Servia.

Sir E. Grey suggests that the four other Powers should mediate at Vienna and St. Petersburg.—Serious riot in Dublin.

July 26. Sunday. Sir E. Grey proposes that the French, Italian, and German Ambassadors should meet him in conference immediately for the purpose of discovering an issue which would prevent complications.

Partial mobilization of Austro–Hungarian army ordered.

Russian Foreign Minister warns German Ambassador that Russia cannot remain indifferent to the fate of Servia.

Sir E. Goschen says the Kaiser is returning to–night.

July 27. Monday. France and Italy accept proposal of a conference. German Secretary of State refuses the proposal of a 'conference.'

Russian Minister for Foreign Affairs proposes direct conversation between Vienna and St. Petersburg.

British Fleet kept assembled after manoeuvres.

Sir E. Grey in the House of Commons makes a statement concerning the attitude of Great Britain.

The *Times* Berlin correspondent reports that the Kaiser returned this afternoon from Kiel to Potsdam.

July 28. Tuesday. Austria–Hungary declares war on Servia.

Why We Are At War

Russia says the key of the situation is to be found at Berlin.

Austria declines any suggestion of negotiations on basis of the Servian reply.

The Kaiser telegraphs to the Tsar.

July 29. Wednesday. Russian mobilization in the four military districts of Odessa, Kiev, Moscow, and Kazan.

Germany offers, in return for British neutrality, to promise territorial integrity of France, but will not extend the same assurance for French colonies.

Sir E. Grey warns the German Ambassador that we should not necessarily stand aside, if all the efforts to maintain the peace failed.

Austria at last realizes that Russia will not remain indifferent.

The Tsar telegraphs to the Kaiser; the latter replies.

July 30. Thursday. Bombardment of Belgrade by Austro–Hungarian forces.

The Prime Minister speaks in the House of Commons on the gravity of the situation, and postpones discussion of the Home Rule Amending Bill.

The Tsar telegraphs to the Kaiser.

July 31. Friday. General Russian mobilization ordered.

Sir E. Grey asks France and Germany whether they will respect neutrality of Belgium.

France promises to respect Belgian neutrality; Germany is doubtful whether any answer will be returned to this request.

Austria declares its readiness to discuss the substance of its ultimatum to Servia.

Fresh telegrams pass between the Kaiser and the Tsar.

Why We Are At War

Germany presents ultimatum to Russia demanding that her mobilization should cease within 12 hours.

Germany presents an ultimatum to France asking her to define her attitude in case of a Russo–German war.

English bankers confer with the Government about the financial situation.

Aug. 1. Saturday. Sir E. Grey protests against detention of English ships at Hamburg.

Orders issued for general mobilization of French army.

Orders issued for general mobilization of German army.

Aug. 2. Sunday. Germans invade Luxemburg.

Sir E. Grey gives France an assurance that the English fleet will protect the North Coast of France against the German fleet.

Germans enter French territory near Cirey.

Aug. 3. Monday. Italy declares itself neutral, as the other members of the Triple Alliance are not engaged in a defensive war.

Germany presents an ultimatum to Belgium.

Sir E. Grey makes an important speech in the House of Commons.

Aug. 4. Tuesday. Germans enter Belgian territory.

Britain presents an ultimatum to Germany demanding an answer by midnight.

The Prime Minister makes a speech in the House of Commons, practically announcing war against Germany and explaining the British position.

Aug. 6. Austria–Hungary declares war on Russia.

Why We Are At War

Aug. 11. The French Ambassador at Vienna demands his passport.

Aug. 12. Great Britain declares war on Austria–Hungary.

Notes:

[Footnote 25: Extracts are printed in the German version of the German White Book (pp. 28–31) from an Austrian official publication of July 27. We print the extracts (the original not being accessible in this country) in Appendix IV.]

[Footnote 26: Full text *infra* in Appendix I (German White Book, pp. 18–23); more correctly in *Correspondence respecting the European Crisis*, No. 4, Count Berchtold to Count Mensdorff, July 24; but the differences between the two versions are immaterial for our present purpose.]

[Footnote 27: See the communication to England in *Correspondence*, No. 4.]

[Footnote 28: *Correspondence*, No. 9, Note communicated by the German Ambassador, July 24.]

[Footnote 29: *Correspondence*, No. 6, Sir G. Buchanan to Sir E. Grey, July 24.]

[Footnote 30: *Correspondence*, No. 13, Note communicated by Russian Ambassador, July 25.]

[Footnote 31: *Correspondence*, No. 17, Sir G. Buchanan to Sir E. Grey, July 25.]

[Footnote 32: For text of Servian note see *infra* Appendix I (German White Book, pp. 23–32). The Austrian comments also are given there.]

[Footnote 33: *Correspondence*, No. 42, Sir F. Bertie to Sir E. Grey, July 27; *ibid*. No. 49, Sir E. Grey to Sir R. Rodd, July 27.]

[Footnote 34: *Correspondence*, No. 43. Sir E. Goschen to Sir E. Grey, July 27.]

[Footnote 35: German White Book, p. 46 (*infra* in Appendix I). The Tsar to His Majesty, July 30.]

[Footnote 36: *Correspondence*, No. 45. Sir G. Buchanan to Sir E. Grey.]

[Footnote 37: Austria declined conversations on July 28 (*Correspondence*, No. 93); but for conversations of July 31 see *Correspondence*, No. III; of August I, see Appendix V.]

[Footnote 38: *Correspondence*, No. 70 (I). M. Sazonof to Russian Ambassador at Berlin, July 28.]

[Footnote 39: *Correspondence*, No. 72. Sir G. Buchanan to Sir E. Grey, July 28.]

[Footnote 40: German White Book, pp. 43, 45 (in Appendix I, *infra*).]

[Footnote 41: *Correspondence*, No. 76. Sir E. Goschen to Sir E. Grey, July 29.]

[Footnote 42: German White Book, p. 42, Exhibit 17 (*infra*, Appendix I).]

[Footnote 43: *Correspondence*, No. 105 (Enclosure 3), July 30.]

[Footnote 44: German White Book, p. 7; the date of the warning seems to be July 27.]

[Footnote 45: German White Book, p. 40, Exhibit II.]

[Footnote 46: *Ibid*. p. 9.]

[Footnote 47: *Ibid*. p. 10.]

[Footnote 48: *Correspondence*, No. 85. Sir E. Goschen to Sir E. Grey, July 29.]

[Footnote 49: *Ibid*. No. 101. Sir E. Grey to Sir E. Goschen, July 30.]

[Footnote 50: *Correspondence*, No. 123. Sir E. Grey to Sir E. Goschen, Aug. 1.]

[Footnote 51: *Ibid*. No. 105. Sir E. Grey to Sir F. Bertie, July 30.]

[Footnote 52: *Ibid*. No. 119. Sir E. Grey to Sir F. Bertie, July 31.]

[Footnote 53: *Ibid*. No. 114, 120, 122.]

[Footnote 54: *Ibid*. No. 148. Sir E. Grey to Sir F. Bertie, Aug. 2.]

[Footnote 55: *Ibid*. No. 153. Sir E. Grey to Sir E. Goschen, Aug. 4.]

[Footnote 56: *Ibid*. No. 159. Sir E. Grey to Sir E. Goschen, Aug. 4]

CHAPTER V. NEGOTIATORS AND NEGOTIATIONS

For purposes of reference the following list of *dramatis personae* may be useful:—

GREAT BRITAIN: King George V, *succ.* 1910. *Foreign Secretary*: Sir Edward Grey. *Ambassadors from France*: M. Paul Cambon.
  Russia: Count Benckendorff.
  Germany: Prince Lichnowsky.
  Austria: Count Albert Mensdorff–Pouilly–Dietrichstein.
  Belgium: Count A. de Lalaing (*Minister*).

RUSSIA: Emperor Nicholas II, *succ.* 1894. *Foreign Secretary* : M. Sazonof. *Ambassadors from Great Britain*: Sir George Buchanan.
  France: M. Paleologue.
  Germany: Count Pourtales.
  Austria: Friedrich Count Szapary.

FRANCE: Raymond Poincare, *President, elected* 1913. *Premier* : M. Viviani. *Acting Foreign Secretary*: M. Doumergue. *Ambassadors from Great Britain*: Sir Francis Bertie.
  Russia: M. Isvolsky.
    M. Sevastopoulo (*Charge d'Affaires*).
  Germany: Baron von Schoen.
  Austria: Count Scezsen.

GERMANY: Emperor William II, *succ.* 1888. *Imperial Chancellor*: Dr. von

Bethmann–Hollweg. *Foreign Secretary*: Herr von Jagow. *Ambassadors from Great Britain*: Sir Edward Goschen.
  Sir Horace Rumbold (*Councillor*).
Russia: M. Swerbeiev.
  M. Bronewsky (*Charge d'Affaires*).
France: M. Jules Cambon.
Austria: Count Ladislaus Szoegyeny–Marich.

AUSTRIA–HUNGARY: Emperor Francis Joseph, *succ.* 1848. *Foreign Secretary*: Count Berchtold. *Ambassadors from Great Britain*: Sir Maurice de Bunsen.
Russia: M. Schebesco.
  M. Kondachev (*Charge d'Affaires*).
France: M. Crozier.
Germany: Herr von Tschirscky–und–Boegendorff.

ITALY: King Victor Emmanuel III, *succ.* 1900. *Foreign Secretary*: Marquis di San Giuliano. *Ambassador from Great Britain*: Sir Rennell Rodd.

BELGIUM: King Albert, *succ.* 1909. *Minister of Great Britain*: Sir Francis Villiers.

SERVIA: King Peter, *succ.* 1903. *Minister of Great Britain* : C.L. des Graz.
  D.M. Crackanthorpe (*First Secretary*). *Russian Charge d'Affaires*: M. Strandtmann.

I

Germany's attitude to Austria and Russia.

From the very beginning of the conversations between the Powers on the assassination of the Archduke Franz Ferdinand at Serajevo, and on the Austrian note to Servia, the German Government took up the attitude that it was a 'matter for settlement between Servia and Austria alone.'[57] Subsequently in their White Book they endeavoured to show that the Servian agitation was part of Russian propagandism.[58] In the negotiations, the cardinal point of their observations is that Russia is not to interfere in this matter, although M. Paul Cambon pointed out that 'Russia would be compelled by her public opinion to take action as soon as Austria attacked Servia'.[59]

Why We Are At War

After the presentation of the Austrian note to Servia, Germany continued to maintain the position that the crisis could be localized, and to reject Sir Horace Rumbold's suggestion that 'in taking military action in Servia, Austria would dangerously excite public opinion in Russia'.[60]

At Vienna Sir Maurice de Bunsen, the British Ambassador, was very frankly told by the German Ambassador that Germany was shielding Austria in the Servian business:—

'As for Germany, she knew very well what she was about in backing up
Austria–Hungary in this matter.... Servian concessions were all a
sham. Servia proved that she well knew that they were insufficient
to satisfy the legitimate demands of Austria–Hungary by the fact
that before making her offer she had ordered mobilization and
retirement of Government from Belgrade.'[61]

M. Sazonof, the Russian Foreign Minister, seems to have divined this policy of Germany pretty soon:—

'My interviews with the German Ambassador confirm my impression that
Germany is, if anything, in favour of the uncompromising attitude
adopted by Austria. The Berlin Cabinet, who could have prevented the
whole of this crisis developing, appear to be exercising no
influence upon their ally.... There is no doubt that the key of the
situation is to be found at Berlin.'[62]

When at the beginning of August the crisis had led to war, it is interesting to observe the opinions expressed by high and well–informed officials about German diplomacy. M. Sazonof summed up his opinion thus:—

'The policy of Austria had throughout been tortuous and immoral, and
she thought she could treat Russia with defiance, secure in the
support of her German ally. Similarly the policy of Germany had been
an equivocal and double–faced policy, and it mattered little whether
the German Government knew or did not know the terms of the Austrian
ultimatum; what mattered was that her intervention with the Austrian
Government had been postponed until the moment had passed when its

influence would have been felt. Germany was unfortunate in her representatives in Vienna and St. Petersburg; the former was a violent Russophobe who had urged Austria on, the latter had reported to his Government that Russia would never go to war.'[63]

And Sir Maurice de Bunsen on the same day wrote that he agreed with his Russian colleague that

'the German Ambassador at Vienna desired war from the first, and his strong personal bias probably coloured his action here. The Russian Ambassador is convinced that the German Government also desired war from the first.'[64]

Sir Maurice does not actually endorse this opinion concerning the attitude of the German Government, but there can be no doubt that this general attitude was most pernicious to the cause of European peace, and that if the German Government had desired war they could scarcely have acted more efficiently towards that end. No diplomatic pressure was put upon Vienna, which under the aegis of Berlin was allowed to go to any lengths against Servia. Over and over again the German diplomats were told that Russia was deeply interested in Servia, but they would not listen. As late as July 28th the German Chancellor himself refused 'to discuss the Servian note', adding that 'Austria's standpoint, and in this he agreed, was that her quarrel with Servia was a purely Austrian concern with which Russia had nothing to do'.[65] Next day the German Ambassador at Vienna was continuing 'to feign surprise that Servian affairs could be of such interest to Russia'.[66] But in their White Book, in order to blacken the character of Russia, the Germans remark that they 'were perfectly aware that a possible warlike attitude of Austria–Hungary against Servia might bring Russia into the field'.[67] Both stories cannot be true: the German Government have, not for the last time in the history of these negotiations, to choose between ineptitude and guilt; the ineptitude of not recognizing an obvious fact, and the guilt of deliberately allowing Austria to act in such a way that Russia was bound to come into the field.

When Austria presented her ultimatum, Sir Edward Grey did all he could to obtain the good offices of Russia for a conciliatory reply by Servia, and to persuade the German Government to use influence with Austria so that she should take a friendly attitude to Servia. On the day of the presentation of the Austrian note he proposed to Prince

Lichnowsky, the German Ambassador, the co–operation of the four Powers, Germany, France, Italy, and Great Britain, in favour of moderation at Vienna and St. Petersburg, and when the Austrians rejected the Servian reply he took the important step of proposing that the French, Italian, and German Ambassadors should meet him in conference immediately 'for the purpose of discovering an issue which would prevent complications'.[68] The proposal was accepted with alacrity by the French and Italian Governments. The German Secretary for Foreign Affairs, Herr von Jagow, on the other hand, was unable or unwilling to understand the proposal, and Sir Edward Goschen seems to have been unable to impress its real character upon the Government of Berlin. For Herr von Jagow, on receipt of the proposal, informed the British Ambassador, Sir Edward Goschen, that the conference suggested

> 'would practically amount to a court of arbitration and could not in
> his opinion be called together except at the request of Austria and
> Russia. He could not therefore fall in with it.'

Sir Edward Goschen not unnaturally pointed out that

> 'the idea had nothing to do with arbitration, but meant that
> representatives of the four nations not directly interested should
> discuss and suggest means for avoiding a dangerous situation'.[69]

Herr von Jagow spoke in the same sense to the French and Italian Ambassadors, who discussed the matter with their British colleague. Some doubt seems to have arisen in their minds as to the sincerity of the German Secretary of State's loudly expressed desire for peace; but, giving him the benefit of the doubt, they concluded that the objection must be to the 'form of the proposal'. 'Perhaps', added Sir Edward Goschen, 'he himself could be induced to suggest lines on which he would find it possible to work with us.'[70] The next day the same idea was pressed by Sir Edward Grey upon Prince Lichnowsky:—

> 'The whole idea of mediation or mediating influence was ready to be
> put into operation by any method that Germany could suggest if mine
> was not acceptable.'[71]

But owing to German dilatoriness in this matter, events had by then gone so far that the very gravest questions had arisen for this country.

With the refusal of the German Government to propose a form of mediation acceptable to themselves before graver events had occurred, the first period of the negotiation comes to an end. The responsibility of rejecting a conference, which, by staving off the evil day, might have preserved the peace of Europe, falls solely on the shoulders of Germany. The reasons advanced by Herr von Jagow were erroneous, and though Dr. von Bethmann–Hollweg, the Imperial Chancellor, was more conciliatory and sympathetic, it may be noted that the German White Book[72] continues to misrepresent Sir Edward Grey's proposal as a conference on the particular question of the Austro–Servian dispute, and not on the general situation of Europe.

In the period that follows come spasmodic attempts at negotiation by direct conversations between the parties concerned, with no advantage, but rather with the growth of mutual suspicion. Down to August 1st both Sir Edward Grey and M. Sazonof were busy trying to find some formula which might be accepted as a basis for postponing hostilities between the Great Powers. And here it may be well to point out that Prince Lichnowsky seems to have been left in the dark by his chiefs. On July 24th, the day after the Austrian note was presented, he was so little acquainted with the true state of affairs, that speaking privately he told Sir Edward Grey 'that a reply favourable on some points must be sent at once by Servia, so that an excuse against immediate action might be afforded to Austria'.[73] And in the matter of the conference, on the very day that Herr von Jagow was making his excuses against entering the proposed conference, Prince Lichnowsky informed Sir Edward Grey, that the German Government accepted in principle mediation between Austria and Russia by the four Powers, reserving, of course, their right as an ally to help Austria if attacked.[74] The mutual incompatibility of the two voices of Germany was pointed out from Rome, where the Marquis di San Giuliano, the Italian Foreign Minister, attempted a reconciliation between them, on information received from Berlin, that 'the difficulty was rather the "conference" than the principle'.[75] But we may ask whether Herr von Jagow's reply to Sir Edward Goschen does not really show that the whole principle of a conference was objected to, seeing that he said that such a 'conference was not practicable', and that 'it would be best to await the outcome of the exchange of views between the Austrian and Russian Governments'.[76] But, if it was not the principle that was objected to, but only the form, where are we? We can do nothing else but assume that the German Government objected to the terms employed by Sir Edward Grey, and that for the sake of a mere quibble they wasted time until other events made the catastrophe inevitable. Impartiality will have to judge whether such action was deliberate or not; whether in this case also it is crime or folly which has to be laid at the door of the

German Government.

The proposed conference having been rejected by Germany, an attempt was then made by several Powers to invite Austria to suspend military action. Although Count Mensdorff, the Austrian Ambassador in London, had made on July 25th a distinction between military preparations and military operations, and had urged that his Government had only the former then in view, it was reported two days later from Rome that there were great doubts 'whether Germany would be willing to invite Austria to suspend military action pending the conference'. Even if she had been willing to do so, it is very doubtful whether, in view of the Austrian declaration of war against Servia on July 28th, and the simultaneous Austrian decree for general mobilization, the position of Europe could have been improved, for on July 29th that declaration was followed by news of the Russian mobilization of the southern districts of Odessa, Kiev, Moscow, and Kazan.[77]

Now the German Secretary of State had argued that 'if Russia mobilized against Germany, latter would have to follow suit'. On being asked what he meant by 'mobilizing against Germany', he said that

> 'if Russia mobilized in the South, Germany would not mobilize, but
> if she mobilized in the north, Germany would have to do so too, and
> Russian system of mobilization was so complicated that it might be
> difficult exactly to locate her mobilization. Germany would
> therefore have to be very careful not to be taken by surprise.'[78]

This was on July 27th, and it cannot be said to have been unreasonable. But when on July 29th Russia mobilized the southern districts no grounds for German mobilization had yet been provided. No secret was made about this mobilization by the Russian Ambassador at Berlin,[79] but it is perhaps as well to point out here the remark made by Sir George Buchanan, the British Ambassador at St. Petersburg, about the language used by his German colleague concerning the mobilization of the four southern districts: 'He accused the Russian Government of endangering the peace of Europe by their mobilization, and said, when I referred to all that had recently been done by Austria, that he could not discuss such matters.'[80] It would perhaps be rash to assume that the German Ambassador, Count Pourtales, used such language to his home Government, for there is no evidence of it in the German White Book. What dispatches appear there from the German Embassy at St. Petersburg are refreshingly honest. The military attache says, 'I deem it certain that mobilization has been ordered for Kiev and Odessa'. He adds: 'it is doubtful at Warsaw and Moscow, and improbable elsewhere'.[81]

There was therefore, according to the evidence produced by the Germans themselves, no mobilization 'against Germany'. The only thing that looks at all like hostile action is contained in the news sent by the Imperial German Consul at Kovno on July 27th, that a 'state of war' (*Kriegszustand*) had been proclaimed in that district. But this is a very different thing from mobilization; it was almost bound to follow in the northern provinces of the Empire as the result of mobilization elsewhere. At any rate the Consul at Kovno announced it on July 27th before any Russian mobilization at all had taken place, and the fact that Germany did not instantly mobilize shows that at the end of July that Government did not consider *Kriegszustand* in Kovno to be equivalent to 'mobilization against Germany'.

Opinion in Berlin seems to have been that Russia would not make war. Perhaps there was no real fear that Russia would take an aggressive attitude, for many people believed that 'Russia neither wanted, nor was in a position to make war'.[82] This attitude of mind was known and deplored in Rome, where the Marquis di San Giuliano said 'there seemed to be a difficulty in making Germany believe that Russia was in earnest'.[83] Such an opinion seems to have been shared by Count Pourtales, who on July 29 reported that the German Government were willing to guarantee that Servian integrity would be respected by Austria. This was held to be insufficient, as Servia might thus become an Austrian vassal, and there would be a revolution in Russia if she were to tolerate such a state of affairs. The next day the Russian Minister for Foreign Affairs told the British and French Ambassadors 'that absolute proof was in the possession of the Russian Government that Germany was making military and naval preparations against Russia—more particularly in the direction of the Gulf of Finland'.[84]

After this, is it difficult to see how German statesmen regarded the situation? Russia, in their eyes, was playing a game of bluff, and strong measures against her were in the interest of Germany. But, though under no illusion as to German preparations, M. Sazonof offered on July 30 to stop all military preparations if Austria 'would eliminate from her ultimatum to Servia points which violate the principle of the sovereignty of Servia'.[85] 'Preparations for general mobilization will be proceeded with if this proposal is rejected by Austria,' wrote Sir George Buchanan.[86] The next day he reported to Sir Edward Grey that all attempts to obtain the consent of Austria to mediation had failed,

56

and that she was moving troops against Russia as well as against Servia.[87]

Face to face therefore with war against another Power, Russia ordered a general mobilization.[88] This was answered on the same day by a proclamation of *Kriegsgefahr* at Berlin, 'as it can only be against Germany that Russian general mobilization is directed'.[89]

Thus on Friday, July 31st, the situation had come to be this, that Russia, feeling herself threatened by the military preparations of Austria and Germany, decided to issue orders for a general mobilization.[90] Meanwhile Sir Edward Grey still clung to the hope that mediation with a view to safeguarding Austrian interests as against Servia might yet be accepted.[91] But his efforts were useless, for Germany had launched an ultimatum (July 31) to Russia, demanding demobilization. As Sir Edward Goschen pointed out, the demand was made 'even more difficult for Russia to accept by asking them to demobilize in the south as well'.[92] The only explanation actually vouchsafed was that this had been asked to prevent Russia pleading that all her mobilization was only directed against Austria. Such a quibble, when such interests are at stake, seems to call for severe comment.

War between the three empires seemed now inevitable, for though the Emperor of Russia and the German Emperor had exchanged telegrams each imploring the other to find a way out of the difficulty, and each saying that matters had gone so far that neither could grant the other's demands,[93] the officials at Berlin were now taking up the position that 'Russia's mobilization had spoilt everything'.[94] This attitude is as inexplicable as it proved disastrous. For it appears that on July 31 Austria and Russia were ready to resume conversations. The Austrians, apparently alarmed at the prospect of a general war, were ready to discuss the substance of the Austrian ultimatum to Servia, and Russia announced that under certain conditions 'she would undertake to preserve her waiting attitude'.[95] Having issued her ultimatum to Russia, Germany naturally mobilized, but what kind of diplomacy is this in which, with the principals both ready to negotiate, a third party issues an ultimatum couched in such terms that a proud country can give but one answer?

The sequence of events seems to be as follows. Austria mobilized against Servia. Russia, rightly or wrongly, took this as a threat to herself, and mobilized all her southern forces against Austria. Then Germany threatened to mobilize unless Russia ceased her military preparations—an inexcusable step, which increased Russia's apprehensions of a general war, and made a general Russian mobilization inevitable.[96] If Russia was the first to mobilize, she took this step in consequence of German threats. We repeat that in spite of the three empires taking this action, discussion was still possible between Russia and Austria,[97] and might have had good results. In fact, the situation was not irretrievable, if Germany had not rendered it so by issuing her ultimatum to Russia. Once again we may ask, was this crime or folly?

II

Germany's attitude to France.

We must now turn our eyes to the West of Europe, and observe the diplomacy of Germany with regard to France and Great Britain. On the 27th of July we are told that the German Government received 'the first intimation concerning the preparatory measures taken by France: the 14th Corps discontinued the manoeuvres and returned to its garrison'.[98] Will it be believed that, except for the assertion 'of rapidly progressing preparations of France, both on water and on land',[99] this is the only shred of evidence that the Germans have produced to prove the aggressive intentions of France? And it may be worth while to point out that on July 29, when the German White Book says that Berlin heard of the 'rapidly progressing preparations of France', the French Ambassador at Berlin informed the Secretary of State that 'they had done nothing more than the German Government had done, namely, recalled the officers on leave'.[100]

The very next day the French Government had 'reliable information that the German troops are concentrated round Thionville and Metz ready for war',[101] and before July 30th German patrols twice penetrated into French territory.[102] With great forbearance the French Government withdrew its troops ten kilometres from the frontier; and, although German reservists had been recalled from abroad 'by tens of thousands', the French Government had not called out a single reservist. Well might the French Minister for Foreign Affairs say 'Germany has done it'.[103]

Having thus invaded France before July 30th, the German Government presented an ultimatum (July 31) demanding what were the French intentions, and on August 1st the French Government replied that it would consult its own interests.[104]

III

Why We Are At War

The Question of British Neutrality.

Even then, nothing had happened to bring this country into the quarrel. If Germany were making war primarily on Russia, and France were only involved as the auxiliary of Russia, Germany would have acted rapidly against Russia, and would have stood on the defensive against France; and England would not have been dragged into war.[105] The question of British neutrality first appears in the British White Book on July 25th, when Sir Edward Grey, in a note to Sir George Buchanan, said: 'if war does take place, the development of other issues may draw us into it, and I am therefore anxious to prevent it'.[106] Two days later he wrote again:—

> 'I have been told by the Russian Ambassador that in German and
> Austrian circles impression prevails that in any event we would
> stand aside ... This impression ought, as I have pointed out, to be
> dispelled by the orders we have given to the First Fleet ... not to
> disperse for manoeuvre leave. But ... my reference to it must not be
> taken to mean that anything more than diplomatic action was
> promised.'[107]

On the 29th the question of our neutrality was seriously discussed at both the Courts of St. James and Berlin independently. Sir Edward Grey, in an interview with Prince Lichnowsky, told him 'he did not wish the Ambassador to be misled ... into thinking we should stand aside'. Developing this, Sir Edward Grey solemnly warned the German Ambassador that

> 'there was no question of our intervening if Germany was not
> involved, or even if France was not involved, but if the issue did
> become such that we thought British interests required us to
> intervene, we must intervene at once, and the decision would have to
> be very rapid.... But ... I did not wish to be open to any reproach
> from him that the friendly tone of all our conversations had misled
> him or his Government into supposing that we should not take
> action.'[108]

Before the news of this had reached Berlin the Imperial Chancellor had made his notorious 'bid for British neutrality' on July 29:—

Why We Are At War

'He said it was clear, so far as he was able to judge the main
principle which governed British policy, that Great Britain would
never stand by and allow France to be crushed in any conflict there
might be. That, however, was not the object at which Germany aimed.
Provided that neutrality of Great Britain were certain, every
assurance would be given to the British Government that the Imperial
Government aimed at no territorial acquisitions at the expense of
France, should they prove victorious in any war that might ensue.

'I questioned his Excellency about the French colonies, and he said
he was unable to give a similar undertaking in that respect. As
regards Holland ... so long as Germany's adversaries respected the
integrity and neutrality of the Netherlands, Germany was ready to
give His Majesty's Government an assurance that she would do
likewise. It depended on the action of France what operations
Germany might be forced to enter upon in Belgium, but when the war
was over, Belgian integrity would be respected if she had not sided
against Germany.'[109]

This request was at once repudiated (July 30) by the British Government:—

'His Majesty's Government cannot for one moment entertain the
Chancellor's proposal that they should bind themselves to neutrality
on such terms.

'What he asks us in effect is to engage to stand by while French
colonies are taken and France is beaten so long as Germany does not
take French territory as distinct from the colonies.

'From the material point of view the proposal is unacceptable, for
France, without further territory in Europe being taken from her,
could be so crushed as to lose her position as a Great Power and
become subordinate to German policy.

'Altogether apart from that, it would be a disgrace for us to make
this bargain with Germany at the expense of France, a disgrace from

which the good name of this country would never recover.

'The Chancellor also in effect asks us to bargain away whatever
obligation or interest we have as regards the neutrality of Belgium.
We could not entertain that bargain either.[110]

He continued by saying that Great Britain must keep her hands absolutely free and hinted
at some scheme for preventing anti–German aggression by the Powers of the Triple
Entente:—

'If the peace of Europe can be preserved, and the present crisis
safely passed, my own endeavour will be to promote some arrangement
to which Germany could be a party, by which she could be assured
that no aggressive or hostile policy would be pursued against her or
her allies by France, Russia, and ourselves, jointly or separately
... The idea has hitherto been too Utopian to form the subject of
definite proposals, but if this crisis ... be safely passed, I am
hopeful that the relief and reaction which will follow will make
possible some more definite rapprochement between the Powers than
has been possible hitherto.'

Thus two points were made clear: we were seriously concerned that France should not be
crushed, and that the neutrality of Belgium should not be violated. It is interesting to note
how this extremely serious warning was received by Dr. von Bethmann–Hollweg:—'His
Excellency was so taken up with the news of the Russian measures along the frontier ...
that he received your communication without a comment.'[111]

But the text of the reply was left with him, so that he could scarcely complain that no
warning had been given to him.

With the data at our disposal, it is not possible to make any deduction as to the effect
which this warning had upon Berlin; but it may be remarked that at Rome that day, the
Marquis di San Giuliano told Sir Rennell Rodd that he had

'good reason to believe that Germany was now disposed to give more
conciliatory advice to Austria, as she seemed convinced that we

should act with France and Russia, and was most anxious to avoid
issue with us.'[112]

As this telegraphic dispatch was not received till the next day, it is not impossible that the
Italian Minister gave this information to Sir Rennell Rodd late in the day, after having
received news from Berlin sent under the impression made by Sir Edward Grey's
warning.

Such an impression, if it ever existed, must have been of short duration, for when the
British Government demanded both of France and Germany whether they were 'prepared
to engage to respect neutrality of Belgium so long as no other Power violates it',[113] the
French gave an unequivocal promise the same day,[114] while the German answer is a
striking contrast:—

'I have seen Secretary of State, who informs me that he must consult
the Emperor and the Chancellor before he can possibly answer. I
gathered from what he said that he thought any reply they might give
could not but disclose a certain amount of their plan of campaign in
the event of war ensuing, and he was therefore very doubtful whether
they would return any answer at all. His Excellency, nevertheless,
took note of your request.

'It appears from what he said that German Government considers that
certain hostile acts have already been committed in Belgium. As an
instance of this, he alleged that a consignment of corn for Germany
had been placed under an embargo already.'[115]

It was now clear that a violation of Belgian neutrality was a contingency that would have
to be faced, and Prince Lichnowsky was warned the next day that 'the neutrality of
Belgium affected feeling in this country', and he was asked to obtain an assurance from
the German Government similar to that given by France:—

'If there were a violation of the neutrality of Belgium by one
combatant, while the other respected it, it would be extremely
difficult to restrain public feeling in this country.'[116]

The Ambassador then, on his own personal responsibility and without authority from his Government, tried to exact a promise that Great Britain would remain neutral 'if Germany gave a promise not to violate Belgian neutrality', but Sir Edward Grey was bound to refuse such an offer, seeing that it left out of account all question of an attack on France and her colonies, about which it had been stated already that there could be no bargaining. Even the guarantee of the integrity of France and her colonies was suggested, but again Sir Edward Grey was bound to refuse, for the reasons he gave to Sir Edward Goschen in rejecting what is now known as Dr. von Bethmann–Hollweg's 'infamous proposal', namely, that France without actually losing territory might be so crushed as to lose her position as a Great Power, and become subordinate to German policy. And if there should be still any doubt about Sir Edward Grey's policy at this moment, we would refer to his statement in the House of Commons on August 27.[117] The important points are that the offers of August 1 were made on the sole responsibility of Prince Lichnowsky, and without authority from his Government; that the Cabinet on August 2 carefully discussed the conditions on which we might remain neutral, and that, on August 3, so far was the German Ambassador from guaranteeing the neutrality of Belgium that he actually had to ask Sir Edward Grey 'not to make the neutrality of Belgium one of our conditions'. Whatever Prince Lichnowsky may have said privately on August 1, the one fact certain is that two days later the German Government were making no concessions on that point; on the contrary they were asking us to withdraw from a position we had taken up on July 30, four days before.

One more effort to preserve peace in Western Europe seems to have been made by Sir Edward Grey. On the telephone he asked Prince Lichnowsky whether, if France remained neutral, Germany would promise not to attack her. The impression seems to have prevailed in Berlin that this was an offer to guarantee French neutrality by the force of British arms, and the German Emperor in his telegram to the King gave evidence of the relief His Imperial Majesty felt at the prospect that the good relations between the two countries would be maintained. Unfortunately for such hopes, France had never been consulted in the matter, nor was there ever any idea of coercing France into neutrality, and even the original proposal had to be abandoned on consideration as unpractical.[118]

Events now marched rapidly. While the Cabinet in London were still discussing whether a violation of Belgian neutrality would be an occasion for war, the news came of the violation of that of Luxemburg. Sir Edward Grey informed M. Cambon[119] that Lord Stanley and Lord Clarendon in 1867 had agreed to a 'collective guarantee' by which it was not intended that every Power was bound single–handed to fight any Government which violated Luxemburg. Although this gross disregard by the Germans of their solemn pledge did not entail the same consequences as the subsequent violation of Belgian neutrality, it is equally reprehensible from the point of view of international law, and the more cowardly in proportion as this state is weaker than Belgium. Against this intrusion Luxemburg protested, but, unlike Belgium, she did not appeal to the Powers.[120]

Two days later, August 4th, the King of the Belgians appealed to the King for 'diplomatic intervention to safeguard the integrity of Belgium'.[121] The German Government had issued an ultimatum to the Belgian, asking for

'a free passage through Belgian territory, and promising to maintain
the independence and integrity of the kingdom and its possessions at
the conclusion of peace, threatening in case of refusal to treat
Belgium as an enemy. An answer was requested within twelve
hours'.[122]

Sir Edward Grey instructed the British Ambassador to protest against this violation of a treaty to which Germany in common with ourselves was a party, and to ask an assurance that the demand made upon Belgium would not be proceeded with. At the same time the Belgian Government was told to resist German aggression by all the means in its power, as Great Britain was prepared to join France and Russia to maintain the independence and integrity of Belgium.[123] On receipt of the protest of Sir Edward Grey, it would seem that Herr von Jagow made one more desperate effort to bid for British neutrality: 'Germany will, under no pretence whatever, annex Belgian territory': to pass through Belgium was necessary because the 'German army could not be exposed to French attack across Belgium, which was planned according to absolutely unimpeachable information'. It was for Germany 'a question of life and death to prevent French advance'.[124] But matters had gone too far: that day (August 4) the Germans violated Belgian territory at Gemmenich, and thereupon the British demand to Germany to respect Belgian neutrality, issued earlier in the day, was converted into an ultimatum:—

'We hear that Germany has addressed note to Belgian Minister for
Foreign Affairs stating that German Government will be compelled to
carry out, if necessary by force of arms, the measures considered

indispensable.

'We are also informed that Belgian territory has been violated at
Gemmenich.

'In these circumstances, and in view of the fact that Germany
declined to give the same assurance respecting Belgium as France
gave last week in reply to our request made simultaneously at Berlin
and Paris, we must repeat that request, and ask that a satisfactory
reply to it and to my telegram of this morning be received here by
12 o'clock to–night. If not, you are instructed to ask for your
passports, and to say that His Majesty's Government feel bound to
take all steps in their power to uphold the neutrality of Belgium
and the observance of a treaty to which Germany is as much a party
as ourselves.'[125]

The effect at Berlin was remarkable. Every sign was given of disappointment and
resentment at such a step being taken, and the 'harangue' of the Chancellor to Sir Edward
Goschen, and his astonishment at the value laid by Great Britain upon the 'scrap of paper'
of 1839 would seem, when coupled with Herr von Jagow's desperate bid for neutrality at
the last moment, to show that the German Government had counted on the neutrality of
this country and had been deeply disappointed. If these outbursts and attempts at the
eleventh hour to bargain for our neutrality were genuine efforts to keep the peace
between Great Britain and Germany, it is our belief that their origin must be found in the
highest authority in the German Empire, whom we believe, in spite of petty signs of
spitefulness exhibited since the war broke out, to have been sincerely and honestly
working in favour of European peace, against obstacles little dreamt of by our
countrymen. But certain signs are not wanting that, in the lower ranks of the German
hierarchy, war with this country had been decided on, and that Sir Edward Grey was not
far wrong when he wrote to Sir Francis Bertie on July 31, 'I believe it to be quite untrue
that our attitude has been a decisive factor in situation. German Government do not
expect our neutrality.'[126] On what other grounds than that orders had been sent out
from Berlin can the fact be explained that the German Customs authorities, three days
before the declaration of war, began detaining British ships,[127] and compulsorily
unloading cargoes of sugar from British vessels? In the former case, indeed, the ships
were ordered to be released; in the latter case, of which the complaint was made

twenty–four hours later, the reply to inquiries was the ominous statement that 'no information was to be had'.[128]

This, however, is a digression from the main question. History will doubtless attribute the outbreak of war between ourselves and Germany to the development of the Belgian question, and, we are confident, will judge that had it not been for the gratuitous attack made on a neutral country by Germany, war with Great Britain would not have ensued on August 4, 1914. The excuses put forward by the German Government for this wanton outrage on international agreements are instructive. In conversation with Sir Edward Goschen, neither Herr von Jagow nor the Chancellor urged that the French had violated the neutrality; the argument is purely and simply that the route by way of the Vosges is difficult, time is everything, and it is a matter of life and death to Germany to crush France as quickly as possible, in order that she may be able to meet the Russians before they reach the German frontier. This excuse does not seem to have been very satisfactory even to those who put it forward, though it was indubitably the real reason; so vice paid homage to virtue, and Herr von Jagow urged to Prince Lichnowsky that he had 'absolutely unimpeachable information' that the German army was exposed to French attack across Belgium. On the other hand, the Chancellor, as late as August 4th, seems to have known nothing of any such action by France; at any rate he made no mention of it in his speech to the Reichstag:—

'We are now in a state of necessity, and necessity knows no law. Our troops have occupied Luxemburg and perhaps are already on Belgian soil. Gentlemen, that is contrary to the dictates of international law. It is true that the French Government has declared at Brussels that France is willing to respect the neutrality of Belgium, as long as her opponent respects it. We knew, however, that France stood ready for invasion. France could wait but we could not wait. A French movement upon our flank upon the Lower Rhine might have been disastrous. So we were compelled to override the just protest of the Luxemburg and Belgian Governments. The wrong—I speak openly—that we are committing we will endeavour to make good as soon as our military goal has been reached. Anybody who is threatened as we are threatened, and is fighting for his highest possessions, can only have one thought—how he is to hack his way through.'[129]

In this double–faced position of the German Government, we have an example either of unsurpassed wickedness or of insurpassable folly. The violation of Belgium must have been designed either in order to bring us into the quarrel, or on the supposition that, in spite of treaties and warnings, we should yet remain neutral. Yet the foolishness of such a calculation is as nothing to that which prompted the excuse that Germany had to violate Belgian neutrality because the French were going to do so, or had done so. In such a case undoubtedly the wisest course for Germany would have been to allow the French to earn the reward of their own folly and be attacked not only by Belgium but also by Great Britain, to whom not five days before they had solemnly promised to observe the neutrality, and whom such a gross violation of the French word must indubitably have kept neutral, if it did not throw her on to the side of Germany. In regard to Belgium the Germans have indeed put forward the plea that the French had already violated its neutrality before war was declared. This plea has been like a snowball. It began with the ineffective accusation that the French were at Givet, a town in French territory, and that this constituted an attack on Germany, though how the presence of the French in a town of their own could be called a violation of their neighbour's neutrality it is difficult to see. From that it has gradually grown into a more formidable story of the French supplying a garrison to Liege. There can be little doubt that all these attempts by Herr von Jagow to claim that the French violated Belgian neutrality are another illustration of Swift's dictum to the effect that 'as universal a practice as lying is, and as easy a one as it seems', it is astonishing that it has been brought to so little perfection, 'even by those who are most celebrated in that faculty'.[130]

IV

England and Servia.

We have seen what attitude was taken by Germany in the crisis which followed upon the Serajevo murders and more definitely upon the presentation of the Austrian note. It is equally important, and to English readers at least more interesting, to realize what attitude was taken by England. Sir Edward Grey throughout maintained the position, which he was so justly praised for adopting in 1912, that England had no direct interest in Balkan disputes, but that it was her bounden duty to prevent a European conflagration. He quickly saw, what Germany would not see, that Russia was so much interested in Servia, for both political and religious reasons, that any attempt by the Austro–Hungarian Government to coerce Servia, to interfere with her territorial integrity or independence as a sovereign state, would inevitably rouse Russia to military action. For Russia had greater interests in the security of Servia than Great Britain had in the security of Belgium. In each case the Great Power was bound by honour and self–interest alike to interfere to protect the smaller Power, but Russia was also bound to Servia by racial and religious bonds. This being so, Sir Edward Grey set himself, not as the German White Book says[131] to localize the conflict, but to prevent if possible a conflict between Austria–Hungary and Servia which would inevitably involve Russia and probably other European powers. He stated his policy with the greatest clearness in the House of Commons on July 27th, but he had already acted on the lines of the policy which he then explained. On July 24th he told Count Mensdorff that he would concern himself

'with the matter simply and solely from the point of view of the
peace of Europe. The merits of the dispute between Austria and
Servia were not the concern of His Majesty's Government[132].'

In similar language, but more fully, on the same day he told the German Ambassador:—

'If the presentation of this ultimatum to Servia did not lead to
trouble between Austria and Russia, we need not concern ourselves
about it; but if Russia took the view of the Austrian ultimatum
which it seemed to me that any Power interested in Servia would
take, I should be quite powerless, in face of the terms of the
ultimatum, to exercise any moderating influence[133].'

Sir Edward Grey at once urged that the four Powers, Germany, Italy, France, and Great Britain, should act together in the interests of peace at the courts of St. Petersburg and Vienna. And he went further and tried to induce Servia to 'express concern and regret' and to 'give Austria the fullest satisfaction', 'if it is proved that Servian officials, however subordinate, were accomplices in the murders at Serajevo[134].' Further than that no British Foreign Minister could go; Sir George Buchanan correctly explained the situation to M. Sazonof when he laid stress on the need of the sanction of British public opinion[135]. Sir Edward Grey re–echoed this when he wrote:—

'I do not consider that public opinion here would or ought to
sanction our going to war over a Servian quarrel. If, however, war
does take place, the development of other issues may draw us into

it, and I am therefore anxious to prevent it.'[136]

However, matters were moving rapidly: the Servian reply[137] was presented on July 25; it was considered unsatisfactory by the Austro–Hungarian Government, and the Minister, with the Legation–staff, withdrew from Belgrade. Next day Sir Edward Grey proposed that a conference of Germany, Italy, France, and Great Britain should meet in London immediately 'for the purpose of discovering an issue which would prevent complications', and 'that all active military operations should be suspended pending results of conference'.[138] This proposal failed, as has been explained in earlier pages (pp. 71–3), and on July 28th Austria–Hungary declared war on Servia. Sir Edward Grey remained firm to his original attitude of non–intervention, and told M. Cambon that 'the dispute between Austria and Servia was not one in which we felt called to take a hand'.[139] And on the same day he declined to discuss with Count Mensdorff 'the merits of the question between Austria and Servia'.[140]

No one can doubt that Sir Edward Grey's attitude was diplomatically correct and consistent. It was also inspired by a genuine desire for peace, and stands out in sharp contrast with the 'equivocal and double–faced' policy of Germany, and with the obstinacy of Austria in refusing to permit the Powers to mediate; for it was with truth that M. Sazonof remarked that

'a refusal to prolong the term of the ultimatum would render
nugatory the proposals made by the Austro–Hungarian Government to
the Powers, and would be in contradiction to the very basis of
international relations.'[141]

V

Great Britain declines 'Solidarity' with Russia and France.

There is however another question which involves the whole foreign policy of Great Britain. Could Sir Edward Grey have prevented the war by boldly declaring at once that England would support Russia and France, if necessary by armed force? It was a policy urged on him from several quarters, and it is possible that such action might have been successful. It is to Sir Edward Grey's credit that he quietly but firmly refused to take so hazardous and unprecedented a step. Let us examine these proposals briefly. As early as

Why We Are At War

July 24th M. Sazonof 'hoped that His Majesty's Government would not fail to proclaim their solidarity with Russia and France.[142]' The French Ambassador at St. Petersburg joined in the request, and M. Sazonof pointed out that

'we would sooner or later be dragged into war if it did break out;
we should have rendered war more likely if we did not from the
outset make common cause with his country and with France[143].'

On July 30th the President of the French Republic expressed his conviction that

'peace between the Powers is in the hands of Great Britain. If His
Majesty's Government announced that England would come to the aid of
France in the event of a conflict between France and Germany, as a
result of the present differences between Austria and Servia, there
would be no war, for Germany would at once modify her
attitude[144].'

Even more important was the opinion of the Italian Minister for Foreign Affairs, whose country was a member of the Triple Alliance:—

'As Germany was really anxious for good relations with ourselves, if
she believed that Great Britain would act with Russia and France, he
thought it would have a great effect.'[145]

Such opinions must, and do, carry great weight, but Sir Edward Grey and the British Ambassadors were equally firm in withstanding them. Sir George Buchanan at once told M. Sazonof that he

'saw no reason to expect any declaration of solidarity from His
Majesty's Government that would entail an unconditional engagement
on their part to support Russia and France by force of arms'.[146]

On July 27th he met the proposal more directly by pointing out that, so far from such a policy conducing to the maintenance of peace, it would merely offend the pride of the Germans and stiffen them in their present attitude.[147] Two days later Sir Edward Grey pointed out to M. Cambon that

'even if the question became one between Austria and Russia, we
should not feel called upon to take a hand in it. It would then be a
question of the supremacy of Teuton or Slav—a struggle for
supremacy in the Balkans; and our idea had always been to avoid
being drawn into a war over a Balkan question'.[148]

That is one answer to the proposal, an answer based on history and on Britain's foreign
policy in past years. Sir Edward Grey had another answer. It was to the effect that
Germany could not, and ought to have known she could not, rely on our neutrality. For
when the Russian Ambassador told him that an impression prevailed in German and
Austrian circles that in any event England would stand aside, he pointed out that

'this impression ought to be dispelled by the orders we have given
to the First Fleet, which is concentrated, as it happens, at
Portland, not to disperse for manoeuvre leave'.[149]

The situation continued to develop unfavourably for the cause of peace owing to the
Austrian declaration of war on Servia, and the consequent mobilizations in Russia,
Germany, and France. On July 31st Sir Edward Grey said:—

'I believe it to be quite untrue that our attitude has been a
decisive factor in situation. German Government do not expect our
neutrality.'[150]

It is not quite clear that Sir Edward Grey's belief was justified. England's attitude may
have been an important factor in the situation, but still in our opinion Sir Edward Grey
was not only right in refusing to commit England to a new Continental policy, but could
not, with due observance of constitutional usages, have taken any other course. Again, it
is doubtful whether the German Government did or did not rely on our neutrality. The
German Chancellor and the German Secretary for Foreign Affairs later affected great
surprise at our action. Germany, however, as we have shown above (p. 82), had been
plainly warned by Sir Edward Grey on July 29th[151] that she could not rely on our
remaining neutral under all circumstances.

Whether Sir Edward Grey was right or wrong in his estimate of Germany's prudence is a
small matter; what is important is that his action was throughout perfectly straightforward

and consistent. And unquestionably he had a very difficult part to play. The near East was like a blazing rick surrounded by farm buildings; Germany was, if not stirring up the conflagration, certainly not attempting to pour water on the flames, while Austria, possibly—and even probably[152] with Germany's knowledge, would allow no one to make the attempt.

It would have aided the Austrian cause more effectively in Europe and elsewhere, if the Government had communicated[153] 'the *dossier* elucidating the Servian intrigues and the connexion between these intrigues and the murder of 28th June', which it said it held at the disposal of the British Government.[154] For even Count Mensdorff 'admitted that, on paper, the Servian reply might seem to be satisfactory'.[155]

To judge whether the Servian reply was satisfactory, it was, and is, necessary to examine the evidence on which the Austro–Hungarian Government based the accusations formulated in its note of July 23rd. But even assuming that the Austrian charges were true, as the German White Book says they are,[156] it is only a stronger reason for allowing the Powers to examine this evidence; and it does not explain the persistent refusal,[157] until July 31st,[158] to permit any negotiations on the basis of the Servian reply.

Such being the situation, it is very difficult to see what more Sir Edward Grey could have done to prevent the outbreak of war between Austria–Hungary and Servia, which did inevitably, as he foresaw from the first, drag in other nations. He urged Servia to moderation and even to submission; he tried to induce the four Powers to mediate jointly at St. Petersburg and Vienna; he proposed a conference of the four Powers to prevent further complications; he did everything in his power to restrain Russia from immediate armed support of Servia; he declined to join Russia and France in eventual military action; and even up to the violation of the neutrality of Belgium he still strove to avert the horrors of war from Europe.

VI

Italy's comments on the situation.

We have already shown (Chap. II) how Italy became a member of the Triple Alliance, and how, in spite of its apparent frailty and of the somewhat divergent aims of its members, that alliance has endured for thirty–two years. It remains to consider what policy Italy adopted in the critical situation created by the presentation of the Austro–Hungarian note to Servia, and to appreciate the significance of that policy. It is supremely significant that Italy, though a member of the Triple Alliance, was not consulted about the terms of the Austrian note to Servia; that she worked persistently side by side with England in endeavouring to prevent an outbreak of war, and, when that failed, to induce the states actually at war, or on the brink of war, to suspend all military operations in order to give diplomatic intervention an opportunity; and it is equally significant that, when the great war broke out, Italy remained neutral, in spite of the pressure from her allies and the tempting bait of a share of the spoil, which, it is said, is even now being offered to her.[159] This is but a bald description of Italy's policy, but it can be substantiated in detail from official documents. As early as July 25th the Italian Ambassador in a conversation with Sir Edward Grey 'made no secret of the fact that Italy was desirous to see war avoided',[160] and he cordially approved the idea of mediation by the four Powers. Two days later Italy again approved the proposed conference of four to be held immediately in London. The Italian Foreign Minister promised to recommend most strongly to the German Government the idea of asking Russia, Austria, and Servia to suspend military operations pending the result of the conference, and went even further in undertaking to ask what procedure Germany thought most likely to be successful at Vienna.[161] He thought it very doubtful whether Germany would consent to ask Austria to suspend military operations, but made a further suggestion that

'Servia may be induced to accept note in its entirety on the advice of the four Powers invited to the conference, and this would enable her to say that she had yielded to Europe and not to Austria–Hungary alone'.[162]

Next day the Marquis di San Giuliano called attention to a point in Servia's reply to Austria which might form a starting–point for mediation.[163] On July 29th he tried to get over Germany's objection to the idea of a 'Conference' by suggesting adherence to the idea of an exchange of views in London.[164] Next day he added to this the practical suggestion that

'Germany might invite Austria to state exactly the terms which she would demand from Servia, and give a guarantee that she would neither deprive her of independence, nor annex territory.... We

might, on the other hand, ascertain from Russia what she would
accept, and, once we knew the standpoints of these two countries,
discussions could be commenced at once.'[165]

Moreover the Italian Ambassador at Vienna, in the hope of pacifying Russia, made the useful suggestion that Austria should

'convert into a binding engagement to Europe the declaration which
has been made at St. Petersburg to the effect that she desires
neither to destroy the independence of Servia, nor to acquire
Servian territory'.[166]

All efforts to preserve peace proved futile; Germany delivered her ultimatum to France and to Russia. Then arose the question, what was Italy to do? The answer to this was given by the Italian Foreign Minister:—

'The war undertaken by Austria, and the consequences which might
result, had, in the words of the German Ambassador himself, an
aggressive object. Both were therefore in conflict with the purely
defensive character of the Triple Alliance; in such circumstances
Italy would remain neutral.'[167]

The German White Book says 'Russia began the war on us'[168] and 'France opened hostilities'[169]; if these statements were true, Italy would have been obliged, if she were to remain faithful to her engagements, to take part in the war side by side with her colleagues of the Triple Alliance. Impartial readers can draw their own conclusions.

NOTE

Austro—Hungarian note to Servia, and Servia's reply.

On July 23rd the Austro—Hungarian Government presented an ultimatum to Servia, demanding unconditional acceptance within 48 hours, an ultimatum which the *Temps* next day described as 'unprecedented in its arrogance and in the extravagance of its demands'. Of it Sir Edward Grey said:—

Why We Are At War

'I had never before seen one State address to another independent
State a document of so formidable a character. Demand No. 5 would be
hardly consistent with the maintenance of Servia's independent
sovereignty, if it were to mean, as it seemed that it might, that
Austria–Hungary was to be invested with a right to appoint officials
who would have authority within the frontiers of Servia.'[170]

It may be true, as the Austrian Ambassador explained,[171] that the Austro–Hungarian
Government did not intend this step to be regarded as an ultimatum, but as a *demarche*
with a time–limit.

In this extraordinary document[172] the Austro–Hungarian Government demanded:—

A. That Servia should publish on the front page of its 'Official Gazette', and in the
'Official Bulletin' of the Army, and should communicate to the Army as the order of the
day a declaration

(1) condemning Serb propaganda against Austria–Hungary;

(2) regretting that Servian officers and functionaries participated in the propaganda;

(3) promising to proceed with the utmost rigour against persons who may be guilty of
such machinations.

B. That Servia should undertake

(1) to suppress any publication inciting to hatred and contempt of Austria–Hungary;

(2) to dissolve the society styled Narodna Odbrana and similar societies and to confiscate
their means of propaganda;

(3) to eliminate from public instruction in Servia all teachers and all methods of
instruction responsible for fomenting opinion against Austria–Hungary;

(4) to remove from the military service and from the administration all officers and
functionaries guilty of such propaganda, whose names and deeds the Austro–Hungarian

Government reserved to itself the right of communicating;

(5) to accept the collaboration in Servia of representatives of Austria–Hungary in the suppression of the subversive anti–Austrian movement;

(6) to take judicial proceedings against accessories to the Serajevo plot, with the co–operation of Austro–Hungarian delegates;

(7) to proceed immediately to the arrest of Major Voija Tankositch and of Milan Ciganovitch, a Servian State employe, who have been compromised by the results of the inquiry at Serajevo;

(8) to stop co–operation of Servian authorities in illicit traffic in arms and explosives, and to dismiss and punish those officials who helped the perpetrators of the Serajevo crime;

(9) to explain the unjustifiable utterances of high Servian officials, at home and abroad, after the Serajevo crime.

On July 25th the Servian reply[173] was presented to the Austro–Hungarian Government. Even to a reader with Austrian sympathies this reply seems to go a long way towards meeting the demands. The Servian Government agreed

A. that Servia should, as demanded, publish a declaration

(1) condemning all propaganda which may be directed against Austria–Hungary;

(2) regretting that, according to the communication from the Imperial and Royal Government, Servian officers and officials participated in the propaganda;

(3) promising to proceed with the utmost rigour against all persons who are guilty of such acts.

B. That Servia would undertake

(1) to introduce a provision into the press law providing for the most severe punishment of incitement to hatred and contempt of Austria–Hungary and to introduce an amendment

to the Constitution providing for the confiscation of such publications;

(2) to dissolve the Narodna Odbrana and similar societies;

(3) to remove at once from their public educational establishments all that serves or could serve to foment propaganda, whenever the Austro–Hungarian Government furnish them with facts and proofs of this propaganda;

(4) to remove from military service all such persons as the judicial inquiry may have proved to be guilty of acts directed against the territorial integrity of Austria–Hungary;

(5) though they do not clearly grasp the meaning or the scope of the demand, to accept the collaboration of Austro–Hungarian officials so far as is consistent with the principle of international law, with criminal procedure and with good neighbourly relations;

(6) to take judicial proceedings against accessories to the Serajevo plot; but they cannot admit the co-operation of Austro–Hungarian officials, as it would be a violation of the Constitution and of the law of criminal procedure;

(7) On this they remark that Major Tankositch was arrested as soon as the note was presented, and that it has not been possible to arrest Ciganovitch, who is an Austro–Hungarian subject, but had been employed (on probation) by the directorate of railways;

(8) to reinforce and extend the measures for preventing illicit traffic of arms and explosives across the frontier;

(9) to give explanations of the remarks made by Servian officials, as soon as the Austro–Hungarian Government have communicated the passages and as soon as they have shown that the remarks were actually made by the said officials.

The Austro–Hungarian Government regarded this reply as unsatisfactory and inadequate; they withdrew their Minister from Belgrade the same evening, and on July 28th declared war on Servia. Meanwhile they published a long official explanation[174] of the grounds on which the Servian reply was considered inadequate; in it they criticized and found unsatisfactory every single article of the reply, except that to demand No. 8. It is not worth while to analyze the whole of this; one sample may be sufficient. Sir Edward Grey commented on demand No. 5 and pointed out[175] that it

'would be hardly consistent with the maintenance of Servia's independent sovereignty, if it were to mean, as it seemed that it might, that Austria–Hungary was to be invested with a right to appoint officials who would have authority within the frontiers of Servia.'

Obviously he was in doubt about the meaning and scope of this demand, and the next was equally vague. The Servian reply to these two demands was necessarily guarded: yet the Austro–Hungarian Government treated this as deliberate misrepresentation:—

'The international law, as well as the criminal law, has nothing to do with this question; it is purely a matter of the nature of state police which is to be solved by way of a special agreement. The reserved attitude of Servia is therefore incomprehensible, and on account of its vague general form it would lead to unbridgeable difficulties.

...

'If the Servian Government misunderstands us here, this is done deliberately, for it must be familiar with the difference between "enquete judiciaire" and simple police researches. As it desired to escape from every control of the investigation which would yield, if correctly carried out, highly undesirable results for it, and as it possesses no means to refuse in a plausible manner the co–operation of our officials (precedents for such police intervention exist in great number), it tries to justify its refusal by showing up our demands as impossible.'[176]

It would have been fairer to Servia to assume that there had been a genuine misunderstanding, and that the explanation here given by Austria might prove satisfactory to Servia, as the Italian Minister for Foreign Affairs suggested.[177] The persistent refusal of Austria–Hungary to permit any discussion on the basis of the Servian reply goes far to justify Sir Maurice de Bunsen's impression

'that the Austro–Hungarian note was so drawn up as to make war inevitable, that their Government are fully resolved to have war with Servia, that they consider their position as a Great Power to be at stake, and that until punishment has been administered to Servia it is unlikely that they will listen to proposals of mediation'.[178]

Notes:

[Footnote 57: *Correspondence respecting the European Crisis*, No. 2. Sir E. Goschen to Sir E. Grey, July 22, 1914.]

[Footnote 58: German White Book, p. 4.]

[Footnote 59: *Correspondence*, No. 10. Sir E. Grey to Sir F. Bertie, July 24.]

[Footnote 60: *Correspondence*, No. 18. Sir H. Rumbold to Sir E. Grey, July 25.]

[Footnote 61: Ibid. No. 32. Sir M. de Bunsen to Sir E. Grey, July 26. See also German White Book, p. 5.]

[Footnote 62: Ibid. No. 54. M. Sazonof to Count Benckendorff, July 15/28, 1914 (communicated by Count Benckendorff, July 28).]

[Footnote 63: *Correspondence*, No. 139. Sir G. Buchanan to Sir E. Grey, August 1.]

[Footnote 64: *Ibid*. No. 141. Sir M. de Bunsen to Sir E. Grey, August 1.]

[Footnote 65: *Ibid*. No. 71. Sir E. Goschen to Sir E. Grey, July 28.]

[Footnote 66: *Correspondence*, No. 94. Sir M. de Bunsen to Sir E. Grey, July 29.]

[Footnote 67: German White Book, p. 4 (see *infra* Appendix I).]

[Footnote 68: *Ibid*. No. 36. Sir E. Grey to Sir F. Bertie, Sir H. Rumbold, and Sir R. Rodd, July 26.]

[Footnote 69: *Correspondence*, No. 43. Sir E. Goschen to Sir E. Grey, July 27.]

[Footnote 70: *Ibid*. No. 60. Sir E. Goschen to Sir E. Grey, July 28.]

[Footnote 71: *Ibid*. No. 84. Sir E. Grey to Sir E. Goschen, July 29.]

[Footnote 72: p. 8 and Exhibit 12 (see *infra* Appendix I).]

[Footnote 73: *Correspondence*, No. 11. Sir E. Grey to Sir II. Rumbold, July 24.]

[Footnote 74: *Correspondence*, No. 46. Sir E. Grey to Sir E. Goschen, July 27.]

[Footnote 75: Ibid. No. 80. Sir R. Rodd to Sir E. Grey, July 29.]

[Footnote 76: Ibid. No. 43. Sir E. Goschen to Sir E. Grey, July 27.]

[Footnote 77: Although the German White Book attempts to make out that Russia mobilized on July 26th, it produces no evidence more satisfactory than the information of the German Imperial attache in Russia, whose account of the Russian military preparations supports only in part the allegations made at Berlin. See German White Book, Exhibits 6 and 7; also *Correspondence*, No. 78, Sir G. Buchanan to Sir E. Grey, July 29. For the Austrian decree of general mobilization, see the Russian Orange Book No. 47 (*infra* in Appendix VI).]

[Footnote 78: *Correspondence*, No. 43. Sir E. Goschen to Sir E. Grey, July 27.]

[Footnote 79: *Ibid*. No. 76. The same to the same, July 29.]

[Footnote 80: *Correspondence*, No. 78. Sir George Buchanan to Sir E. Grey, July 29, 1914.]

[Footnote 81: German White Book, p. 38, and Exhibit No. 7, July 26.]

[Footnote 82: *Correspondence*, No. 71. Sir E. Goschen to Sir E. Grey, July 28. See also quotation in *Times* of July 29, p. 8, col. 2, from the *Militaer–Wochenblatt*: 'The fighting power of Russia is usually over–estimated, and numbers are far less decisive than *moral*, the higher command, armaments.... All military preparations for war, of whatever sort, have been taken with that attention to detail and that order which marks Germany. It can therefore be said, without exaggeration, that Germany can face the advent of grave events with complete calm, trusting to God and her own might.']

[Footnote 83: *Correspondence*, No. 80. Sir R. Rodd to Sir E. Grey, July 29.]

[Footnote 84: *Ibid*. No. 97. Sir G. Buchanan to Sir E. Grey, July 30. Cf. Russian Orange Book, Nos. 61, 62 (*infra* in Appendix VI).]

[Footnote 85: *Ibid*.]

[Footnote 86: *Correspondence*, No. 97. Sir G. Buchanan to Sir E. Grey, July 30.]

[Footnote 87: *Ibid*. No. 113. Sir G. Buchanan to Sir E. Grey, July 31.]

[Footnote 88: *Ibid*.]

[Footnote 89: *Ibid*. No. 112. Sir E. Goschen to Sir E. Grey, July 31.]

[Footnote 90: *Ibid*. No. 113, *ut sup*. On August 1 *The Times* published a semi–official telegram from Berlin, dated Eydtkuhnen, July 31, that 'the second and third Russian cavalry divisions are on the frontier between Wirballen, Augustof, and Allenstein'.]

[Footnote 91: *Ibid*. No. 111. Sir E. Grey to Sir E. Goschen, July 31.]

[Footnote 92: *Ibid*. No. 121. Sir E. Goschen to Sir E. Grey, July 31.]

[Footnote 93: See German White Book, pp. 12 and 13, and Exhibits 20, 21, 22, 23, 23a (see *infra* Appendix I).]

[Footnote 94: *Correspondence*, No. 121. Sir E. Goschen to Sir E. Grey, July 31.]

[Footnote 95: *Ibid*. Nos. 131, 133, 135.]

[Footnote 96: Russian Orange Book, No. 58 (*infra* Appendix VI).]

[Footnote 97: *Ibid*. No. 133. Sir E. Grey to Sir E. Goschen, August 1, encloses a telegram of July 31, to the effect that 'The Austro–Hungarian Ambassador declared the readiness of his Government to discuss the substance of the Austrian ultimatum to Servia. M. Sazonof replied by expressing his satisfaction, and said it was desirable that the discussions should take place in London with the participation of the Great Powers.']

[Footnote 98: German White Book, p. 8.]

[Footnote 99: *Ibid*. p. 9, Exhibit No. 17.]

[Footnote 100: *Correspondence*, No. 76. Sir E. Goschen to Sir E. Grey, July 29: 'His Excellency denied German Government had done this. Nevertheless it is true.']

[Footnote 101: Ibid. No. 99. Sir F. Bertie to Sir E. Grey, July 30.]

[Footnote 102: *Correspondence*. Enclosure 3 in No. 105. French Minister for Foreign Affairs to M. Cambon.]

[Footnote 103: *Ibid*.]

[Footnote 104: German White Book, p. 48 (see *infra*, Appendix I).]

[Footnote 105: *Correspondence*, No. 138. Sir E. Goschen to Sir E. Grey, Aug. 1.]

[Footnote 106: *Correspondence*, No. 24. Sir E. Grey to Sir G. Buchanan, July 25.]

[Footnote 107: *Correspondence*, No. 47. Sir E. Grey to Sir G. Buchanan, July 27.]

[Footnote 108: *Ibid*. No. 89. Sir E. Grey to Sir E. Goschen, July 29.]

[Footnote 109: *Correspondence*, No. 85. Sir E. Goschen to Sir E. Grey, July 29 (received July 29).]

[Footnote 110: *Ibid*. No. 101. Sir E. Grey to Sir E. Goschen, July 30.]

[Footnote 111: *Correspondence*, No. 109. Sir E. Goschen to Sir E. Grey, July 31.]

[Footnote 112: *Ibid*. No. 106. Sir R. Rodd to Sir E. Grey, July 30.]

[Footnote 113: *Correspondence*, No. 114. Sir E. Grey to Sir F. Bertie and Sir E. Goschen, July 31.]

[Footnote 114: *Ibid*. No. 125. Sir F. Bertie to Sir E. Grey, July 31.]

[Footnote 115: *Ibid*. No. 122. Sir E. Goschen to Sir E. Grey, July 31. It may be observed that by the Hague Convention of 1907, Belgium was bound to impose this embargo after the ultimatum of Germany to Russia (Art. 2).]

[Footnote 116: *Correspondence*, No. 123. Sir E. Grey to Sir E. Goschen, August 1.]

[Footnote 117: *The Times*, August 28, 1914, p. 9, cols. 5 and 6.]

[Footnote 118: See *The Times*, August 27, 1914. The Imperial Chancellor telegraphed to Prince Lichnowsky: 'Germany is ready to take up the English proposal if England guarantees with her forces the absolute neutrality of France in a Russo–German conflict.... We promise that the French frontier shall not be passed by our troops before 7 p.m. on Monday, August 3, if England's consent is given in the meantime.']

[Footnote 119: *Correspondence*, No. 148. Sir E. Grey to Sir F. Bertie, August 2.]

[Footnote 120: *Correspondence*, No. 147. Minister of State, Luxemburg, to Sir E. Grey, August 2.]

[Footnote 121: *Ibid*. No. 153. Sir E. Grey to Sir E. Goschen, August 4.]

[Footnote 122: *Ibid*.]

[Footnote 123: *Ibid*. No. 155. Sir E. Grey to Sir F. Villiers, August 4.]

[Footnote 124: *Correspondence*, No. 157. German Foreign Secretary to Prince Lichnowsky, August 4.]

[Footnote 125: *Ibid*. No. 159. Sir E. Grey to Sir E. Goschen, August 4.]

[Footnote 126: *Correspondence*, No. 116, July 31.]

[Footnote 127: *Ibid*. Nos. 130, 143, 145.]

[Footnote 128: *Ibid*. Nos. 149, 150, August 2 and 3.]

[Footnote 129: *The Times*, August 11, p. 5, col. 1.]

[Footnote 130: *Thoughts on Various Subjects, Moral and Diverting* (October, 1706).]

[Footnote 131: p. 6.]

[Footnote 132: *Correspondence*, No. 5. Sir E. Grey to Sir M. de Bunsen, July 24.]

[Footnote 133: *Ibid*. No. 10. Sir E. Grey to Sir F. Bertie, July 24. Cf. No. 24, Sir E. Grey to Sir G. Buchanan, July 25: 'The sudden, brusque, and peremptory character of the Austrian *demarche* makes it almost inevitable that in a very short time both Russia and Austria will have mobilized against each other.']

[Footnote 134: *Ibid*. No. 12. Sir E. Grey to Mr. Crackanthorpe, July 24.]

[Footnote 135: *Ibid*. No. 6. Sir G. Buchanan to Sir E. Grey, July 24: 'I said ... direct British interests in Servia were *nil*, and a war on behalf of that country would never be sanctioned by British public opinion.']

[Footnote 136: *Correspondence*, No. 24. Sir E. Grey to Sir G. Buchanan, July 25.]

[Footnote 137: See note at the end of this chapter.]

[Footnote 138: *Correspondence*, No. 36. Sir E. Grey to Sir F. Bertie, July 26.]

[Footnote 139: *Ibid*. No. 87. Sir E. Grey to Sir F. Bertie, July 29.]

[Footnote 140: *Ibid*. No. 91. Sir E. Grey to Sir M. de Bunsen, July 29.]

[Footnote 141: *Ibid*. No. 13. Note communicated to Sir E. Grey by the Russian Ambassador, July 25.]

[Footnote 142: *Correspondence*, No. 6. Sir G. Buchanan to Sir E. Grey, July 24.]

[Footnote 143: *Ibid*.]

[Footnote 144: *Ibid*. No. 99. Sir F. Bertie to Sir E. Grey, July 30. Cf. No. 119, Sir E. Grey to Sir F. Bertie, July 31.]

[Footnote 145: *Correspondence*, No. 80. Sir R. Rodd to Sir E. Grey, July 29.]

[Footnote 146: *Ibid*. No. 6. Sir G. Buchanan to Sir E. Grey, July 24.]

[Footnote 147: *Ibid*. No. 44. Sir G. Buchanan to Sir E. Grey, July 27: 'Their (sc. the German) attitude would merely be stiffened by such a menace, and we could only induce her (sc. Germany) to use her influence at Vienna to avert war by approaching her in the capacity of a friend who was anxious to preserve peace.']

[Footnote 148: *Ibid*. No. 87. Sir E. Grey to Sir F. Bertie, July 29.]

[Footnote 149: *Correspondence*, No. 47. Sir E. Grey to Sir G. Buchanan, July 27.]

[Footnote 150: *Ibid*. No. 116. Sir E. Grey to Sir F. Bertie, July 31.]

[Footnote 151: *Ibid*. No. 89. Sir E. Grey to Sir E. Goschen, July 29.]

[Footnote 152: *Correspondence*, No. 95. Sir M. de Bunsen to Sir E. Grey, July 30: 'Although I am not able to verify it, I have private information that the German Ambassador knew the text of the Austrian ultimatum to Servia before it was despatched, and telegraphed it to the German Emperor. I know from the German Ambassador himself that he endorses every line of it.']

[Footnote 153: But see Appendix IV.]

[Footnote 154: *Correspondence*, No. 4, p. 8.]

[Footnote 155: *Ibid*. No. 48. Sir E. Grey to Sir M. de Bunsen, July 27.]

[Footnote 156: pp. 3 to 5 and Exhibits 1 and 2 (see *infra* Appendix I).]

[Footnote 157: *Correspondence*, No. 61, Sir M. de Bunsen to Sir E. Grey, July 28; No. 78, Sir G. Buchanan to Sir E. Grey, July 29; No. 96, Sir M. de Bunsen to Sir E. Grey, July 30.]

[Footnote 158: *Correspondence*, No. 110, Sir E. Grey to Sir G. Buchanan, July 31; No. 137, Sir E. Grey to Sir M. de Bunsen, August 1.]

[Footnote 159: *The Times*, September 3, p. 7. For Italy's ignorance of the contents of the Austrian note, see App. V.]

[Footnote 160: *Correspondence*, No. 29. Sir E. Grey to Sir R. Rodd, July 25.]

[Footnote 161: *Ibid*. No. 49. Sir E. Grey to Sir R. Rodd, July 27.]

[Footnote 162: *Ibid*. No. 57. Sir R. Rodd to Sir E. Grey, July 27. Cf. No. 78, Sir G. Buchanan to Sir E. Grey, July 29.]

[Footnote 163: *Correspondence*, No. 64. Sir R. Rodd to Sir E. Grey, July 28. Cf. *supra*, p. 99.]

[Footnote 164: *Ibid*. No. 80. Sir R. Rodd to Sir E. Grey, July 29. Cf. No. 92, Sir E. Grey to Sir R. Rodd, July 29.]

[Footnote 165: *Ibid*. No. 106. Sir R. Rodd to Sir E. Grey, July 30.]

[Footnote 166: *Ibid*. No. 79. Sir M. de Bunsen to Sir E. Grey, July 29.]

[Footnote 167: *Ibid*. No. 152. Sir E. Grey to Sir F. Bertie, August 3.]

[Footnote 168: p. 15 (see Appendix I *infra*).]

[Footnote 169: p. 16 (*ibid.*).]

[Footnote 170: *Correspondence*, No. 5. Sir E. Grey to Sir M. de Bunsen, July 24. The text is also given in the German White Book (pp. 18–23), which will be found in Appendix I.]

[Footnote 171: *Ibid*. No. 14. Sir E. Grey to Sir F. Bertie, July 25.]

[Footnote 172: *Ibid*. No. 4. Communicated by Count Mensdorff, July 24.]

[Footnote 173: *Correspondence*, No. 39. Communicated by the Servian Minister, July 27. See also German White Book (pp. 23–32), *infra* in Appendix I.]

[Footnote 174: German White Book, pp. 24 *et sqq.*; see *infra* Appendix I.]

[Footnote 175: *Correspondence*, No. 5. Sir E. Grey to Sir M. de Bunsen, July 24.]

[Footnote 176: German White Book, pp. 29 *et sqq.*; see *infra* Appendix I.]

[Footnote 177: *Correspondence*, No. 64. Sir R. Rodd to Sir E. Grey, July 28.]

[Footnote 178: *Ibid*. No. 41. Sir M. de Bunsen to Sir E. Grey, July 27.]

CHAPTER VI. THE NEW GERMAN THEORY OF THE STATE

The war in which England is now engaged with Germany is fundamentally a war between two different principles—that of *raison d'etat*, and that of the rule of law. The antagonism between these two principles appeared in our own internal history as far back as the seventeenth century, when the Stuarts championed the theory of state–necessity and the practice of a prerogative free to act outside and above the law in order to meet the demands of state–necessity, and when Parliament defended the rule of law and sought to include the Crown under that law. The same antagonism now appears externally in a struggle between two nations, one of which claims a prerogative to act outside and above the public law of Europe in order to secure the 'safety' of its own state, while the other stands for the rule of public law. The one regards international covenants to which it has pledged its own word as 'scraps of paper' when they stand in the way of *salus populi*; the other regards the maintenance of such covenants as a grave and inevitable obligation.

Taught by Treitschke, whom they regard as their great national historian, and whose lectures on *Politik* have become a gospel, the Germans of to–day assume as an ultimate end and a final standard what they regard as the national German state.[179] 'The state', says Treitschke, 'is the highest thing in the external society of man: above it there is nothing at all in the history of the world.' There is here no room for comity of nations; for a *societas totius humani generis* ; for international law in any true sense. What really exists is the exclusive state—*der geschlossene Staat*—and in another sense than that of Fichte. This state is rigorously national: it excludes all foreign words from its vocabulary, and it would fain exclude all foreign articles from its shores in order to found a real 'national' economy such as List preached. Further, in the teaching of Treitschke this exclusive state is, 'as Machiavelli first clearly saw', essentially power: *der Staat ist Macht*. It may be defined as 'the public might for defence and offence'. As the highest duty of the individual is self–perfection, the highest duty of the state is self–preservation; and self–preservation means power. 'To care for its power is the highest moral duty of the state.' 'Of all political weaknesses that of feebleness is the most abominable and despicable: it is the sin against the Holy Spirit of Politics.' This may seem the mere worship of might, and it is in effect nothing else than the mere worship of might; but we should misrepresent Treitschke if we did not add that power is not conceived by him as mere or bare power. The power of the state is precious and ultimate because the state is a vehicle of culture: the armed sword of the German state is precious because that state is the *colporteur* of German culture. And thus Treitschke holds that Machiavelli, the great apostle of might, is only wrong in so far as he failed to see that might must justify itself by having a content, that is to say, by being used to spread the highest moral culture. It is naturally assumed by German nationalists that this is German culture.

Two results flow from this philosophy, one negative, the other positive. The negative result is the repudiation of any idea of the final character of international obligation; the other is the praise of the glory of war.

Salus populi suprema lex; and to it all international 'law' so called must bend. The absolute sovereignty of the state is necessary for its absolute power; and that absolute sovereignty cannot be bound by *any* obligation, even of its own making. Every treaty or promise made by a state, Treitschke holds, is to be understood as limited by the proviso *rebus sic stantibus*. 'A state cannot bind its will for the future over against other states.' International treaties are no absolute limitation, but a voluntary self–limitation of the state, and only for such time as the state may find to be convenient. The state has no judge set over it, and any 'legal' obligation it may incur is in the last resort subject to its own decision—in other words, to its own repudiation.[180] That the end justifies the means (in other words, that the maintenance of the German Empire as it stands justifies the violation of an international obligation) 'has a certain truth'. 'It is ridiculous to advise a state which is in competition with other states to start by taking the catechism into its hands.' All these hints of his master were adopted and expanded by Bernhardi, the faithful disciple of Treitschke, whose Berlin lectures were attended in the last quarter of the nineteenth century by soldiers and officials as well as by students. There is no such thing, Bernhardi feels, as universal international law. 'Each nation evolves its own conception of Right (*Recht*): none can say that one nation has a better conception than another.' 'No self–respecting nation would sacrifice its own conception of Right' to any international rule: 'by so doing it would renounce its own highest ideals.' The ardent nationalism which will reject foreign words and foreign wares will reject international law as something 'foreign'. Again, Bernhardi makes play with the proviso *rebus sic stantibus* ; and this, curiously enough, he does in reference to Belgium. Things are altered in Belgium, and therefore the plighted word of Germany may no longer be binding. 'When Belgium was proclaimed neutral, no one contemplated that she would lay claim to a large and valuable region of Africa. It may well be asked whether the acquisition of such territory is not *ipso facto* a breach of neutrality.'[181]

But it is the glorification of war—war aggressive as well as war defensive—which is the most striking result of the doctrine of the all–sufficing, all–embracing national state. In the index to Treitschke's *Politik*, under the word War, one reads the following headings—'its sanctity'; 'to be conceived as an ordinance set by God'; 'is the most powerful maker of nations'; 'is politics *par excellence*'. Two functions, says Treitschke, the state exists to discharge; and these are to administer law, and to make war. Of the two war, since it is politics *par excellence*, would appear to be the greater. War cannot be thought or wished out of the world: it is the only medicine for a sick nation. When we are sunk in the selfish individualism of peace, war comes to make us realize that we are members one of another. 'Therein lies the majesty of war, that the petty individual altogether vanishes before the great thought of the state.' War alone makes us realize the social organism to which we belong: 'it is political idealism which demands war.' And again, 'what a perversion of morality it were, if one struck out of humanity heroism'(*Heldentum*)—as if *Heldentum* could not exist in peace! 'But the living God will see to it that war shall always recur as a terrible medicine for humanity.'

Thus the idealization of the state as power results in the idealization of war. As we have seen that the state must be 'power' in order to preserve itself at all, we now find that it must be a war–state to preserve itself from 'sickness'. If it does not fight, individualism will triumph over the social organism; heroism will perish out of the world. Hence Bernhardi writes: 'the maintenance of peace never can or may be the goal of a policy'. War, war—the 'strong medicine', the teacher of heroism, and, as Bernhardi adds to Treitschke, the inevitable biological law, the force that spreads the finest culture—war is the law of humanity. And this war is offensive as well as defensive— primarily, indeed, offensive. For the growing nation must preserve all its new members in its bosom: it must not let them slip away by emigration to foreign soils. It must therefore find for itself colonies; and since the world is already largely occupied, it must find them by conquest from other powers.[182] Treitschke already cried the watchwords—'Colonies!' 'Sea–power to gain colonies!' Treitschke already designated England as the object of German attack, and began to instil in Germany a hatred of England. England blocked the way to the growth of Germany from a European into a World–power; Germany, to preserve intact for German culture the surplus of the growing population, must be a World–power or perish. And besides, England was a 'sick' state—a sham, an hypocrisy.[183]

The whole philosophy seems paganism, or rather barbarism, with a moral veneer. It seems barbarism, because it brings us back to the good old days when mere might was right. Bernhardi, speaking of the right of conquest of new territory inherent in a growing people, tells us that in such cases 'might is at once the supreme right, and the dispute as to what is right is decided by the arbitrament of war', which gives a 'biologically just decision'! And he expresses wonder and surprise at those who think that 'the weak nation is to have the same right to live as the powerful and vigorous nation'. In a word, then, might is right. The doctrine has in itself a rude barbaric simplicity: what is utterly revolting in the neo–Germanic presentment is its moral veneer—the talk of war as the fruit of 'political idealism' and the expression of the 'social organism': the talk of 'historical development' as invalidating supposed 'rights' like the neutrality of Belgium; above all, the talk of power as 'the vehicle of the highest culture'. Treitschke, a stern

Protestant, seeks to reconcile the doctrine with Christianity; but the doctrine is all the same pagan. It is the worship of brute force disguised as *Heldentum*, and of vicious cunning disguised as political morality: it is a mixture of Nietzsche[184] and of Machiavelli. It is a doctrine of the omnipotence of the super–nation, which 'to maintain its state', as Machiavelli said, 'will go to work against faith and charity and humanity and religion', and which will stride ruthlessly to war when 'the day' comes. And when it goes to war, all the veneer of culture goes. 'Have a care', Mommsen once said, 'lest in this state, which has been at once a power in arms and a power in intelligence, the intelligence should vanish, and nothing but the pure military state should remain.' Mommsen's warning has come true in August, 1914. By their fruits ye shall know them. The fruits of *Heldentum* are Louvain smoking in ashes to the sky.

It has seemed worth while to describe this philosophy of life, because it is not only the philosophy of a professor like Treitschke, but also that of a soldier like Bernhardi; and not only so, but it is the philosophy of the Prussian Government. Even the Imperial Chancellor himself used this doctrine (with some qualms, it is true) to justify Germany in 'hewing its way' through Belgium. Let us only remember, in justice to a great people, that it is not really the doctrine of Germany, but rather the doctrine of Prussia (though Treitschke will tell us that Germany is 'just merely an extended Prussia'). And let us remember, in extenuation of Prussia, that she has suffered from two things—geographical pressure springing from her mid–European situation, and an evil tradition of ruthless conquest perpetuated by her Hohenzollern rulers since the days of the Great Elector, and especially since Frederic the Great. Geographical pressure on all sides has made Prussia feel herself in a state of chronic strangulation; and a man who feels strangled will struggle ruthlessly for breath. To get breathing space, to secure frontiers which would ease an intolerable pressure, Frederic the Great could seize Silesia in time of peace in spite of his father's guarantee of the Pragmatic Sanction, and could suggest the partition of Poland. Frontier pressure thus led to ruthless conquest irrespective of rights; and that tradition has sunk deep. It has been easier for England, an island state in the West exempt from pressure, to think in other terms: it has been possible for Russia, secure in the East, to think, and to think nobly (as the present Tsar has done), of international obligation. Nor is it an accident that sees England and Russia united in the common cause of Europe to-day—that sees both championing the cause of small nations, one in the East, the other in the West.[185]

But in whatever way we may excuse Prussia we must fight Prussia; and we fight it in the noblest cause for which men can fight. That cause is the public law of Europe, as a sure shield and buckler of all nations, great and small, and especially the small. To the doctrine of the almightiness of the state—to the doctrine that all means are justified which are, or seem, necessary to its self–preservation, we oppose the doctrine of a European society, or at least a European comity of nations, within which all states stand; we oppose the doctrine of a public law of Europe, by which all states are bound to respect the covenants they have made. We will not and cannot tolerate the view that nations are 'in the state and posture of gladiators' in their relations one with another; we stand for the reign of law.

Our cause, as one would expect from a people that has fought out its own internal struggles under the forms of law, is a legal cause. We are a people in whose blood the cause of law is the vital element. It is no new thing in our history that we should fight for that cause. When England and Revolutionary France went to war in 1793, the cause, on the side of England, was a legal cause. We fought for the public law of Europe, as it had stood since the Peace of Westphalia in 1648. We did not fight in 1870, because neither France nor Germany had infringed the public law of Europe by attacking the neutrality of Belgium, but we were ready to fight if they did. A fine cartoon in *Punch*, of August, 1870, shows armed England encouraging Belgium, who stands ready with spear and shield, with the words—'Trust me! Let us hope that they won't trouble you, dear friend. But if they do——' To–day they have; and England has drawn her sword. How could she have done otherwise, with those traditions of law so deep in all Anglo–Saxon blood—traditions as real and as vital to Anglo–Saxon America as to Anglo–Saxon England; traditions which are the fundamental basis of Anglo–Saxon public life all the world over? America once fought and beat England, in long–forgotten days, on the ground of law. That very ground of law—that law–abidingness which is as deeply engrained in the men of Massachusetts to–day as it is in any Britisher—is a bond of sympathy between the two in this great struggle of the nations.

To Germans our defence of public law may seem part of the moral hypocrisy of which in their view we are full. What we are doing, they feel, is to strike at Germany, our competitor for 'world–empire', with its dangerous navy, while Germany is engaged in a life and death struggle with France and Russia. We too, they feel, are Machiavellians; but we have put on what Machiavelli called 'the mantle of superstition', the pretence of morality and law, to cover our craft. It is true that we are fighting for our own interest.

Why We Are At War

But what is our interest? We are fighting for Right, because Right is our supreme interest. The new German political theory enunciates that 'our interest is our right'. The old—the very old—English political theory is, 'The Right is our interest'. It is true that we have everything to gain by defending the cause of international law. Should that prevent us from defending that cause? What do we not lose of precious lives in the defence?

This is the case of England. England stands for the idea of a public law of Europe, and for the small nations which it protects. She stands for her own preservation, which is menaced when public law is broken, and the 'ages' slow−bought gain' imperilled.

(Treitschke's *Politik*, lectures delivered in Berlin during the years 1875 to 1895, was published in two volumes in 1899. General Bernhardi's book, *Deutschland und der naechste Krieg*, was published in 1911, and has been translated into English under the title *Germany and the Next War*. See also J.A. Cramb, *England and Germany*, 1914.)

Notes:

[Footnote 179: The unity of the German state is in no small measure a matter of artificial Prussianization. Of this Prussianization Treitschke was the great advocate, though he was himself ultimately of Slavonic origin, and immediately of Saxon birth.]

[Footnote 180: We are reminded of the famous sentence in *The Prince*:—*Dove non e giudizio da richiamare si guarda al fine*.]

[Footnote 181: Bernhardi adds: 'The conception of permanent neutrality is entirely contrary to the essential nature of the state, which can only attain its highest moral aims in competition with other states.' It would seem to follow that by violating the neutrality of Belgium Germany is helping that country to attain its highest moral aims. The suggestion that Belgium is no longer a neutral Power was not adopted by the German Government before the war, nor by Dr. von Bethmann−Hollweg in his speech to the Reichstag on the Belgian question (see *supra*, p. 91).]

[Footnote 182: It was significant that Germany, while offering to England at the end of July a guarantee of the integrity of the soil of France, would not offer any guarantee of the integrity of French colonies (*supra*, p. 82).]

[Footnote 183: Nothing has here been said, though much might be said, of the distortion of history and ethnology by German nationalism, or Pan–Germanism. It is well known that the Pan–Germans regard England as Teutonic, and destined to be gathered into the German fold. In these last few weeks we have been reproached as a people for being traitors to our 'Teutonic' blood. Better be traitors to blood than to plain duty; but as a matter of fact our mixed blood has many other strains than the Teutonic. On the aims of the Pan–Germanists readers may with profit consult a book by Paul Vergnet, *La France en danger* (Oct. 1913).]

[Footnote 184: In fairness to Nietzsche it should be said that in his later years he revolted against the Prussian military system.]

[Footnote 185: German professors have recently reproached England for being allied with 'Muscovite barbarism'. Is Russia so barbarous, whose sovereign convened the first Peace Conference? Have not England and Russia striven together in peace (as they now strive together in war) for a great common cause? The German White Book, which seeks to fasten on Russia the blame of the present war, is oblivious of all that has happened in these matters since 1898. The reader may with advantage refer, on this subject, to a pamphlet by Professor Vinogradoff, *Russia: the Psychology of a Nation* (Oxford, 1914).]

EPILOGUE

In conclusion something must be said of the process by which our understanding with France, still so elastic in 1912 and 1913, became the solid alliance which now, on sea and land alike, confronts the German forces. England gave France no positive engagements until the eleventh hour; it may be argued that England gave them far too late, and that the war might never have occurred if England had been less obstinately and judicially pacific. But the English case for the delay is clear. We hesitated to throw in our lot with France, because France would not stand neutral while Germany made war on Russia. We shrank from the incalculable entanglements which seemed to lie before us if we allied ourselves with a power which was so committed. Why, we were asking ourselves, should we fight the battles of Russia in the Balkans?

We were perhaps too cautious in suspecting that France might contemplate this policy. She could not define beforehand the limits which she would observe in defending Russia's cause. But she knew, as we now know, that a war with Russia meant, to German statesmen, only a pretext for a new attack on France, even more deadly in intention than that of 1870. France could not do without the help of Russia. How then could she afford to forfeit Russia's friendship by declaring, at Germany's command, that she would do nothing to help Russia?

This loyalty to the Dual Alliance left France during the last days before the war in a cruel dilemma. Russia, however well disposed, could not help her ally in the first weeks of a war; and for France these were the critical weeks, the weeks upon which her own fate must depend. She appealed urgently to England for support.

But, even on July 31st, the English Cabinet replied that it could make no definite engagement. This answer, it is true, had been foreshadowed in earlier communications. Sir Edward Grey had made it abundantly clear that there could be no prospect of common action unless France were exposed to 'an unprovoked attack', and no certainty of such action even in that case. But France had staked everything upon the justice of her cause. She had felt that her pacific intentions were clear to all the world; and that England could not, with any self–respect, refuse assistance. The French mobilization had been delayed until July 31st, to convince the British Cabinet of French good faith; and the French fleet had been left in the Mediterranean to guard the interests of England no less than those of France. We can imagine how bitter was the disappointment with which France received the English answer of July 31st.

But we were loyal to our obligations as we understood them. If our answers to France were guarded, our answers to the German overtures of July 29th and August 1st show that we were fighting the battle of France with diplomatic weapons. On August 2nd we went still further, by undertaking to defend the French coasts and shipping, if the German fleet should come into the Channel or through the North Sea. To justify our position of reserve from July 31st to August 4th we may quote what Mr. Asquith said the other day (September 4th):—

'No one who has not been in that position can realize the strength,
the energy, and the persistence with which we laboured for peace. We
persevered by every expedient that diplomacy could suggest,
straining almost to breaking–point our most cherished friendships
and obligations.'

Those efforts failed. We know to–day that mediation had never any prospects of success, because Germany had resolved that it should not succeed. Ought we to have known this from the first? It is easy to be wise after the event. But in England we have Cabinet government and we have Parliamentary government. Before an English minister can act, in a matter of national importance, no matter how positive his own convictions may be, he must convince his colleagues, and they must feel certain of convincing a democracy which is essentially pacific, cautious, slow to move. Nothing short of the German attack on Belgium would have convinced the ordinary Englishman that German statesmanship had degenerated into piracy. That proof was given us on August 4th; and on that day we sent our ultimatum to Berlin.

To–day all England is convinced; and we are fighting back to back with the French for their national existence and our own. Our own, because England's existence depends not only on her sea–power, but upon the maintenance of European state–law. The military spirit which we have described above (Chap. VI) tramples upon the rights of nations because it sees a foe in every equal; because it regards the prosperity of a neighbour as a national misfortune; because it holds that national greatness is only to be realized in the act of destroying or absorbing other nationalities. To those who are not yet visibly assailed, and who possibly believe themselves secure, we can only give the warning: *Tua res agitur, paries cum proximus ardet.*

Of the issue England is not afraid. The most unfavourable issue would find her still convinced that she has taken the only course compatible with honour and with public law. Military anarchism shall be destroyed if England, France, and Russia can destroy it. On this object England and France have staked their last ship and their last soldier. But, it may be asked, what state–system do we hope to establish, if and when we are successful in this great crusade?

What England not only desires but needs, and needs imperatively, is, first, the restitution to Belgium of her former status and whatever else can be restored of all that she has sacrificed. This is the indispensable preliminary to any form of settlement. The next essential is an adequate guarantee to France that she shall never experience such another invasion as we have seen in August, 1914; without a France which is prosperous, secure, and independent, European civilization would be irreparably maimed and stunted. The third essential, as essential as the other two, is the conservation of those other nations which can only exist on sufferance so long as *Realpolitik* is practised with impunity.

Why We Are At War

To minor nationalities it should be clear that England is their friend, and cannot choose but stand their friend. Three times in her history she has made war upon a would–be despot of the Continent, treating the 'Balance of Power' as a principle for which no sacrifice could be too great. In these struggles she assisted the small Powers, less from altruism than because their interest was her own. She supported Holland against Philip II of Spain and against Louis XIV; against Napoleon she supported not Holland only, but also Portugal and, to the best of her power, Switzerland and Piedmont.

We do not argue—it would be absurd to argue—that England has always been free from reproach in her dealings with the smaller states. Holland may well remember the naval conflicts of the seventeenth century and the English Navigation Laws. But Holland should also remember that, in the seventeenth century, England was not yet a great Power; Holland and England fought as rivals and on equal terms, in a feud which subsequent alliances have healed, over a policy which England has long since renounced as mischievous and futile. On Denmark we inflicted a great wrong in 1807; it can only be extenuated by the fact, which Denmark knows now though she did not know it then, that Napoleon had conspired with Russia to seize the Danish fleet and use it against England. Denmark, indeed, has better cause to complain that we gave her no assistance in 1864. That mistake—for it was a mistake of weakness, not deliberate treachery—has brought its own nemesis. We are still paying for that particular mistake, and we are not likely to forget the lesson. The case of Schleswig–Holstein shows how the losses of such a state as Denmark may react on such a state as England.

England cannot afford that her weaker neighbours should become less prosperous or less independent than they are. So far as the long arm of naval power reaches, England is bound to give them whatever help she can. From motives of self–preservation, if on no other ground, she could not tolerate their subordination to such a power as Germany aspires to found. Her quarrel is not with the German people, but with the political system for which the German Empire, in its present temper, stands. That system England is bound to resist, no matter by what power it is adopted.

English sympathies and English traditions are here at one with English interests. England is proud to recollect how she befriended struggling nationalities in the nineteenth century. She did not support Greece and Italy for the sake of any help that they could give her. The goodwill of England to Holland, to Switzerland, to the Scandinavian states, is largely based upon their achievements in science and art and literature. They have proved that they can serve the higher interests of humanity. They have contributed to the growth of that common civilization which links together the small powers and the great with bonds more sacred and more durable than those of race, of government, of material interest. In this fraternity each nation has a duty to the rest. If we have harped on England's interest, it must not for a moment be supposed that we have forgotten England's duty. But England stands to–day in this fortunate position, that her duty and her interest combine to impel her in the same direction.

APPENDIX I. GERMANY'S REASONS

FOR

WAR WITH RUSSIA

How Russia and her Ruler betrayed Germany's confidence and thereby made the European War.

WITH THE ORIGINAL TELEGRAMS AND NOTES.

Druck und Verlag: Liebheit &Thiesen, Berlin.

Foreign Office, Berlin, August 1914.

On June 28th the Austro–Hungarian successor to the throne, Arch–Duke Franz Ferdinand, and his wife, the Duchess of Hohenberg, were assassinated by a member of a band of servian conspirators. The investigation of the crime through the Austro–Hungarian authorities has yielded the fact that the conspiracy against the life of the Arch–Duke and successor to the throne was prepared and abetted in Belgrade with the cooperation of Servian officials, and executed with arms from the Servian State arsenal. This crime must have opened the eyes of the entire civilized world, not only in regard to the aims of the Servian policies directed against the conservation and integrity of the Austro–Hungarian monarchy, but also concerning the criminal means which the pan–Serb propaganda in Servia had no hesitation in employing for the achievement of these aims.

Why We Are At War

The goal of these policies was the gradual revolutionizing and final separation of the south–easterly districts from the Austro–Hungarian monarchy and their union with Servia. This direction of Servias policy has not been altered in the least in spite of the repeated and solemn declarations of Servia in which it vouchsafed a change in these policies toward Austria–Hungary as well as the cultivation of good and neighborly relations.

In this manner for the third time in the course of the last 6 years Servia has led Europe to the brink of a world–war.

It could only do this because it believed itself supported in its intentions by Russia.

Russia soon after the events brought about by the Turkish revolution of 1908, endeavored to found a union of the Balcan states under Russian patronage and directed against the existence of Turkey. This union which succeeded in 1911 in driving out Turkey from a greater part of her European possessions, collapsed over the question of the distribution of spoils. The Russian policies were not dismayed over this failure. According to the idea of the Russian statesmen a new Balcan union under Russian patronage should be called into existence, headed no longer against Turkey, now dislodged from the Balcan, but against the existence of the Austro–Hungarian monarchy. It was the idea that Servia should cede to Bulgaria those parts of Macedonia which it had received during the last Balcan war, in exchange for Bosnia and the Herzegovina which were to be taken from Austria. To oblige Bulgaria to fall in with this plan it was to be isolated, Roumania attached to Russia with the aid of French propaganda, and Servia promised Bosnia and the Herzegovina.

Under these circumstances it was clear to Austria that it was not compatible with the dignity and the spirit of self–preservation of the monarchy to view idly any longer this agitation across the border. The Imperial and Royal Government appraised Germany of this conception and asked for our opinion. With all our heart we were able to agree with our allys estimate of the situation, and assure him that any action considered necessary to end the movement in Servia directed against the conservation of the monarchy would meet with our approval.

We were perfectly aware that a possible warlike attitude of Austria–Hungary against Servia might bring Russia upon the field, and that it might therefore involve us in a war, in accordance with our duty as allies. We could not, however, in these vital interests of Austria—Hungary, which were at stake, advise our ally to take a yielding attitude not compatible with his dignity, nor deny him our assistance in these trying days. We could do this all the less as our own interests were menaced through the continued Serb agitation. If the Serbs continued with the aid of Russia and France to menace the existence of Austria—Hungary, the gradual collapse of Austria and the subjection of all the Slavs under one Russian sceptre would be the consequence, thus making untenable the position of the Teutonic race in Central Europe. A morally weakened Austria under the pressure of Russian pan—slavism would be no longer an ally on whom we could count and in whom we could have confidence, as we must be able to have, in view of the ever more menacing attitude of our easterly and westerly neighbors. We, therefore, permitted Austria a completely free hand in her action towards Servia but have not participated in her preparations.

Austria chose the method of presenting to the Servian Government a note, in which the direct connection between the murder at Sarajevo and the pan—Serb movement, as not only countenanced but actively supported by the Servian Government, was explained, and in which a complete cessation of this agitation, as well as a punishment of the guilty, was requested. At the same time Austria—Hungary demanded as necessary guarantee for the accomplishment of her desire the participation of some Austrian officials in the preliminary examination on Servian territory and the final dissolution of the pan—Serb societies agitating against Austria—Hungary. The Imperial and Royal Government gave a period of 48 hours for the unconditional acceptance of its demands.

The Servian Government started the mobilization of its army one day after the transmission of the Austro—Hungarian note.

As after the stipulated date the Servian Government rendered a reply which, though complying in some points with the conditions of Austria—Hungary, yet showed in all essentials the endeavor through procrastination and new negotiations to escape from the just demands of the monarchy, the latter discontinued her diplomatic relations with Servia without indulging in further negotiations or accepting further Servian assurances, whose value, to its loss, she had sufficiently experienced.

From this moment Austria was in fact in a state of war with Servia, which it proclaimed officially on the 28th of July by declaring war.

Why We Are At War

[Sidenote: see exhibits 1 &2.]

From the beginning of the conflict we assumed the position that there were here concerned the affairs of Austria alone, which it would have to settle with Servia. We therefore directed our efforts toward the localizing of the war, and toward convincing the other powers that Austria–Hungary had to appeal to arms in justifiable self–defence, forced upon her by the conditions. We emphatically took the position that no civilized country possessed the right to stay the arm of Austria in this struggle with barbarism and political crime, and to shield the Servians against their just punishment. In this sense we instructed our representatives with the foreign powers.

[Sidenote: see exhibit 3.]

Simultaneously the Austro–Hungarian Government communicated to the Russian Government that the step undertaken against Servia implied merely a defensive measure against the Serb agitation, but that Austria–Hungary must of necessity demand guarantees for a continued friendly behavior of Servia towards the monarchy. Austria–Hungary had no intention whatsoever to shift the balance of power in the Balcan.

In answer to our declaration that the German Government desired, and aimed at, a localization of the conflict, both the French and the English Governments promised an action in the same direction. But these endeavors did not succeed in preventing the interposition of Russia in the Austro–Servian disagreement.

[Sidenote: see exhibits 4 &5.]

The Russian Government submitted an official communique on July 24th, according to which Russia could not possibly remain indifferent in the Servio–Austrian conflict. The same was declared by the Russian Secretary of Foreign Affairs, M. Sasonow, to the German Ambassador, Count Pourtales, in the afternoon of July 26th. The German Government declared again, through its Ambassador at St. Petersburg, that Austria–Hungary had no desire for conquest and only wished peace at her frontiers. After the official explanation by Austria–Hungary to Russia that it did not claim territorial gain in Servia, the decision concerning the peace of the world rested exclusively with St. Petersburg.

Why We Are At War

[Sidenote: see exhibits 6, 7, 8, 9.]

The same day the first news of Russian mobilization reached Berlin in the evening.

[Sidenote: see exhibits 10, 10a, 10b.]

The German Ambassadors at London, Paris, and St. Petersburg were instructed to energetically point out the danger of this Russian mobilization. The Imperial Ambassador at St. Petersburg was also directed to make the following declaration to the Russian Government:

> "Preparatory military measures by Russia will force us to counter–measures which must consist in mobilizing the army.

> "But mobilization means war.

> "As we know the obligations of France towards Russia, this mobilization would be directed against both Russia and France. We cannot assume that Russia desires to unchain such a European war. Since Austria–Hungary will not touch the existence of the Servian kingdom, we are of the opinion that Russia can afford to assume an attitude of waiting. We can all the more support the desire of Russia to protect the integrity of Servia as Austria–Hungary does not intend to question the latter. It will be easy in the further development of the affair to find a basis for an understanding."

[Sidenote: see exhibit 11.]

On July 27th the Russian Secretary of War, M. Ssuchomlinow, gave the German military attache his word of honor that no order to mobilize had been issued, merely preparations were being made, but not a horse mustered, nor reserves called in. If Austria–Hungary crossed the Servian frontier, the military districts directed towards Austria, i.e. Kiev, Odessa, Moscow, Kazan, would be mobilized, under no circumstances those situated on the German frontier, i.e. St. Petersburg, Vilna, and Warsaw. Upon inquiry into the object of the mobilization against Austria–Hungary, the Russian Minister of War replied by shrugging his shoulders and referring to the diplomats. The military attache then pointed to these mobilization measures against Austria–Hungary as extremely menacing also for Germany.

In the succeeding days news concerning Russian mobilization came at a rapid rate. Among it was also news about preparations on the German–Russian frontier, as for instance the announcement of the state of war in Kovno, the departure of the Warsaw garrison, and the strengthening of the Alexandrovo garrison.

On July 27th, the first information was received concerning preparatory measures taken by France: the 14th Corps discontinued the manoeuvres and returned to its garrison.

In the meantime we had endeavored to localize the conflict by most emphatic steps.

[Sidenote: see exhibit 12.]

On July 26th, Sir Edward Grey had made the proposal to submit the differences between Austria–Hungary and Servia to a conference of the Ambassadors of Germany, France, and Italy under his chairmanship. We declared in regard to this proposal that we could not, however much we approved the idea, participate in such a conference, as we could not call Austria in her dispute with Servia before a European tribunal.

France consented to the proposal of Sir Edward Grey, but it foundered upon Austria's declining it, as was to be expected.

[Sidenote: see exhibit 13.]

Faithful to our principle that mediation should not extend to the Austro–Servian conflict, which is to be considered as a purely Austro–Hungarian affair, but merely to the relations between Austria–Hungary and Russia, we continued our endeavors to bring about an understanding between these two powers.

[Sidenote: see exhibits 15 & 16.]

We further declared ourselves ready, after failure of the conference idea, to transmit a second proposal of Sir Edward Grey's to Vienna in which he suggested Austria–Hungary should decide that either the Servian reply was sufficient, or that it be used as a basis for further negotiations. The Austro–Hungarian Government remarked with full appreciation of our action that it had come too late, the hostilities having already been opened.

In spite of this we continued our attempts to the utmost, and we advised Vienna to show every possible advance compatible with the dignity of the monarchy.

Unfortunately, all these proposals were overtaken by the military preparations of Russia and France.

[Sidenote: see exhibit 17.]

On July 29th, the Russian Government made the official notification in Berlin that four army districts had been mobilized. At the same time further news was received concerning rapidly progressing military preparations of France, both on water and on land.

On the same day the Imperial Ambassador in St. Petersburg had an interview with the Russian Foreign Secretary, in regard to which he reported by telegraph, as follows:

"The Secretary tried to persuade me that I should urge my Government to participate in a quadruple conference to find means to induce Austria–Hungary to give up those demands which touch upon the sovereignty of Servia. I could merely promise to report the conversation and took the position that, after Russia had decided upon the baneful step of mobilization, every exchange of ideas appeared now extremely difficult, if not impossible. Besides, Russia now was demanding from us in regard to Austria–Hungary the same which Austria–Hungary was being blamed for with regard to Servia, i.e. an infraction of sovereignty. Austria–Hungary having promised to consider the Russian interests by disclaiming any territorial aspiration,—a great concession on the part of a state engaged in war—should therefore be permitted to attend to its affair with Servia alone. There would be time at the peace conference to return to the matter of forbearance towards the sovereignty of Servia.

Why We Are At War

"I added very solemnly that at this moment the entire Austro–Servian affair was eclipsed by the danger of a general European conflagration, and I endeavored to present to the Secretary the magnitude of this danger.

"It was impossible to dissuade Sasonow from the idea that Servia could not now be deserted by Russia".

On July 29th, the German Military Attache at St. Petersburg wired the following report on a conversation with the Chief of the General Staff of the Russian army:

"The Chief of the General Staff has asked me to call on him, and he has told me that he has just come from His Majesty. He has been requested by the Secretary of War to reiterate once more that everything had remained as the Secretary had informed me two days ago. He offered confirmation in writing and gave me his word of honor in the most solemn manner that nowhere there had been a mobilization, viz. calling in of a single man or horse up to the present time, i.e. 3 o'clock in the afternoon. He could not assume a guaranty for the future, but he could emphasize that in the fronts directed towards our frontiers His Majesty desired no mobilization.

"As, however, I had received here many pieces of news concerning the calling in of the reserves in different parts of the country also in Warsaw and in Vilna, I told the general that his statements placed me before a riddle. On his officers word of honor he replied that such news was wrong, but that possibly here and there a false alarm might have been given.

"I must consider this conversation as an attempt to mislead us as to the extent of the measures hitherto taken in view of the abundant and positive information about the calling in of reserves."

In reply to various inquiries concerning reasons for its threatening attitude, the Russian Government repeatedly pointed out that Austria–Hungary had commenced no conversation in St. Petersburg. The Austro–Hungarian Ambassador in St. Petersburg was therefore instructed on July 29th, at our suggestion, to enter into such conversation with Sasonow. Count Szapary was empowered to explain to the Russian minister the note to Servia though it had been overtaken by the state of war, and to accept any suggestion on the part of Russia as well as to discuss with Sasonow all questions touching directly upon the Austro–Russian relations.

[Sidenote: see exhibit 19.]

Shoulder to shoulder with England we labored incessantly and supported every proposal in Vienna from which we hoped to gain the possibility of a peaceable solution of the conflict. We even as late as the 30th of July forwarded the English proposal to Vienna, as basis for negotiations, that Austria–Hungary should dictate her conditions in Servia, i.e. after her march into Servia. We thought that Russia would accept this basis.

During the interval from July 29th to July 31st there appeared renewed and cumulative news concerning Russian measures of mobilization. Accumulation of troops on the East Prussian frontier and the declaration of the state of war over all important parts of the Russian west frontier allowed no further doubt that the Russian mobilization was in full swing against us, while simultaneously all such measures were denied to our representative in St. Petersburg on word of honor.

Nay, even before the reply from Vienna regarding the Anglo–German mediation whose tendencies and basis must have been known in St. Petersburg, could possibly have been received in Berlin, Russia ordered a general mobilization.

[Sidenote: see exhibits 18, 20, 21, 22, 23.]

During the same days, there took place between His Majesty the Kaiser, and Czar Nicolas an exchange of telegrams in which His Majesty called the attention of the Czar to the menacing character of the Russian mobilization during the continuance of his own mediating activities.

On July 31st, the Czar directed the following telegram to His Majesty the Kaiser:

> "I thank You cordially for Your mediation which permits the hope
> that everything may yet end peaceably. It is technically impossible

106

to discontinue our military preparations which have been made
necessary by the Austrian mobilization. It is far from us to want
war. As long as the negotiations between Austria and Servia
continue, my troops will undertake no provocative action. I give You
my solemn word thereon. I confide with all my faith in the grace of
God, and I hope for the success of Your mediation in Vienna for the
welfare of our countries and the peace of Europe.

"Your cordially devoted

"Nicolas."

This telegram of the Czar crossed with the following, sent by H.M. the Kaiser, also on
July 31st, at 2 p.m.:

"Upon Your appeal to my friendship and Your request for my aid I
have engaged in mediation between Your Government and the Government
of Austria–Hungary. While this action was taking place, Your troops
were being mobilized against my ally Austria–Hungary, whereby, as I
have already communicated to You, my mediation has become almost
illusory. In spite of this, I have continued it, and now I receive
reliable news that serious preparations for war are going on on my
eastern frontier. The responsibility for the security of my country
forces me to measures of defence. I have gone to the extreme limit
of the possible in my efforts for the preservation of the peace of
the world. It is not I who bear the responsibility for the
misfortune which now threatens the entire civilized world. It rests
in Your hand to avert it. No one threatens the honor and peace of
Russia which might well have awaited the success of my mediation.
The friendship for You and Your country, bequeathed to me by my
grand–father on his deathbed, has always been sacred to me, and I
have stood faithfully by Russia while it was in serious affliction,
especially during its last war. The peace of Europe can still be
preserved by You if Russia decides to discontinue those military
preparations which menace Germany and Austria–Hungary."

Why We Are At War

Before this telegram reached its destination, the mobilization of all the Russian forces, obviously directed against us and already ordered during the afternoon of the 31st of July, was in full swing. Notwithstanding, the telegram of the Czar was sent at 2 o'clock that same afternoon.

[Sidenote: see exhibit 24.]

After the Russian general mobilization became known in Berlin, the Imperial Ambassador at St. Petersburg was instructed on the afternoon of July 31st to explain to the Russian Government that Germany declared the state of war as counter–measure against the general mobilization of the Russian army and navy which must be followed by mobilization if Russia did not cease its military measures against Germany and Austria–Hungary within 12 hours, and notified Germany thereof.

[Sidenote: see exhibit 25.]

At the same time the Imperial Ambassador in Paris was instructed to demand from the French Government a declaration within 18 hours, whether it would remain neutral in a Russo–German war.

The Russian Government destroyed through its mobilization, menacing the security of our country, the laborious action at mediation of the European cabinets. The Russian mobilization in regard to the seriousness of which the Russian Government was never allowed by us to entertain a doubt, in connection with its continued denial, shows clearly that Russia wanted war.

The Imperial Ambassador at St. Petersburg delivered his note to M. Sasonow on July 31st at 12 o'clock midnight.

The reply of the Russian Government has never reached us.

Two hours after the expiration of the time limit the Czar telegraphed to H.M. the Kaiser, as follows:

"I have received Your telegram. I comprehend that You are forced to
mobilize, but I should like to have from You the same guaranty which

108

Why We Are At War

I have given You, viz., that these measures do not mean war, and that we shall continue to negotiate for the welfare of our two countries and the universal peace which is so dear to our hearts. With the aid of God it must be possible to our long tried friendship to prevent the shedding of blood. I expect with full confidence Your urgent reply."

To this H.M. the Kaiser replied:

"I thank You for Your telegram. I have shown yesterday to Your Government the way through which alone war may yet be averted. Although I asked for a reply by to–day noon, no telegram from my Ambassador has reached me with the reply of Your Government. I therefore have been forced to mobilize my army. An immediate, clear and unmistakable reply of Your Government is the sole way to avoid endless misery. Until I receive this reply I am unable, to my great grief, to enter upon the subject of Your telegram. I must ask most earnestly that You, without delay, order Your troops to commit, under no circumstances, the slightest violation of our frontiers."

As the time limit given to Russia had expired without the receipt of a reply to our inquiry, H.M. the Kaiser ordered the mobilization of the entire German Army and Navy on August 1st at 5 p.m.

[Sidenote: see exhibit 25.]

The German Ambassador at St. Petersburg was instructed that, in the event of the Russian Government not giving a satisfactory reply within the stipulated time, he should declare that we considered ourselves in a state of war after the refusal of our demands. However, before a confirmation of the execution of this order had been received, that is to say, already in the afternoon of August 1st, i.e., the same afternoon on which the telegram of the Czar, cited above, was sent, Russian troops crossed our frontier and marched into German territory.

Thus Russia began the war against us.

Meanwhile the Imperial Ambassador in Paris put our question to the French Cabinet on July 31st at 7 p.m.

[Sidenote: see exhibit 27.]

The French Prime Minister gave an equivocal and unsatisfactory reply on August 1st at 1. p.m. which gave no clear idea of the position of France, as he limited himself to the explanation that France would do that which her interests demanded. A few hours later, at 5 p.m., the mobilization of the entire French army and navy was ordered.

On the morning of the next day France opened hostilities.

THE ORIGINAL TELEGRAMS AND NOTES.

THE NOTE OF AUSTRIA–HUNGARY TO SERVIA.

Presented July 23rd in Belgrade.

"On March 31st, 1909, the Royal Servian Minister to the Court of Vienna made the following statement, by order of his Government:

"Servia declares that she is not affected in her rights by the situation established in Bosnia, and that she will therefore adapt herself to the decisions which the powers are going to arrive at in reference to Art. 25 of the Berlin Treaty. By following the councils of the powers, Servia binds herself to cease the attitude of protest and resistance which she has assumed since last October, relative to the annexation, and she binds herself further to change the direction of her present policies towards Austria–Hungary, and, in the future, to live with the latter in friendly and neighborly relations.

"The history of the last years, and especially the painful events of June 28th, have demonstrated the existence of a subversive movement in Servia whose aim it is to separate certain territories from the Austro–Hungarian monarchy. This movement, which developed under the eyes of the Servian Government, has found expression subsequently beyond the territory of the kingdom, in acts of terrorism, a series of assassinations and murders.

Why We Are At War

"Far from fulfilling the formal obligations contained in the declaration of March 31st, 1909, the Royal Servian Government has done nothing to suppress this movement. She suffered the criminal doings of the various societies and associations directed against the monarchy, the unbridled language of the press, the glorification of the originators of assassinations, the participation of officers and officials in subversive intrigues; she suffered the unwholesome propaganda in public education, and lastly permitted all manifestations which would mislead the Servian people into hatred of the monarchy and into contempt for its institutions.

"This sufferance of which the Royal Servian Government made itself guilty, has lasted up to the moment in which the events of June 28th demonstrated to the entire world the ghastly consequences of such sufferance.

"*It becomes plain from the evidence and confessions of the criminal authors of the outrage of June 28th, that the murder at Sarajevo was conceived in Belgrade, that the murderers received the arms and bombs with which they were equipped, from Servian officers and officials who belonged to the Narodna Odbrana, and that, lastly, the transportation of the criminals and their arms to Bosnia was arranged and carried out by leading Servian frontier officials.*

"The cited results of the investigation do not permit the Imperial and Royal Government to observe any longer the attitude of waiting, which it has assumed for years towards those agitations which have their centre in Belgrade, and which from there radiate into the territory of the monarchy. These results, on the contrary, impose upon the Imperial and Royal Government the duty to terminate intrigues which constitute a permanent menace for the peace of the monarchy.

"In order to obtain this purpose, the Imperial and Royal Government is forced to demand official assurance from the Servian Government that it condemns the propaganda directed against Austria–Hungary, i.e. the entirety of the machinations whose aim it is to separate parts from the monarchy which belong to it, and that she binds herself to suppress with all means this criminal and terrorizing propaganda.

"In order to give to these obligations a solemn character, the Royal Servian Government will publish on the first page of its official organ of July 26th, 1914, the following declaration:

Why We Are At War

"The Royal Servian Government condemns the propaganda directed against Austria–Hungary, i.e. the entirety of those machinations whose aim it is to separate from the Austro–Hungarian monarchy territories belonging thereto, and she regrets sincerely the ghastly consequences of these criminal actions.

"The Royal Servian Government regrets that Servian officers and officials have participated in the propaganda, cited above, and have thus threatened the friendly and neighborly relations which the Royal Government was solemnly bound to cultivate by its declaration of March 31st, 1909.

"The Royal Government which disapproves and rejects every thought or every attempt at influencing the destinations of the inhabitants of any part of Austria–Hungary, considers it its duty to call most emphatically to the attention of its officers and officials, and of the entire population of the kingdom, that it will hence–forward proceed with the utmost severity against any persons guilty of similar actions, to prevent and suppress which it will make every effort."

"This explanation is to be brought simultaneously to the cognizance of the Royal Army through an order of H.M. the King, and it is to be published in the official organ of the Army.

"The Royal Servian Government binds itself, in addition, as follows:

"1. to suppress any publication which fosters hatred of, and contempt for, the Austro–Hungarian monarchy, and whose general tendency is directed against the latters territorial integrity;

"2. to proceed at once with the dissolution of the society Narodna Odbrana, to confiscate their entire means of propaganda, and to proceed in the same manner against the other societies and associations in Servia which occupy themselves with the propaganda against Austria–Hungary. The Royal Government will take the necessary measures, so that the dissolved societies may not continue their activities under another name or in another form;

"3. without delay to eliminate from the public instruction in Servia, so far as the corps of instructors, as well as the means of instruction are concerned, that which serves, or may serve, to foster the propaganda against Austria–Hungary;

"4. to remove from military service and the administration in general all officers and officials who are guilty of propaganda against Austria–Hungary, and whose names, with a communication of the material which the Imperial and Royal Government possesses against them, the Imperial and Royal Government reserves the right to communicate to the Royal Government;

"5. to consent that in Servia officials of the Imperial and Royal Government co–operate in the suppression of a movement directed against the territorial integrity of the monarchy;

"6. to commence a judicial investigation against the participants of the conspiracy of June 28th, who are on Servian territory. Officials, delegated by the Imperial and Royal Government will participate in the examinations;

"7. to proceed at once with all severity to arrest Major Voja Tankosic and a certain Milan Ciganowic, Servian State officials, who have been compromised through the result of the investigation;

"8. to prevent through effective measures the participation of the Servian authorities in the smuggling of arms and explosives across the frontier and to dismiss those officials of Shabatz and Loznica, who assisted the originators of the crime of Sarajevo in crossing the frontier;

"9. to give to the Imperial and Royal Government explanations in regard to the unjustifiable remarks of high Servian functionaries in Servia and abroad who have not hesitated, in spite of their official position, to express themselves in interviews in a hostile manner against Austria–Hungary after the outrage of June 28th;

"10. The Imperial and Royal Government expects a reply from the Royal Government at the latest until Saturday 25th inst., at 6 p.m. A memoir concerning the results of the investigations at Sarajevo, so far as they concern points 7. and 8. is enclosed with this note."

ENCLOSURE.

Why We Are At War

The investigation carried on against Gabrilo Princip and accomplices in the Court of Sarajevo, on account of the assassination on June 28th has, so far, yielded the following results:

1. The plan to murder Arch-Duke Franz Ferdinand during his stay in Sarajevo was conceived in Belgrade by Gabrilo Princip, Nedeljko, Gabrinowic, and a certain Milan Ciganowic and Trifko Grabez, with the aid of Major Voja Tankosic.

2. The six bombs and four Browning pistols which were used by the criminals, were obtained by Milan Ciganowic and Major Tankosic, and presented to Princip Gabrinowic in Belgrade.

3. The bombs are hand grenades, manufactured at the arsenal of the Servian Army in Kragujevac.

4. To insure the success of the assassination, Milan Ciganowic instructed Princip Gabrinowic in the use of the grenades and gave instructions in shooting with Browning pistols to Princip Grabez in a forest near the target practice field of Topshider—(outside Belgrade).

5. In order to enable the crossing of the frontier of Bosnia and Herzegovina by Princip Gabrinowic and Grabez, and the smuggling of their arms, a secret system of transportation was organized by Ciganowic. The entry of the criminals with their arms into Bosnia and Herzegovina was effected by the frontier captains of Shabatz (Rade Popowic) and of Loznica, as well as by the custom house official Rudivoy Grbic of Loznica with the aid of several other persons.

THE SERVIAN ANSWER.

Presented at Vienna, July 25th, 1914. (With Austria's commentaries in italics.)

The Royal Government has received the communication of the Imperial and Royal Government of the 23rd inst. and is convinced that its reply will dissipate any misunderstanding which threatens to destroy the friendly and neighborly relations between the Austrian monarchy and the kingdom of Servia.

Why We Are At War

The Royal Government is conscious that nowhere there have been renewed protests against the great neighborly monarchy like those which at one time were expressed in the Skuptschina, as well as in the declaration and actions of the responsible representatives of the state at that time, and which were terminated by the Servian declaration of March 31st 1909; furthermore that since that time neither the different corporations of the kingdom, nor the officials have made an attempt to alter the political and judicial condition created in Bosnia and the Herzegovina. The Royal Government states that the I. and R. Government has made no protestation in this sense excepting in the case of a text book, in regard to which the I. and R. Government has received an entirely satisfactory explanation. Servia has given during the time of the Balcan crisis in numerous cases evidence of her pacific and moderate policy, and it is only owing to Servia and the sacrifices which she has brought in the interest of the peace of Europe that this peace has been preserved.

The Royal Servian Government limits itself to establishing that since the declaration of March 31st 1909, there has been no attempt on the part of the Servian Government to alter the position of Bosnia and the Herzegovina.

With this she deliberately shifts the foundation of our note, as we have not insisted that she and her officials have undertaken anything official in this direction. Our gravamen is that in spite of the obligation assumed in the cited note, she has omitted to suppress the movement directed against the territorial integrity of the monarchy.

Her obligation consisted in changing her attitude and the entire direction of her policies, and in entering into friendly and neighborly relations with the Austro—Hungarian monarchy, and not only not to interfere with the possession of Bosnia.

The Royal Government cannot be made responsible for expressions of a private character, as for instance newspaper articles and the peaceable work of societies, expressions which are of very common appearance in other countries, and which ordinarily are not under the control of the state. This, all the less, as the Royal Government has shown great courtesy in the solution of a whole series of questions which have arisen between Servia and Austria—Hungary, whereby it has succeeded to solve the greater number thereof, in favor of the progress of both countries.

The assertion of the Royal Servian Government that the expressions of the press and the activity of Servian associations possess a private character and thus escape governmental control, stands in full contrast with the institutions of modern states and even the most liberal of press and society laws, which nearly everywhere subject the press and the societies to a certain control of the state. This is also provided for by the Servian institutions. The rebuke against the Servian Government consists in the fact that it has totally omitted to supervise its press and its societies, in so far as it knew their direction to be hostile to the monarchy.

The Royal Government was therefore painfully surprised by the assertions that citizens of Servia had participated in the preparations of the outrage in Sarajevo. The Government expected to be invited to cooperate in the investigation of the crime, and it was ready in order to prove its complete correctness, to proceed against all persons in regard to whom it would receive information.

This assertion is incorrect. The Servian Government was accurately informed about the suspicion resting upon quite definite personalities and not only in the position, but also obliged by its own laws to institute investigations spontaneously. The Servian Government has done nothing in this direction.

According to the wishes of the I. and R. Government, the Royal Government is prepared to surrender to the court, without regard to position and rank, every Servian citizen, for whose participation in the crime of Sarajevo it should have received proof. It binds itself particularly on the first page of the official organ of the 26th of July to publish the following enunciation:

"The Royal Servian Government condemns every propaganda which should be directed against Austria–Hungary, i. e. the entirety of such activities as aim towards the separation of certain territories from the Austro–Hungarian monarchy, and it regrets sincerely the lamentable consequences of these criminal machinations."

The Austrian demand reads:

"The Royal Servian Government condemns the propaganda against Austria–Hungary...."

Why We Are At War

The alteration of the declaration as demanded by us, which has been made by the Royal Servian Government, is meant to imply that a propaganda directed against Austria–Hungary does not exist, and that it is not aware of such. This formula is insincere, and the Servian Government reserves itself the supterfuge for later occasions that it had not disavowed by this declaration the existing propaganda, nor recognized the same as hostile to the monarchy, whence it could deduce further that it is not obliged to suppress in the future a propaganda similar to the present one.

The Royal Government regrets that according to a communication of the I. and R. Government certain Servian officers and functionaries have participated in the propaganda just referred to, and that these have therefore endangered the amicable relations for the observation of which the Royal Government had solemnly obliged itself through the declaration of March 31st, 1909.

The Government ... identical with the demanded text.

The formula as demanded by Austria reads:

"The Royal Government regrets that Servian officers and functionaries ... have participated...."

Also with this formula and the further addition "according to the declaration of the I. and R. Government", the Servian Government pursues the object, already indicated above, to preserve a free hand for the future.

The Royal Government binds itself further:

1. During the next regular meeting of the Skuptschina to embody in the press laws a clause, to wit, that the incitement to hatred of, and contempt for, the monarchy is to be must severely punished, as well as every publication whose general tendency is directed against the territorial integrity of Austria–Hungary.

It binds itself in view of the coming revision of the constitution to embody an amendment into Art. 22 of the constitutional law which permits the confiscation of such publications as is at present impossible according to the clear definition of Art. 22 of the constitution.

Why We Are At War

Austria had demanded:

1. To suppress every publication which incites to hatred and contempt for the monarchy, and whose tendency is directed against the territorial integrity of the monarchy.

We wanted to bring about the obligation for Servia to take care that such attacks of the press would cease in the future.

Instead Servia offers to pass certain laws which are meant as means towards this end, viz.:

a) A law according to which the expressions of the press hostile to the monarchy can be individually punished, a matter, which is immaterial to us, all the more so, as the individual prosecution of press intrigues is very rarely possible and as, with a lax enforcement of such laws, the few cases of this nature would not be punished. The proposition, therefore, does not meet our demand in any way, and it offers not the least guarantee for the desired success.

b) An amendment to Art. 22 of the constitution, which would permit confiscation, a proposal, which does not satisfy us, as the existence of such a law in Servia is of no use to us. For we want the obligation of the Government to enforce it and that has not been promised us.

These proposals are therefore entirely unsatisfactory and evasive as we are not told within what time these laws will be passed, and as in the event of the notpassing of these laws by the Skuptschina everything would remain as it is, excepting the event of a possible resignation of the Government.

2. The Government possesses no proofs and the note of the I. and R. Government does not submit them that the society Narodna Odbrana and other similar societies have committed, up to the present, any criminal actions of this manner through anyone of their members. Notwithstanding this, the Royal Government will accept the demand of the I. and R. Government and dissolve the society Narodna Odbrana, as well as every society which should act against Austria–Hungary.

Why We Are At War

The propaganda of the Narodna Odbrana and affiliated societies hostile to the monarchy fills the entire public life of Servia; it is therefore an entirely inacceptable reserve if the Servian Government asserts that it knows nothing about it. Aside from this, our demand is not completely fulfilled, as we have asked besides:

"To confiscate the means of propaganda of these societies to prevent the reformation of the dissolved societies under another name and in another form."

In these two directions the Belgrade Cabinet is perfectly silent, so that through this semi−concession there is offered us no guarantee for putting an end to the agitation of the associations hostile to the Monarchy, especially the Narodna Odbrana.

3. The Royal Servian Government binds itself without delay to eliminate from the public instruction in Servia anything which might further the propaganda directed against Austria−Hungary provided the I. and R. Government furnishes actual proofs.

Also in this case the Servian Government first demands proofs for a propaganda hostile to the Monarchy in the public instruction of Servia while it must know that the text books introduced in the Servian schools contain objectionable matter in this direction and that a large portion of the teachers are in the camp of the Narodna Odbrana and affiliated societies.

Furthermore, the Servian Government has not fulfilled a part of our demands, as we have requested, as it omitted in its text the addition desired by us: "as far as the body of instructors is concerned, as well as the means of instruction"—a sentence which shows clearly where the propaganda hostile to the Monarchy is to be found in the Servian schools.

4. The Royal Government is also ready to dismiss those officers and officials from the military and civil services in regard to whom it has been proved by judicial investigation that they have been guilty of actions against the territorial integrity of the monarchy; it expects that the I. and R. Government communicate to it for the purpose of starting the investigation the names of these officers and officials, and the facts with which they have been charged.

By promising the dismissal from the military and civil services of those officers and officials who are found guilty by judicial procedure, the Servian Government limits its assent to those cases, in which these persons have been charged with a crime according to the statutory code. As, however, we demand the removal of such officers and officials as indulge in a propaganda hostile to the Monarchy, which is generally not punishable in Servia, our demands have not been fulfilled in this point.

5. The Royal Government confesses that it is not clear about the sense and the scope of that demand of the I. and R. Government which concerns the obligation on the part of the Royal Servian Government to permit the cooperation of officials of the I. and R. Government on Servian territory, but it declares that it is willing to accept every cooperation which does not run counter to international law and criminal law, as well as to the friendly and neighborly relations.

The international law, as well as the criminal law, has nothing to do with this question; it is purely a matter of the nature of state police which is to be solved by way of a special agreement. The reserved attitude of Servia is therefore incomprehensible and on account of its vague general form it would lead to unbridgeable difficulties.

6. The Royal Government considers it its duty as a matter of course to begin an investigation against all those persons who have participated in the outrage of June 28th and who are in its territory. As far as the cooperation in this investigation of specially delegated officials of the I. and R. Government is concerned, this cannot be accepted, as this is a violation of the constitution and of criminal procedure. Yet in some cases the result of the investigation might be communicated to the Austro–Hungarian officials.

The Austrian demand was clear and unmistakable:

1. To institute a criminal procedure against the participants in the outrage.

2. Participation by I. and R. Government officials in the examinations ("Recherche" in contrast with "enquete judiciaire").

3. It did not occur to us to let I. and R. Government officials participate in the Servian court procedure; they were to cooperate only in the police researches which had to furnish and fix the material for the investigation.

If the Servian Government misunderstands us here, this is done deliberately, for it must be familiar with the difference between "enquete judiciaire" and simple police researches. As it desired to escape from every control of the investigation which would yield, if correctly carried out, highly undesirable results for it, and as it possesses no means to refuse in a plausible manner the cooperation of our officials (precedents for such police intervention exist in great number) it tries to justify its refusal by showing up our demands as impossible.

7. The Royal Government has ordered on the evening of the day on which the note was received the arrest of Major Voislar Tankosic. However, as far as Milan Ciganowic is concerned who is a citizen of the Austro–Hungarian Monarchy and who has been employed till June 28th with the Railroad Department, it has as yet been impossible to locate him, wherefor a warrant has been issued against him.

The I. and R. Government is asked to make known, as soon as possible, for the purpose of conducting the investigation, the existing grounds for suspicion and the proofs of guilt, obtained in the investigation at Sarajevo.

This reply is disingenuous. According to our investigation, Ciganowic, by order of the police prefect in Belgrade, left three days after the outrage for Ribari, after it had become known that Ciganowic had participated in the outrage. In the first place, it is therefore incorrect that Ciganowic left the Servian service on June 28th. In the second place, we add that the prefect of police at Belgrade who had himself caused the departure of this Ciganowic and who knew his whereabout, declared in an interview that a man by the name of Milan Ciganowic did not exist in Belgrade.

8. The Servian Government will amplify and render more severe the existing measures against the suppression of smuggling of arms and explosives.

It is a matter of course that it will proceed at once against, and punish severely, those officials of the frontier service on the line Shabatz–Loznica who violated their duty and who have permitted the perpetrators of the crime to cross the frontier.

9. The Royal Government is ready to give explanations about the expressions which its officials in Servia and abroad have made in interviews after the outrage and which, according to the assertion of the I. and R. Government, were hostile to the Monarchy. As

soon as the I. and R. Government points out in detail where those expressions were made and succeeds in proving that those expressions have actually been made by the functionaries concerned, the Royal Government itself will take care that the necessary evidences and proofs are collected therefor.

The Royal Servian Government must be aware of the interviews in question. If it demands of the I. and R. Government that it should furnish all kinds of detail about the said interviews and if it reserves for itself the right of a formal investigation, it shows that it is not its intention seriously to fulfill the demand.

10. The Royal Government will notify the I. and R. Government, so far as this has not been already done by the present note, of the execution of the measures in question as soon as one of those measures has been ordered and put into execution.

The Royal Servian Government believes it to be to the common interest not to rush the solution of this affair and it is therefore, in case the I. and R. Government should not consider itself satisfied with this answer, ready, as ever, to accept a peaceable solution, be it by referring the decision of this question to the International Court at the Hague or by leaving it to the decision of the Great Powers who have participated in the working out of the declaration given by the Servian Government on March 31st 1909.

The Servian Note, therefore, is entirely a play for time.

EXHIBIT I.

The Chancellor to the Imperial Ambassadors at Paris, London, and St. Petersburg, on Juli 23rd 1914.

The publications of the Austro–Hungarian Government concerning the circumstances under which the Assassination of the Austrian successor to the throne and his consort took place, disclose clearly the aims which the pan–Serb propaganda has set itself and the means which it utilizes for their realization. Through the published facts the last doubt must disappear that the center of action of the efforts for the separation of the south slavic provinces from the Austro–Hungarian Monarchy and their union with the Servian Kingdom must be sought in Belgrade where it displays its activity with the connivance of members of the Government and of the Army.

Why We Are At War

The Serb intrigues may be traced back through a series of years. In a specially marked manner the pan–Serb chauvinism showed itself during the Bosnian crisis. Only to the far–reaching self–restraint and moderation of the Austro–Hungarian Government and the energetic intercession of the powers is it to be ascribed that the provocations to which at that time Austria–Hungary was exposed on the part of Servia, did not lead to a conflict. The assurance of future well–behaviour which the Servian Government gave at that time, it has not kept. Under the very eyes, at least with the tacit sufferance of official Servia, the pan–Serb propaganda has meanwhile increased in scope and intensity; at its door is to be laid the latest crime the threads of which lead to Belgrade. It has become evident that it is compatible neither with the dignity nor with the self–preservation of the Austro–Hungarian Monarchy to view any longer idly the doings across the border through which the safety and the integrity of the Monarchy are permanently threatened. With this state of affairs, the action as well as the demands of the Austro–Hungarian government can be viewed only as justifiable. Nevertheless, the attitude assumed by public opinion as well as by the government in Servia does not preclude the fear that the Servian government will decline to meet these demands and that it will allow itself to be carried away into a provocative attitude toward Austria–Hungary. Nothing would remain for the Austro–Hungarian government, unless it renounced definitely its position as a great power, but to press its demands with the Servian government and, if need be, enforce the same by appeal to military measures, in regard to which the choice of means must be left with it.

I have the honor to request you to express yourself in the sense indicated above to (the present representative of M. Viviani) (Sir Edward Grey) (M. Sasonow) and therewith give special emphasis to the view that in this question there is concerned an affair which should be settled solely between Austria–Hungary and Servia, the limitation to which it must be the earnest endeavor of the powers to insure. We anxiously desire the localisation of the conflict because every intercession of another power on account of the various treaty–alliances would precipitate inconceivable consequences.

I shall look forward with interest to a telegraphic report about the course of your interview.

EXHIBIT 2.

The Chancellor to the Governments of Germany. Confidential. Berlin, July 28, 1914.

Why We Are At War

You will make the following report to the Government to which you are accredited:

In view of the facts which the Austrian Government has published in its note to the Servian Government, the last doubt must disappear that the outrage to which the Austro–Hungarian successor to the throne has fallen a victim, was prepared in Servia, to say the least with the connivance of members of the Servian government and army. It is a product of the pan–Serb intrigues which for a series of years have become a source of permanent disturbance for the Austro–Hungarian Monarchy and for the whole of Europe.

The pan–Serb chauvinism appeared especially marked during the Bosnian crisis. Only to the far–reaching self–restraint and moderation of the Austro–Hungarian government and the energetic intercession of the powers is it to be ascribed that the provocations to which Austria–Hungary was exposed at that time, did not lead to a conflict. The assurance of future well–behaviour, which the Servian government gave at that time, it has not kept. Under the very eyes, at least with the tacit sufferance of official Servia, the pan–Serb propaganda has meanwhile continued to increase in scope and intensity. It would be compatible neither with its dignity nor with its right to self–preservation if the Austro–Hungarian government persisted to view idly any longer the intrigues beyond the frontier, through which the safety and the integrity of the monarchy are permanently threatened. With this state of affairs, the action as well as the demands of the Austro–Hungarian Government can be viewed only as justifiable.

The reply of the Servian government to the demands which the Austro–Hungarian government put on the 23rd inst. through its representative in Belgrade, shows that the dominating factors in Servia are not inclined to cease their former policies and agitation. There will remain nothing else for the Austro–Hungarian government than to press its demands, if need be through military action, unless it renounces for good its position as a great power.

Some Russian personalities deem it their right as a matter of course and a task of Russia's to actively become a party to Servia in the conflict between Austria–Hungary and Servia. For the European conflagration which would result from a similar step by Russia, the "Nowoje Wremja" believes itself justified in making Germany responsible in so far as it does not induce Austria–Hungary to yield.

Why We Are At War

The Russian press thus turns conditions upside down. It is not Austria–Hungary which has called forth the conflict with Servia, but it is Servia which, through unscrupulous favor toward pan–Serb aspirations, even in parts of the Austro–Hungarian monarchy, threatens the same in her existence and creates conditions, which eventually found expression in the wanton outrage at Sarajevo. If Russia believes that it must champion the cause of Servia in this matter, it certainly has the right to do so. However, it must realize that it makes the Serb activities its own, to undermine the conditions of existence of the Austro–Hungarian monarchy, and that thus it bears the sole responsibility if out of the Austro–Servian affair, which all other great powers desire to localize, there arises a European war. This responsibility of Russia's is evident and it weighs the more heavily as Count Berchtold has officially declared to Russia that Austria–Hungary has no intention to acquire Servian territory or to touch the existence of the Servian Kingdom, but only desires peace against the Servian intrigues threatening its existence.

The attitude of the Imperial government in this question is clearly indicated. The agitation conducted by the pan–Slavs in Austria–Hungary has for its goal, with the destruction of the Austro–Hungarian monarchy, the scattering or weakening of the triple alliance with a complete isolation of the German Empire in consequence. Our own interest therefore calls us to the side of Austria–Hungary. The duty, if at all possible, to guard Europe against a universal war, points to the support by ourselves of those endeavors which aim at the localization of the conflict, faithful to the course of those policies which we have carried out successfully for forty–four years in the interest of the preservation of the peace of Europe.

Should, however, against our hope, through the interference of Russia the fire be spread, we should have to support, faithful to our duty as allies, the neighbor–monarchy with all the power at our command. We shall take the sword only if forced to it, but then in the clear consciousness that we are not guilty of the calamity which war will bring upon the peoples of Europe.

EXHIBIT 3.

Telegram of the Imperial Ambassador at Vienna to the Chancellor on July 24th 1914.

Count Berchtold has asked to–day for the Russian Charge d'affaires in order to explain to him thoroughly and cordially Austria–Hungary's point of view toward Servia. After recapitulation of the historical development of the past few years, he emphasized that the Monarchy entertained no thought of conquest toward Servia. Austria–Hungary would not claim Servian territory. It insisted merely that this step was meant as a definite means of checking the Serb intrigues. Impelled by force of circumstance, Austria–Hungary must have a guaranty for continued amicable relations with Servia. It was far from him to intend to bring about a change in the balance of powers in the Balcan. The Charge d'affaires who had received no instructions from St. Petersburg, took the discussion of the Secretary "ad referendum" with the promise to submit it immediately to Sasonow.

EXHIBIT 4.

Telegram of the Imperial Ambassador at St. Petersburg to the Chancellor on July 24th 1914.

I have just utilized the contents of Order 592 in a prolonged interview with Sasonow. The Secretary (Sasonow) indulged in unmeasured accusations toward Austria–Hungary and he was very much agitated. He declared most positively that Russia could not permit under any circumstances that the Servo–Austrian difficulty be settled alone between the parties concerned.

EXHIBIT 5.

The Imperial Ambassador at St. Petersburg to the Chancellor. Telegram of July 26th 1914.

The Austro–Hungarian Ambassador had an extended interview with Sasonow this afternoon. Both parties had a satisfactory impression as they told me afterwards. The assurance of the Ambassador that Austria–Hungary had no idea of conquest but wished to obtain peace at last at her frontiers, greatly pacified the Secretary.

EXHIBIT 6.

Telegram of the Imperial Ambassador at St. Petersburg, to the Chancellor on July 25th 1914.

Message to H.M. from General von Chelius (German honorary aide de camp to the Czar).

The manoeuvres of the troops in the Krasnoe camp were suddenly interrupted and the regiments returned to their garrisons at once. The manoeuvres have been cancelled. The military pupils were raised to-day to the rank of officers instead of next fall. At headquarters there obtains great excitement over the procedure of Austria. I have the impression that complete preparations for mobilization against Austria are being made.

EXHIBIT 7.

Telegram of the Imperial Ambassador at St. Petersburg, to the Chancellor on July 26th 1914.

The military attache requests the following message to be sent to the general staff:

I deem it certain that mobilisation has been ordered for Kiev and Odessa. It is doubtful at Warsaw and Moscow and improbable elsewhere.

EXHIBIT 8.

Telegram of the Imperial Consulate at Kovno to the Chancellor on July 27th 1914.

Kovno has been declared to be in a state of war.

(Note that the official translator means *Kriegszustand*.)

EXHIBIT 9.

Telegram of the Imperial Minister at Berne to the Chancellor on July 27th 1914.

Have learned reliably that French XIVth corps has discontinued manoeuvres.

EXHIBIT 10.

Telegram of the Chancellor to the Imperial Ambassador at London. Urgent. July 26th 1914.

Austria–Hungary has declared in St. Petersburg officially and solemnly that it has no desire for territorial gain in Servia; that it will not touch the existence of the Kingdom, but that it desires to establish peaceful conditions. According to news received here, the call for several classes of the reserves is expected immediately which is equivalent to mobilization.[186] If this news proves correct, we shall be forced to contermeasures very much against our own wishes. Our desire to localize the conflict and to preserve the peace of Europe remains unchanged. We ask to act in this sense at St. Petersburg with all possible emphasis.

[Footnote 186: The German text inserts *auch gegen uns*, i.e. also against us.]

EXHIBIT 10a.

Telegram of the Imperial Chancellor to the Imperial Ambassador at Paris. July 26th 1914.

After officially declaring to Russia that Austria–Hungary has no intention to acquire territorial gain and to touch the existence of the Kingdom, the decision whether there is to be a European war rests solely with Russia which has to bear the entire responsibility. We depend upon France with which we are at one in the desire for the preservation of the peace of Europe that it will exercise its influence at St. Petersburg in favour of peace.

EXHIBIT 10b.

Telegram of the Chancellor to the Imperial Ambassador at St. Petersburg on July 26th, 1914.

After Austria's solemn declaration of its territorial dis–interestedness, the responsibility for a possible disturbance of the peace of Europe through a Russian intervention rests solely upon Russia. We trust still that Russia will undertake no steps which will threaten seriously the peace of Europe.

EXHIBIT 11.

Telegram of the Imperial Ambassador at St. Petersburg to the Chancellor on July 27th, 1914.

Why We Are At War

Military Attache reports a conversation with the Secretary of War:

Sasonow has requested the latter to enlighten me on the situation. The Secretary of War has given me his word of honor that no order to mobilize has as yet been issued. Though general preparations are being made, no reserves were called and no horses mustered. If Austria crossed the Servian frontier, such military districts as are directed toward Austria, viz., Kiev, Odessa, Moscow, Kazan, are to be mobilized. Under no circumstances those on the German frontier, Warsaw, Vilna, St. Petersburg. Peace with Germany was desired very much. Upon my inquiry into the object of mobilization against Austria he shrugged his shoulders and referred to the diplomats. I told the Secretary that we appreciated the friendly intentions, but considered mobilization even against Austria as very menacing.

EXHIBIT 12.

Telegram of the Chancellor to the Imperial Ambassador at London on July 27th, 1914.

We know as yet nothing of a suggestion of Sir Edward Grey's to hold a quadruple conference in London. It is impossible for us to place our ally in his dispute with Servia before a European tribunal. Our mediation must be limited to the danger of an Austro–Russian conflict.

EXHIBIT 13.

Telegram of the Chancellor to the Imperial Ambassador at London on July 25th, 1914.

The distinction made by Sir Edward Grey between an Austro–Servian and an Austro–Russian conflict is perfectly correct. We do not wish to interpose in the former any more than England, and as heretofore we take the position that this question must be localized by virtue of all powers refraining from intervention. It is therefore our hope that Russia will refrain from any action in view of her responsibility and the seriousness of the situation. We are prepared, in the event of an Austro–Russian controversy, quite apart from our known duties as allies, to intercede between Russia and Austria jointly with the other powers.

EXHIBIT 14.

Telegram of the Chancellor to the Imperial Ambassador at St. Petersburg on July 28th, 1914.

We continue in our endeavor to induce Vienna to elucidate in St. Petersburg the object and scope of the Austrian action in Servia in a manner both convincing and satisfactory to Russia. The declaration of war which has meanwhile ensued alters nothing in this matter.

EXHIBIT 15.

Telegram of the Chancellor to the Imperial Ambassador in London on July 27th, 1914.

We have at once started the mediation proposal in Vienna in the sense as desired by Sir Edward Grey. We have communicated besides to Count Berchtold the desire of M. Sasonow for a direct parley with Vienna.

EXHIBIT 16.

Telegram of the Imperial Ambassador at Vienna to the Chancellor on July 28th, 1914.

Count Berchtold requests me to express to Your Excellency his thanks for the communication of the English mediation proposal. He states, however, that after the opening of hostilities by Servia and the subsequent declaration of war, the step appears belated.

EXHIBIT 17.

Telegram of the Chancellor to the Imperial Ambassador at Paris on July 29th, 1914.

News received here regarding French preparations of war multiplies from hour to hour. I request that You call the attention of the French Government to this and accentuate that such measures would call forth counter–measures on our part. We should have to proclaim threatening state of war (drohende Kriegsgefahr), and while this would not mean a call for the reserves or mobilization, yet the tension would be aggravated. We continue to hope for the preservation of peace.

EXHIBIT 18.

Telegram of the Military Attache at St. Petersburg to H. M. the Kaiser on July 30th, 1914.

Prince Troubetzki said to me yesterday, after causing Your Majesty's telegram to be delivered at once to Czar Nicolas: Thank God that a telegram of Your Emperor has come. He has just told me the telegram has made a deep impression upon the Czar but as the mobilization against Austria had already been ordered and Sasonow had convinced His Majesty that it was no longer possible to retreat, His Majesty was sorry he could not change it any more. I then told him that the guilt for the measureless consequences lay at the door of premature mobilization against Austria–Hungary which after all was involved merely in a local war with Servia, for Germany's answer was clear and the responsibility rested upon Russia which ignored Austria–Hungary's assurance that it had no intentions of territorial gain in Servia. Austria–Hungary mobilized against Servia and not against Russia and there was no ground for an immediate action on the part of Russia. I further added that in Germany one could not understand any more Russia's phrase that "she could not desert her brethren in Servia", after the horrible crime of Sarajevo. I told him finally he need not wonder if Germany's army were to be mobilized.

EXHIBIT 19.

Telegram of the Chancellor to the Imperial Ambassador at Rome on July 31st, 1914.

We have continued to negotiate between Russia and Austria–Hungary through a direct exchange of telegrams between His Majesty the Kaiser and His Majesty the Czar, as well as in conjunction with Sir Edward Grey. Through the mobilization of Russia all our efforts have been greatly handicapped if they have not become impossible. In spite of pacifying assurances Russia is taking such far–reaching measures against us that the situation is becoming continually more menacing.

EXHIBIT 20.

I. His Majesty to the Czar.

July 28th, 10.45 p.m.

Why We Are At War

I have heard with the greatest anxiety of the impression which is caused by the action of Austria–Hungary against Servia. The inscrupulous agitation which has been going on for years in Servia, has led to the revolting crime of which Archduke Franz Ferdinand has become a victim. The spirit which made the Servians murder their own King and his consort, still dominates that country. Doubtless You will agree with me that both of us, You as well as I, and all other sovereigns, have a common interest to insist that all those who are responsible for this horrible murder, shall suffer their deserved punishment.

On the other hand I by no means overlook the difficulty encountered by You and Your Government to stem the tide of public opinion. In view of the cordial friendship which has joined us both for a long time with firm ties, I shall use my entire influence to induce Austria–Hungary to obtain a frank and satisfactory understanding with Russia. I hope confidently that You will support me in my efforts to overcome all difficulties which may yet arise.

Your most sincere and devoted friend and cousin

signed: Wilhelm.

EXHIBIT 21.

II. The Czar to His Majesty.

Peterhof Palace, July 29th, 1 p.m.

I am glad that You are back in Germany. In this serious moment I ask You earnestly to help me. An ignominious war has been declared against a weak country and in Russia the indignation which I fully share is tremendous. I fear that very soon I shall be unable to resist the pressure exercised upon me and that I shall be forced to take measures which will lead to war. To prevent a calamity as a European war would be, I urge You in the name of our old friendship to do all in Your power to restrain Your ally from going too far.

signed: Nicolas.

EXHIBIT 22.

Why We Are At War

III. His Majesty to the Czar.

July 29th, 6.30 p.m.

I have received Your telegram and I share Your desire for the conservation of peace. However: I cannot—as I told You in my first telegram—consider the action of Austria–Hungary as an "ignominious war". Austria–Hungary knows from experience that the promises of Servia as long as they are merely on paper are entirely unreliable.

According to my opinion the action of Austria–Hungary is to be considered as an attempt to receive full guaranty that the promises of Servia are effectively translated into deeds. In this opinion I am strengthened by the explanation of the Austrian cabinet that Austria–Hungary intended no territorial gain at the expense of Servia. I am therefore of opinion that it is perfectly possible for Russia to remain a spectator in the Austro–Servian war without drawing Europe into the most terrible war it has ever seen. I believe that a direct understanding is possible and desirable between Your Government and Vienna, an understanding which—as I have already telegraphed You—my Government endeavors to aid with all possible effort. Naturally military measures by Russia, which might be construed as a menace by Austria–Hungary, would accelerate a calamity which both of us desire to avoid and would undermine my position as mediator which—upon Your appeal to my friendship and aid—I willingly accepted.

signed: Wilhelm.

EXHIBIT 23.

IV. His Majesty to the Czar.

July 30th, 1 a.m.

My Ambassador has instructions to direct the attention of Your Government to the dangers and serious consequences of a mobilization; I have told You the same in my last telegram. Austria–Hungary has mobilized only against Servia, and only a part of her army. If Russia, as seems to be the case according to Your advice and that of Your Government, mobilizes against Austria–Hungary, the part of the mediator with which You have entrusted me in such friendly manner and which I have accepted upon Your express desire, is threatened if not made impossible. The entire weight of decision now rests upon Your shoulders, You have to bear the responsibility for war or peace.

signed: Wilhelm.

EXHIBIT 23a.

V. The Czar to His Majesty.

Peterhof, July 30th, 1914, 1.20 p.m.

I thank You from my heart for Your quick reply. I am sending to-night Tatisheft (Russian honorary aide to the Kaiser) with instructions. The military measures now taking form were decided upon five days ago, and for the reason of defence against the preparations of Austria. I hope with all my heart that these measures will not influence in any manner Your position as mediator which I appraise very highly. We need Your strong pressure upon Austria so that an understanding can be arrived at with us.

Nicolas.

EXHIBIT 24.

Telegram of the Chancellor to the Imperial Ambassador at St. Petersburg on July 31st, 1914. Urgent.

In spite of negotiations still pending and although we have up to this hour made no preparations for mobilization, Russia has mobilized her entire army and navy, hence also against us. On account of these Russian measures we have been forced, for the safety of the country, to proclaim the threatening state of war, which does not yet imply mobilization. Mobilization, however, is bound to follow if Russia does not stop every measure of war against us and against Austria–Hungary within 12 hours and notifies us definitely to this effect. Please to communicate this at once to M. Sasonow and wire hour of communication.

EXHIBIT 25.

Why We Are At War

Telegram of the Chancellor to the Imperial Ambassador in Paris on July 31st, 1914. Urgent.

Russia has ordered mobilization of her entire army and fleet, therefore also against us in spite of our still pending mediation. We have therefore declared the threatening state of war which is bound to be followed by mobilization unless Russia stops within 12 hours all measures of war against us and Austria. Mobilization inevitably implies war. Please ask French Government whether it intends to remain neutral in a Russo–German war. Reply must be made in 18 hours. Wire at once hour of inquiry. Utmost speed necessary.

EXHIBIT 26.

Telegram of the Chancellor to the Imperial Ambassador in St. Petersburg on August 1st, 12.52 p.m. Urgent.

If the Russian Government gives no satisfactory reply to our demand, Your Excellency will please transmit this afternoon 5 o'clock (mid–European time) the following statement:

"Le Gouvernement Imperial s'est efforce des les debuts de la crise de la mener a une solution pacifique. Se rendant a un desir que lui en avail ete exprime par Sa Majeste l'Empereur de Russie, Sa Majeste l'Empereur d'Allemagne d'accord avec l'Angleterre etait applique a accomplir un role mediateur aupres des Cabinets de Vienne et de St. Petersbourg, lorsque la Russie, sans en attendre le resultat, proceda a la mobilisation de la totalite de ses forces de terre et de mer.

"A la suite de cette mesure menacante motivee par aucun preparatif militaire de la part de l'Allemagne, l'Empire Allemand se trouva vis–a–vis d'un danger grave et imminent. Si le Gouvernement Imperial eut manque de parer a ce peril il aurait compromis la securite et l'existence meme de l'Allemagne. Par consequent le Gouvernement Allemand se vit force de s'adresser au Gouvernement de Sa Majeste l'Empereur de toutes les Russies en sistant sur la cessation des dits actes militaires. La Russie ayant refuse de faire droit a cette demande et ayant manifeste par ce refus, que son action etait dirigee contre l'Allemande, j'ai l'honneur d'ordre de mon Gouvernement de faire savoir a Votre Excellence ce qui suit:

"Sa Majeste l'Empereur, mon auguste Souverain, an nom de l'Empire releve le defi et Se considere en etat de guerre avec la Russie."

Please wire urgent receipt and time of carrying out this instruction by Russian time.

Please ask for Your passports and turn over protection and affairs to the American Embassy.

EXHIBIT 27.

Telegram of the Imperial Ambassador in Paris to the Chancellor on August 1st 1.05 p. m.

Upon my repeated definite inquiry whether France would remain neutral in the event of a Russo–German war, the Prime Minister declared that France would do that which her interests dictated.

APPENDIX II. EXTRACTS FROM

SIR EDWARD GREY'S

CORRESPONDENCE

RESPECTING THE EUROPEAN

CRISIS

For the complete Correspondence see White Paper Miscellaneous No. 6 (1914) (Cd. 7467), presented to both Houses of Parliament by Command of His Majesty, August 1914

No. 13.

Note communicated by Russian Ambassador, July 25.

(Translation.)

Why We Are At War

M. Sazionof telegraphs to the Russian Charge d'Affaires at Vienna on the 11th (24th) July, 1914:

"The communication made by Austria–Hungary to the Powers the day after the presentation of the ultimatum at Belgrade leaves a period to the Powers which is quite insufficient to enable them to take any steps which might help to smooth away the difficulties that have arisen.

"In order to prevent the consequences, equally incalculable and fatal to all the Powers, which may result from the course of action followed by the Austro–Hungarian Government, it seems to us to be above all essential that the period allowed for the Servian reply should be extended. Austria–Hungary, having declared her readiness to inform the Powers of the results of the enquiry upon which the Imperial and Royal Government base their accusations, should equally allow them sufficient time to study them.

"In this case, if the Powers were convinced that certain of the Austrian demands were well founded, they would be in a position to offer advice to the Servian Government.

"A refusal to prolong the term of the ultimatum would render nugatory the proposals made by the Austro–Hungarian Government to the Powers, and would be in contradiction to the very bases of international relations.

"Prince Kudachef is instructed to communicate the above to the Cabinet at Vienna.

"M. Sazonof hopes that His Britannic Majesty's Government will adhere to the point of view set forth above, and he trusts that Sir E. Grey will see his way to furnish similar instructions to the British Ambassador at Vienna."

No. 17.

Sir G. Buchanan to Sir Edward Grey.—(Received July 25.)

(Telegraphic.) *St. Petersburgh, July 25, 1914.*

I Saw the Minister for Foreign Affairs this morning....

Why We Are At War

The Minister for Foreign Affairs said that Servia was quite ready to do as you had suggested and to punish those proved to be guilty, but that no independent State could be expected to accept the political demands which had been put forward. The Minister for Foreign Affairs thought, from a conversation which he had with the Servian Minister yesterday, that, in the event of the Austrians attacking Servia, the Servian Government would abandon Belgrade, and withdraw their forces into the interior, while they would at the same time appeal to the Powers to help them. His Excellency was in favour of their making this appeal. He would like to see the question placed on an international footing, as the obligations taken by Servia in 1908, to which reference is made in the Austrian ultimatum, were given not to Austria, but to the Powers.

If Servia should appeal to the Powers, Russia would be quite ready to stand aside and leave the question in the hands of England, France, Germany, and Italy. It was possible, in his opinion, that Servia might propose to submit the question to arbitration.

On my expressing the earnest hope that Russia would not precipitate war by mobilising until you had had time to use your influence in favour of peace, his Excellency assured me that Russia had no aggressive intentions, and she would take no action until it was forced on her. Austria's action was in reality directed against Russia. She aimed at overthrowing the present *status quo* in the Balkans, and establishing her own hegemony there. He did not believe that Germany really wanted war, but her attitude was decided by ours. If we took our stand firmly with France and Russia there would be no war. If we failed them now, rivers of blood would flow, and we would in the end be dragged into war. I said that England could play the role of mediator at Berlin and Vienna to better purpose as friend who, if her counsels of moderation were disregarded, might one day be converted into an ally, than if she were to declare herself Russia's ally at once. His Excellency said that unfortunately Germany was convinced that she could count upon our neutrality.

I said all I could to impress prudence on the Minister for Foreign Affairs, and warned him that if Russia mobilised, Germany would not be content with mere mobilisation, or give Russia time to carry out hers, but would probably declare war at once. His Excellency replied that Russia could not allow Austria to crush Servia and become the predominant Power in the Balkans, and, if she feels secure of the support of France, she will face all the risks of war. He assured me once more that he did not wish to precipitate a conflict, but that unless Germany could restrain Austria I could regard the situation as desperate.

138

Why We Are At War

No. 18.

Sir H. Rumbold to Sir Edward Grey.—(Received July 25.)

(Telegraphic.) *Berlin, July 25, 1914.*

Your telegram of the 24th July acted on.

Secretary of State for Foreign Affairs says that on receipt of a telegram at 10 this morning from German Ambassador at London, he immediately instructed German Ambassador at Vienna to pass on to Austrian Minister for Foreign Affairs your suggestion for an extension of time limit, and to speak to his Excellency about it. Unfortunately it appeared from press that Count Berchtold is at Ischl, and Secretary of State thought that in these circumstances there would be delay and difficulty in getting time limit extended. Secretary of State said that he did not know what Austria–Hungary had ready on the spot, but he admitted quite freely that Austro–Hungarian Government wished to give the Servians a lesson, and that they meant to take military action. He also admitted that Servian Government could not swallow certain of the Austro–Hungarian demands.

Secretary of State said that a reassuring feature of situation was that Count Berchtold had sent for Russian representative at Vienna and had told him that Austria–Hungary had no intention of seizing Servian territory. This step should, in his opinion, exercise a calming influence at St. Petersburgh. I asked whether it was not to be feared that, in taking military action against Servia, Austria would dangerously excite public opinion in Russia. He said he thought not. He remained of opinion that crisis could be localised. I said that telegrams from Russia in this morning's papers did not look very reassuring, but he maintained his optimistic view with regard to Russia. He said that he had given the Russian Government to understand that last thing Germany wanted was a general war, and he would do all in his power to prevent such a calamity. If the relations between Austria and Russia became threatening, he was quite ready to fall in with your suggestion as to the four Powers working in favour of moderation at Vienna and St. Petersburgh.

Secretary of State confessed privately that he thought the note left much to be desired as a diplomatic document. He repeated very earnestly that, though he had been accused of knowing all about the contents of that note, he had in fact had no such knowledge.

Why We Are At War

No. 41.

Sir M. de Bunsen to Sir Edward Grey.—(Received July 27.)

(Telegraphic.) *Vienna, July* 27, 1914.

I have had conversations with all my colleagues representing the Great Powers. The impression left on my mind is that the Austro–Hungarian note was so drawn up as to make war inevitable; that the Austro–Hungarian Government are fully resolved to have war with Servia; that they consider their position as a Great Power to be at stake; and that until punishment has been administered to Servia it is unlikely that they will listen to proposals of mediation. This country has gone wild with joy at the prospect of war with Servia, and its postponement or prevention would undoubtedly be a great disappointment.

I propose, subject to any special directions you desire to send me, to express to the Austrian Minister for Foreign Affairs the hope of His Majesty's Government that it may yet be possible to avoid war, and to ask his Excellency whether he cannot suggest a way out even now.

No. 43.

Sir E. Goschen to Sir Edward Grey.—(Received July 27.)

(Telegraphic.) *Berlin, July* 27, 1914.

Your telegram of 26th July.

Secretary of State says that conference you suggest would practically amount to a court of arbitration and could not, in his opinion, be called together except at the request of Austria and Russia. He could not therefore fall in with your suggestion, desirous though he was to co–operate for the maintenance of peace. I said I was sure that your idea had nothing to do with arbitration, but meant that representatives of the four nations not directly interested should discuss and suggest means for avoiding a dangerous situation. He maintained, however, that such a conference as you proposed was not practicable. He added that news he had just received from St. Petersburgh showed that there was an intention on the part of M. de Sazonof to exchange views with Count Berchtold. He thought that this method of procedure might lead to a satisfactory result, and that it would be best, before doing anything else, to await outcome of the exchange of views between the Austrian and Russian Governments.

In the course of a short conversation Secretary of State said that as yet Austria was only partially mobilising, but that if Russia mobilised against Germany latter would have to follow suit. I asked him what he meant by "mobilising against Germany." He said that if Russia only mobilised in south, Germany would not mobilise, but if she mobilised in north, Germany would have to do so too, and Russian system of mobilisation was so complicated that it might be difficult exactly to locate her mobilisation. Germany would therefore have to be very careful not to be taken by surprise.

Finally, Secretary of State said that news from St. Petersburgh had caused him to take more hopeful view of the general situation.

No. 56.

Sir M. de Bunsen to Sir Edward Grey.—(Received July 28.)

(Telegraphic.) *Vienna, July* 27, 1914.

The Russian Ambassador had to-day a long and earnest conversation with Baron Macchio, the Under-secretary of State for Foreign Affairs. He told him that, having just come back from St. Petersburgh, he was well acquainted with the views of the Russian Government and the state of Russian public opinion. He could assure him that if actual war broke out with Servia it would be impossible to localise it, for Russia was not prepared to give way again, as she had done on previous occasions, and especially during the annexation crisis of 1909. He earnestly hoped that something would be done before Servia was actually invaded. Baron Macchio replied that this would now be difficult, as a skirmish had already taken place on the Danube, in which the Servians had been the aggressors. The Russian Ambassador said that he would do all he could to keep the Servians quiet pending any discussions that might yet take place, and he told me that he would advise his Government to induce the Servian Government to avoid any conflict as long as possible, and to fall back before an Austrian advance. Time so gained should suffice to enable a settlement to be reached. He had just heard of a satisfactory conversation which the Russian Minister for Foreign Affairs had yesterday with the

Austrian Ambassador at St. Petersburgh. The former had agreed that much of the Austro–Hungarian note to Servia had been perfectly reasonable, and in fact they had practically reached an understanding as to the guarantees which Servia might reasonably be asked to give to Austria–Hungary for her future good behaviour. The Russian Ambassador urged that the Austrian Ambassador at St. Petersburgh should be furnished with full powers to continue discussion with the Russian Minister for Foreign Affairs, who was very willing to advise Servia to yield all that could be fairly asked of her as an independent Power. Baron Macchio promised to submit this suggestion to the Minister for Foreign Affairs.

No. 62.

Sir M. de Bunsen to Sir Edward Grey.—(Received July 28.)

(Telegraphic.) *Vienna, July 28*, 1914.

I spoke to Minister for Foreign Affairs to–day in the sense of your telegram of 27th July to Berlin. I avoided the word "mediation," but said that, as mentioned in your speech,[187] which he had just read to me, you had hopes that conversations in London between the four Powers less interested might yet lead to an arrangement which Austro–Hungarian Government would accept as satisfactory and as rendering actual hostilities unnecessary. I added that you had regarded Servian reply as having gone far to meet just demands of Austria–Hungary; that you thought it constituted a fair basis of discussion during which warlike operations might remain in abeyance, and that Austrian Ambassador in Berlin was speaking in this sense. Minister for Foreign Affairs said quietly, but firmly, that no discussion could be accepted on basis of Servian note; that war would be declared to–day, and that well–known pacific character of Emperor, as well as, he might add, his own, might be accepted as a guarantee that war was both just and inevitable. This was a matter that must be settled directly between the two parties immediately concerned. I said that you would hear with regret that hostilities could not now be arrested, as you feared that they might lead to complications threatening the peace of Europe.

In taking leave of his Excellency, I begged him to believe that, if in the course of present grave crisis our point of view should sometimes differ from his, this would arise, not from want of sympathy with the many just complaints which Austria–Hungary had against Servia, but from the fact that, whereas Austria–Hungary put first her quarrel with Servia, you were anxious in the first instance for peace of Europe. I trusted this larger aspect of the question would appeal with equal force to his Excellency. He said he had it also in mind, but thought that Russia ought not to oppose operations like those impending, which did not aim at territorial aggrandisement and which could no longer be postponed.

[Footnote 187: "Hansard," Vol. 65, No. 107, Columns 931, 932, 933.]

No. 85.

Sir E. Goschen to Sir Edward Grey.—(Received July 29.)

(Telegraphic.) *Berlin, July* 29, 1914.

I was asked to call upon the Chancellor to–night. His Excellency had just returned from Potsdam.

He said that should Austria be attacked by Russia a European conflagration might, he feared, become inevitable, owing to Germany's obligations as Austria's ally, in spite of his continued efforts to maintain peace. He then proceeded to make the following strong bid for British neutrality. He said that it was clear, so far as he was able to judge the main principle which governed British policy, that Great Britain would never stand by and allow France to be crushed in any conflict there might be. That, however, was not the object at which Germany aimed. Provided that neutrality of Great Britain were certain, every assurance would be given to the British Government that the Imperial Government aimed at no territorial acquisitions at the expense of France should they prove victorious in any war that might ensue.

I questioned his Excellency about the French colonies, and he said that he was unable to give a similar undertaking in that respect. As regards Holland, however, his Excellency said that, so long as Germany's adversaries respected the integrity and neutrality of the Netherlands, Germany was ready to give His Majesty's Government an assurance that she would do likewise. It depended upon the action of France what operations Germany might be forced to enter upon in Belgium, but when the war was over, Belgian integrity would be respected if she had not sided against Germany.

His Excellency ended by saying that ever since he had been Chancellor the object of his policy had been, as you were aware, to bring about an understanding with England; he trusted that these assurances might form the basis of that understanding which he so much desired. He had in mind a general neutrality agreement between England and Germany, though it was of course at the present moment too early to discuss details, and an assurance of British neutrality in the conflict which present crisis might possibly produce, would enable him to look forward to realisation of his desire.

In reply to his Excellency's enquiry how I thought his request would appeal to you, I said that I did not think it probable that at this stage of events you would care to bind yourself to any course of action and that I was of opinion that you would desire to retain full liberty.

Our conversation upon this subject having come to an end, I communicated the contents of your telegram of to-day to his Excellency, who expressed his best thanks to you.

No. 87.

Sir Edward Grey to Sir F. Bertie.

Sir, *Foreign Office, July* 29, 1914.

After telling M. Cambon to-day how grave the situation seemed to be, I told him that I meant to tell the German Ambassador to-day that he must not be misled by the friendly tone of our conversations into any sense of false security that we should stand aside if all the efforts to preserve the peace, which we were now making in common with Germany, failed. But I went on to say to M. Cambon that I thought it necessary to tell him also that public opinion here approached the present difficulty from a quite different point of view from that taken during the difficulty as to Morocco a few years ago. In the case of Morocco the dispute was one in which France was primarily interested, and in which it appeared that Germany, in an attempt to crush France, was fastening a quarrel on France on a question that was the subject of a special agreement between France and us. In the present case the dispute between Austria and Servia was not one in which we felt called to take a hand. Even if the question became one between Austria and Russia we should not feel called upon to take a hand in it. It would then be a question of the supremacy of Teuton or Slav—a struggle for supremacy in the Balkans; and our idea had always been to avoid being drawn into a war over a Balkan question. If Germany became involved and France became involved, we had not made up our minds what we should do; it was a case that we should have to consider. France would then have been drawn into a quarrel which was not hers, but in which, owing to her alliance, her honour and interest obliged her to engage. We were free from engagements, and we should have to decide what British interests required us to do. I thought it necessary to say that, because, as he knew, we were taking all precautions with regard to our fleet, and I was about to warn Prince Lichnowsky not to count on our standing aside, but it would not be fair that I should let M. Cambon be misled into supposing that this meant that we had decided what to do in a contingency that I still hoped might not arise.

M. Cambon said that I had explained the situation very clearly. He understood it to be that in a Balkan quarrel, and in a struggle for supremacy between Teuton and Slav we should not feel called to intervene; should other issues be raised, and Germany and France become involved, so that the question became one of the hegemony of Europe, we should then decide what it was necessary for us to do. He seemed quite prepared for this announcement, and made no criticism upon it.

He said French opinion was calm, but decided. He anticipated a demand from Germany that France would be neutral while Germany attacked Russia. This assurance France, of course, could not give; she was bound to help Russia if Russia was attacked.

I am, &c.

E. GREY.

No. 89.

Sir Edward Grey to Sir E. Goschen.

Sir, *Foreign Office, July* 29, 1914.

After speaking to the German Ambassador this afternoon about the European situation, I said that I wished to say to him, in a quite private and friendly way, something that was on my mind. The situation was very grave. While it was restricted to the issues at present actually involved we had no thought of interfering in it. But if Germany became involved in it, and then France, the issue might be so great that it would involve all European interests; and I did not wish him to be misled by the friendly tone of our conversation—which I hoped would continue—into thinking that we should stand aside.

He said that he quite understood this, but he asked whether I meant that we should, under certain circumstances, intervene?

I replied that I did not wish to say that, or to use anything that was like a threat or an attempt to apply pressure by saying that, if things became worse, we should intervene. There would be no question of our intervening if Germany was not involved, or even if France was not involved. But we knew very well that, if the issue did become such that we thought British interests required us to intervene, we must intervene at once, and the decision would have to be very rapid, just as the decisions of other Powers had to be. I hoped that the friendly tone of our conversations would continue as at present, and that I should be able to keep as closely in touch with the German Government in working for peace. But if we failed in our efforts to keep the peace, and if the issue spread so that it involved practically every European interest, I did not wish to be open to any reproach from him that the friendly tone of all our conversations had misled him or his Government into supposing that we should not take action, and to the reproach that, if they had not been so misled, the course of things might have been different.

The German Ambassador took no exception to what I had said; indeed, he told me that it accorded with what he had already given in Berlin as his view of the situation.

I am, &c.

E. GREY.

No. 98.

Sir E. Goschen to Sir Edward Grey.—(Received July 30.)

(Telegraphic.) *Berlin, July* 30, 1914.

Secretary of State informs me that immediately on receipt of Prince Lichnowsky's telegram recording his last conversation with you he asked Austro−Hungarian

Government whether they would be willing to accept mediation on basis of occupation by Austrian troops of Belgrade or some other point and issue their conditions from there. He has up till now received no reply, but he fears Russian mobilisation against Austria will have increased difficulties, as Austria–Hungary, who has as yet only mobilised against Servia, will probably find it necessary also against Russia. Secretary of State says if you can succeed in getting Russia to agree to above basis for an arrangement and in persuading her in the meantime to take no steps which might be regarded as an act of aggression against Austria he still sees some chance that European peace may be preserved.

He begged me to impress on you difficulty of Germany's position in view of Russian mobilisation and military measures which he hears are being taken in France. Beyond recall of officers on leave—a measure which had been officially taken after, and not before, visit of French Ambassador yesterday—Imperial Government had done nothing special in way of military preparations. Something, however, would have soon to be done, for it might be too late, and when they mobilised they would have to mobilise on three sides. He regretted this, as he knew France did not desire war, but it would be a military necessity.

His Excellency added that telegram received from Prince Lichnowsky last night contains matter which he had heard with regret, but not exactly with surprise, and at all events he thoroughly appreciated frankness and loyalty with which you had spoken.

He also told me that this telegram had only reached Berlin very late last night; had it been received earlier Chancellor would, of course, not have spoken to me in way he had done.

No. 101.

Sir Edward Grey to Sir E. Goschen.

(Telegraphic.) *Foreign Office, July* 30, 1914.

Your telegram of 29th July.[188]

His Majesty's Government cannot for a moment entertain the Chancellor's proposal that they should bind themselves to neutrality on such terms.

What he asks us in effect is to engage to stand by while French colonies are taken and France is beaten so long as Germany does not take French territory as distinct from the colonies.

From the material point of view such a proposal is unacceptable, for France, without further territory in Europe being taken from her, could be so crushed as to lose her position as a Great Power, and become subordinate to German policy.

Altogether, apart from that, it would be a disgrace for us to make this bargain with Germany at the expense of France, a disgrace from which the good name of this country would never recover.

The Chancellor also in effect asks us to bargain away whatever obligation or interest we have as regards the neutrality of Belgium. We could not entertain that bargain either.

Having said so much, it is unnecessary to examine whether the prospect of a future general neutrality agreement between England and Germany offered positive advantages sufficient to compensate us for tying our hands now. We must preserve our full freedom to act as circumstances may seem to us to require in any such unfavourable and regrettable development of the present crisis as the Chancellor contemplates.

You should speak to the Chancellor in the above sense, and add most earnestly that the one way of maintaining the good relations between England and Germany is that they should continue to work together to preserve the peace of Europe; if we succeed in this object, the mutual relations of Germany and England will, I believe, be *ipso facto* improved and strengthened. For that object His Majesty's Government will work in that way with all sincerity and good–will.

And I will say this: If the peace of Europe can be preserved, and the present crisis safely passed, my own endeavour will be to promote some arrangement to which Germany could be a party, by which she could be assured that no aggressive or hostile policy would be pursued against her or her allies by France, Russia, and ourselves, jointly or separately. I have desired this and worked for it, as far as I could, through the last Balkan crisis, and, Germany having a corresponding object, our relations sensibly improved. The idea has hitherto been too Utopian to form the subject of definite proposals, but if this present crisis, so much more acute than any that Europe has gone through for generations, be safely passed, I am hopeful that the relief and reaction which will follow may make possible some more definite rapprochement between the Powers than has been possible hitherto.

[Footnote 188: See No. 85.]

Enclosure 1 in No. 105.

Sir Edward Grey to M. Cambon.

My dear Ambassador, *Foreign Office, November 22*, 1912.

From time to time in recent years the French and British naval and military experts have consulted together. It has always been understood that such consultation does not restrict the freedom of either Government to decide at any future time whether or not to assist the other by armed force. We have agreed that consultation between experts is not, and ought not to be regarded as, an engagement that commits either Government to action in a contingency that has not arisen and may never arise. The disposition, for instance, of the French and British fleets respectively at the present moment is not based upon an engagement to co–operate in war.

You have, however, pointed out that, if either Government had grave reason to expect an unprovoked attack by a third Power, it might become essential to know whether it could in that event depend upon the armed assistance of the other.

I agree that, if either Government had grave reason to expect an unprovoked attack by a third Power, or something that threatened the general peace, it should immediately discuss with the other whether both Governments should act together to prevent aggression and to preserve peace, and, if so, what measures they would be prepared to take in common. If these measures involved action, the plans of the General Staffs would at once be taken into consideration, and the Governments would then decide what effect should be given to them.

Yours, &c.

E. GREY.

Why We Are At War

No. 119.

Sir Edward Grey to Sir F. Bertie.

Sir, *Foreign Office, July* 31, 1914.

M. Cambon referred to–day to a telegram that had been shown to Sir Arthur Nicolson this morning from the French Ambassador in Berlin, saying that it was the uncertainty with regard to whether we would intervene which was the encouraging element in Berlin, and that, it we would only declare definitely on the side of Russia and France, it would decide the German attitude in favour of peace.

I said that it was quite wrong to suppose that we had left Germany under the impression that we would not intervene. I had refused overtures to promise that we should remain neutral. I had not only definitely declined to say that we would remain neutral, I had even gone so far this morning as to say to the German Ambassador that, if France and Germany became involved in war, we should be drawn into it. That, of course, was not the same thing as taking an engagement to France, and I told M. Cambon of it only to show that we had not left Germany under the impression that we would stand aside.

M. Cambon then asked me for my reply to what he had said yesterday.

I said that we had come to the conclusion, in the Cabinet to–day, that we could not give any pledge at the present time. Though we should have to put our policy before Parliament, we could not pledge Parliament in advance. Up to the present moment, we did not feel, and public opinion did not feel, that any treaties or obligations of this country were involved. Further developments might alter this situation and cause the Government and Parliament to take the view that intervention was justified. The preservation of the neutrality of Belgium might be, I would not say a decisive, but an important factor, in determining our attitude. Whether we proposed to Parliament to intervene or not to intervene in a war, Parliament would wish to know how we stood with regard to the neutrality of Belgium, and it might be that I should ask both France and Germany whether each was prepared to undertake an engagement that she would not be the first to violate the neutrality of Belgium.

M. Cambon repeated his question whether we would help France if Germany made an attack on her.

I said that I could only adhere to the answer that, as far as things had gone at present, we could not take any engagement.

M. Cambon urged that Germany had from the beginning rejected proposals that might have made for peace. It could not be to England's interest that France should be crushed by Germany. We should then be in a very diminished position with regard to Germany. In 1870 we had made a great mistake in allowing an enormous increase of German strength, and we should now be repeating the mistake. He asked me whether I could not submit his question to the Cabinet again.

I said that the Cabinet would certainly be summoned as soon as there was some new development, but at the present moment the only answer I could give was that we could not undertake any definite engagement.

I am, &c.

E. GREY.

No. 122.

Sir E. Goschen to Sir Edward Grey.—(Received August 1.)

(Telegraphic.) *Berlin, July* 31, 1914.

Neutrality of Belgium, referred to in your telegram of 31st July to Sir F. Bertie.

I have seen Secretary of State, who informs me that he must consult the Emperor and the Chancellor before he could possibly answer. I gathered from what he said that he thought any reply they might give could not but disclose a certain amount of their plan of campaign in the event of war ensuing, and he was therefore very doubtful whether they would return any answer at all. His Excellency, nevertheless, took note of your request.

It appears from what he said that German Government consider that certain hostile acts have already been committed by Belgium. As an instance of this, he alleged that a consignment of corn for Germany had been placed under an embargo already.

I hope to see his Excellency to-morrow again to discuss the matter further, but the prospect of obtaining a definite answer seems to me remote.

In speaking to me to-day the Chancellor made it clear that Germany would in any case desire to know the reply returned to you by the French Government.

No. 123.

Sir Edward Grey to Sir E. Goschen.

Sir, *Foreign Office, August* 1, 1914.

I told the German Ambassador to-day that the reply[189] of the German Government with regard to the neutrality of Belgium was a matter of very great regret, because the neutrality of Belgium affected feeling in this country. If Germany could see her way to give the same assurance as that which had been given by France it would materially contribute to relieve anxiety and tension here. On the other hand, if there were a violation of the neutrality of Belgium by one combatant while the other respected it, it would be extremely difficult to restrain public feeling in this country. I said that we had been discussing this question at a Cabinet meeting, and as I was authorised to tell him this I gave him a memorandum of it.

He asked me whether, if Germany gave a promise not to violate Belgian neutrality, we would engage to remain neutral.

I replied that I could not say that; our hands were still free, and we were considering what our attitude should be. All I could say was that our attitude would be determined largely by public opinion here, and that the neutrality of Belgium would appeal very strongly to Public opinion here. I did not think that we could give a promise of neutrality on that condition alone.

The Ambassador pressed me as to whether I could not formulate conditions on which we would remain neutral. He even suggested that the integrity of France and her colonies might be guaranteed.

I said that I felt obliged to refuse definitely any promise to remain neutral on similar terms, and I could only say that we must keep our hands free.

I am, &c.

E. GREY.

[Footnote 189: See No. 122.]

No. 133.

Sir Edward Grey to Sir E. Goschen.

(Telegraphic.) *Foreign Office, August* 1, 1914.

M. De Etter came to–day to communicate the contents of a telegram from M. Sazonof, dated the 31st July, which are as follows:—

"The Austro–Hungarian Ambassador declared the readiness of his Government to discuss the substance of the Austrian ultimatum to Servia. M. Sazonof replied by expressing his satisfaction, and said it was desirable that the discussions should take place in London with the participation of the Great Powers.

"M. Sazonof hoped that the British Government would assume the direction of these discussions. The whole of Europe would be thankful to them. It would be very important that Austria should meanwhile put a stop provisionally to her military action on Servian territory."

(The above has been communicated to the six Powers.)

No. 134.

Why We Are At War

Sir F. Bertie to Sir Edward Grey.—(Received August 1.)

(Telegraphic.) *Paris, August 1, 1914.*

President of the Republic has informed me that German Government were trying to saddle Russia with the responsibility; that it was only after a decree of general mobilisation had been issued in Austria that the Emperor of Russia ordered a general mobilisation; that, although the measures which the German Government have already taken are in effect a general mobilisation, they are not so designated; that a French general mobilisation will become necessary in self–defence, and that France is already forty–eight hours behind Germany as regards German military preparations; that the French troops have orders not to go nearer to the German frontier than a distance of 10 kilom. so as to avoid any grounds for accusations of provocation to Germany, whereas the German troops, on the other hand, are actually on the French frontier and have made incursions on it; that, notwithstanding mobilisations, the Emperor of Russia has expressed himself ready to continue his conversations with the German Ambassador with a view to preserving the peace; that French Government, whose wishes are markedly pacific, sincerely desire the preservation of peace and do not quite despair, even now, of its being possible to avoid war.

No. 148.

Sir Edward Grey to Sir F. Bertie.

(Telegraphic.) *Foreign Office, August 2, 1914.*

After the Cabinet this morning I gave M. Cambon the following memorandum:—

"I am authorised to give an assurance that, if the German fleet comes into the Channel or through the North Sea to undertake hostile operations against French coasts or shipping, the British fleet will give all the protection in its power.

"This assurance is of course subject to the policy of His Majesty's Government receiving the support of Parliament, and must not be taken as binding His Majesty's Government to take any action until the above contingency of action by the German fleet takes place."

Why We Are At War

I pointed out that we had very large questions and most difficult issues to consider, and that Government felt that they could not bind themselves to declare war upon Germany necessarily if war broke out between France and Germany to-morrow, but it was essential to the French Government, whose fleet had long been concentrated in the Mediterranean, to know how to make their dispositions with their north coast entirely undefended. We therefore thought it necessary to give them this assurance. It did not bind us to go to war with Germany unless the German fleet took the action indicated, but it did give a security to France that would enable her to settle the disposition of her own Mediterranean fleet.

M. Cambon asked me about the violation of Luxemburg. I told him the doctrine on that point laid down by Lord Derby and Lord Clarendon in 1867. He asked me what we should say about the violation of the neutrality of Belgium. I said that was a much more important matter; we were considering what statement we should make in Parliament to-morrow—in effect, whether we should declare violation of Belgian neutrality to be a *casus belli*. I told him what had been said to the German Ambassador on this point.

No. 153.

Sir Edward Grey to Sir E. Goschen.

(Telegraphic.) *Foreign Office, August* 4, 1914.

The King of the Belgians has made an appeal to His Majesty the King for diplomatic intervention on behalf of Belgium in the following terms:—

"Remembering the numerous proofs of your Majesty's friendship and that of your predecessor, and the friendly attitude of England in 1870 and the proof of friendship you have just given us again, I make a supreme appeal to the diplomatic intervention of your Majesty's Government to safeguard the integrity of Belgium."

His Majesty's Government are also informed that the German Government has delivered to the Belgian Government a note proposing friendly neutrality entailing free passage through Belgian territory, and promising to maintain the independence and integrity of the kingdom and its possessions at the conclusion of peace, threatening in case of refusal to treat Belgium as an enemy. An answer was requested within twelve hours.

We also understand that Belgium has categorically refused this as a flagrant violation of the law of nations.

His Majesty's Government are bound to protest against this violation of a treaty to which Germany is a party in common with themselves, and must request an assurance that the demand made upon Belgium will not be proceeded with and that her neutrality will be respected by Germany. You should ask for an immediate reply.

APPENDIX III. Extract from the Dispatch from His Majesty's Ambassador at Berlin respecting the Rupture of Diplomatic Relations with the German Government.

(Cd. 7445.)

Sir E. Goschen to Sir Edward Grey.

Sir, *London, August* 8, 1914.

In accordance with the instructions contained in your telegram of the 4th instant I called upon the Secretary of State that afternoon and enquired, in the name of His Majesty's Government, whether the Imperial Government would refrain from violating Belgian neutrality. Herr von Jagow at once replied that he was sorry to say that his answer must be "No," as, in consequence of the German troops having crossed the frontier that morning, Belgian neutrality had been already violated. Herr von Jagow again went into the reasons why the Imperial Government had been obliged to take this step, namely, that they had to advance into France by the quickest and easiest way, so as to be able to get well ahead with their operations and endeavour to strike some decisive blow as early as possible. It was a matter of life and death for them, as if they had gone by the more southern route they could not have hoped, in view of the paucity of roads and the strength of the fortresses, to have got through without formidable opposition entailing great loss of time. This loss of time would have meant time gained by the Russians for bringing up their troops to the German frontier. Rapidity of action was the great German asset, while that of Russia was an inexhaustible supply of troops. I pointed out to Herr von Jagow that this *fait accompli* of the violation of the Belgian frontier rendered, as he would readily understand, the situation exceedingly grave, and I asked him whether there was not still time to draw back and avoid possible consequences, which both he and I would deplore. He replied that, for the reasons he had given me, it was now impossible for them to draw back.

During the afternoon I received your further telegram of the same date, and, in compliance with the instructions therein contained, I again proceeded to the Imperial Foreign Office and informed the Secretary of State that unless the Imperial Government could give the assurance by 12 o'clock that night that they would proceed no further with their violation of the Belgian frontier and stop their advance, I had been instructed to demand my passports and inform the Imperial Government that His Majesty's Government would have to take all steps in their power to uphold the neutrality of Belgium and the observance of a treaty to which Germany was as much a party as themselves.

Herr von Jagow replied that to his great regret he could give no other answer than that which he had given me earlier in the day, namely, that the safety of the Empire rendered it absolutely necessary that the Imperial troops should advance through Belgium. I gave his Excellency a written summary of your telegram and, pointing out that you had mentioned 12 o'clock as the time when His Majesty's Government would expect an answer, asked him whether, in view of the terrible consequences which would necessarily ensue, it were not possible even at the last moment that their answer should be reconsidered. He replied that if the time given were even twenty–four hours or more, his answer must be the same. I said that in that case I should have to demand my passports. This interview took place at about 7 o'clock. In a short conversation which ensued Herr von Jagow expressed his poignant regret at the crumbling of his entire policy and that of the Chancellor, which had been to make friends with Great Britain and then, through Great Britain, to get closer to France. I said that this sudden end to my work in Berlin was to me also a matter of deep regret and disappointment, but that he must understand that under the circumstances and in view of our engagements, His Majesty's Government could not possibly have acted otherwise than they had done.

I then said that I should like to go and see the Chancellor, as it might be, perhaps, the last time I should have an opportunity of seeing him. He begged me to do so. I found the Chancellor very agitated. His Excellency at once began a harangue, which lasted for about 20 minutes. He said that the step taken by His Majesty's Government was terrible to a degree; just for a word—"neutrality," a word which in war time had so often been disregarded—just for a scrap of paper Great Britain was going to make war on a kindred nation who desired nothing better than to be friends with her. All his efforts in that direction had been rendered useless by this last terrible step, and the policy to which, as I knew, he had devoted himself since his accession to office had tumbled down like a house of cards. What we had done was unthinkable; it was like striking a man from behind while he was fighting for his life against two assailants. He held Great Britain responsible for all the terrible events that might happen. I protested strongly against that statement, and said that, in the same way as he and Herr von Jagow wished me to understand that for strategical reasons it was a matter of life and death to Germany to advance through Belgium and violate the latter's neutrality, so I would wish him to understand that it was, so to speak, a matter of "life and death" for the honour of Great Britain that she should keep her solemn engagement to do her utmost to defend Belgium's neutrality if attacked. That solemn compact simply had to be kept, or what confidence could anyone have in engagements given by Great Britain in the future? The Chancellor said, "But at what price will that compact have been kept. Has the British Government thought of that?" I hinted to his Excellency as plainly as I could that fear of consequences could hardly be regarded as an excuse for breaking solemn engagements, but his Excellency was so excited, so evidently overcome by the news of our action, and so little disposed to hear reason that I refrained from adding fuel to the flame by further argument. As I was leaving he said that the blow of Great Britain joining Germany's enemies was all the greater that almost up to the last moment he and his Government had been working with us and supporting our efforts to maintain peace between Austria and Russia. I said that this was part of the tragedy which saw the two nations fall apart just at the moment when the relations between them had been more friendly and cordial than they had been for years. Unfortunately, notwithstanding our efforts to maintain peace between Russia and Austria, the war had spread and had brought us face to face with a situation which, if we held to our engagements, we could not possibly avoid, and which unfortunately entailed our separation from our late fellow—workers. He would readily understand that no one regretted this more than I.

After this somewhat painful interview I returned to the embassy and drew up a telegraphic report of what had passed. This telegram was handed in at the Central Telegraph Office a little before 9 P.M. It was accepted by that office, but apparently never despatched.[190]

[Footnote 190: This telegram never reached the Foreign Office.]

APPENDIX IV. THE CRIME OF SERAJEVO

SELECTIONS FROM THE AUSTRIAN *dossier* OF THE CRIME

The following document is contained in the German Version of the German White Book (pp. 28–31); and though it adds little to our knowledge of the Austrian case against Servia, it deserves to be reprinted, as it is omitted altogether in the official version in English of the German White Book. The authorship of the document is uncertain. It has the appearance of an extract from a German newspaper.

Aus dem oesterreich–ungarischen Material.

Wien, 27. Juli. Das in der oesterreichisch–ungarischen Zirkularnote an die auswaertigen Botschaften in Angelegenheit des serbischen Konflikts erwaehnte Dossier wird heute veroeffentlicht.

In diesem Memoire wird darauf hingewiesen, dass die von Serbien ausgegangene Bewegung, die sich zum Ziele gesetzt hat, die suedlichen Teile Oesterreich–Ungarns von der Monarchie loszureiszen, um sie mit Serbien zu einer staatlichen Einheit zu verbinden, weit zurueckgreist. Diese in ihren Endzielen stets gleichbleibende und nur in ihren Mitteln und an Intensitaet wechselnde Propaganda erreichte zur Zeit der Unnerionskrise ihren Hoehepunkt und trat damals ossen mit ihren Tendenzen hervor. Waehrend einerjeits die gesamte serbische Bresse zum Kampfe gegen die Monarchie ausrief, bildeten sich—von anderen Propagandamitteln abgesehen—Ussoziationen, die diese Kaempfe vorbereiteten, unter denen die Harodna Odbrana an Bedeutung hervorragte. Aus einem revolutionaeren Komitee hervorgegangen, fonstituierte sich diese vom Belgrader Auswaertigen Amte voellig abhaengige Organisation unter Leitung von Staatsmaennern und Offizieren, darunter dem General Tantovic und dem ehemaligen Minister Ivanovic. Auch Major Oja Jantovic und Milan Pribicevic gehoeren zu diesen Gruendern. Dieser Berein hatte sich die Bildung und Ausruestung von Freischaren fuer den bevorstehenden Krieg gegen die oefterreichisch–ungarische Monarchie zum Ziele gesetzt. In einer dem Memoire angefuegten Anlage wird ein Auszug aus dem vom Zentralausschusse der Narodna Odbrana herausgegebenen Vereinsorgane gleichen Namens veroeffentlicht, worin in mehreren Artikeln die Taetigfelt und Ziele dieses Vereins ausfuehrlich dargelegt werden. Es heisst darin, dass zu der Hauptaufgabe der Narodna Odbrana die Verbindung

159

mit ihren nahen und ferneren Bruedern jenseits der Grenze und unseren uebrigen Freunden in der Welt gehoeren.

Oesterreich ist als erster und groesster Feind bezeichnet. Wie die Narodna Odbrana die Notwendigkeit des Kampfes mit Oesterreich predigt, predigt sie eine heilige Wahrheit unserer nationalen Lage. Das Schlusskapitel enthaelt einen Apell an die Regierung und das Volk Serbiens, sich mit allen Mitteln fuer den Kampf vorzubereiten, den die Annexion vorangezeigt hat.

Das Memoire schildert nach einer Aussage eines von der Narodna Odbrana angeworbenen Komitatschis die damalige Taetigkeit der Narodna Odbrana, die eine von zwei Hauptleuten, darunter Jankovic, geleitete *Schule zur Ausbildung von Banden* unterhielt, Schulen, welche von General Jankovic und von Hauptmann Milan Pribicevic regelmaessig inspiziert wurden. Weiter wurden die Komitatschis im *Schiessen und Bombenwerfen, im Minenlegen, Sprengen von Eisenbahnbruecken* usw. unterrichtet. Nach der feierlichen Erklaerung der Serbischen Regierung vom Jahre 1909 schien auch das Ende dieser Organisation gekommen zu sein. Diese Erwartungen haben sich aber nicht nur nicht erfuellt, sondern die Propaganda wurde durch die serbische Presse fortgesetzt. Das Memoire fuehrt als Beispiel die Art und Weise an, wie das Attentat gegen den bosnischen Landeschef Varesanin publizistisch verwertet wurde, indem der Attentaeter als serbischer Nationalheld gefeiert und seine Tat verherrlicht wurde. Diese Blaetter wurden nicht nur in Serbien verbreitet, sondern auch auf wohlorganisierten Schleichwegen in die Monarchie hineingeschmuggelt.

Unter der gleichen Leitung wie bei ihrer Gruendung wurde die Narodna Odbrana neuerlich der zentralpunkt einer Agitation welcher der *Schuetzenbund mit 762 Vereinen, ein Sokolbund mit 3500 Mitgliedern, und verschiedene andere Vereine angehoerten.*

Im Kleide eines Kulturvereins auftretend, dem nur die geistige und die fueoerperliche Entwickelung der Bevoelkerung Serbiens sowie deren materielle Kraeftigung am Herzen liegt, enthullt die Narodna Oobrana ihr wahres reorganisiertes Programm in vorzitiertem Auszug aus ihrem Vereinsorgan, in welchem "die heilige Wahrheit" gepredigt wird, dass es eine unerlaessliche Notwendigkeit ist, gegen Oesterreich, seinen ersten groessten Feind, diesen Ausrottungskampf mit Gewehr und Kanone zu fuehren, und das Volk mit allen Mitteln auf den Kampf vorzubereiten, zur Befreiung der unterworfenen Gebiete, in denen viele Millionen unterjochter Brueder schmachten. Die in dem Memoire zitierten

Why We Are At War

Aufrufe und Reden aehnlichen Charakters beleuchten die vielseitige auswaertige Taetigkeit der Narodna Oobrana und ihrer affilierten Vereine, die in Vortragsreifen, in der Teilnahme an Festen von bosnischen Vereinen, bei denen offen Mitglieder fuer die erwaehnte serbische Vereinigung geworben wurden, besteht. Gegenwaertig ist noch die Untersuchung darueber im Zuge, dass die Sokolvereine Serbiens analoge Vereinigungen der Monarchie bestimmten, sich mit ihnen in einem bisher geheim gehaltenen Verbande zu vereinigen. Durch Vertrauensmaenner und Missionaere wurde die Aufwiegelung in die Kreise Erwachsener und der urteilslosen Jugend gebracht. So wurden von Milan Pribicewitsch ehmalige honvedoffiziere und ein Gendarmerieleutnant zum Verlassen des Heeresdienstes in der Monarchie unter bedenklichen Umstaenden verleitet. In den Schulen der Lehrerbildungsanstalten wurde eine weitgehende Agitation entwickelt. Der gewuenschte Krieg gegen die Monarchie wurde militaerisch auch insofern vorbereitet, als serbische Emissaere im Falle des Ausbruchs der Feindseligkeiten mit der Zerstoerung von Transportmitteln usw., der Anfachung von Revolten und Paniken betraut wurden. Alles dies wird in einer besonderen Beilage belegt.

Das Memoire schildert ferner den Zusammenhang zwischen dieser Taetigkeit der Narodna Oobrana und den affilierten Organisationen mit den Attentaten gegen den Koeniglichen Kommissaer in Agram Cuvaj im Juli 1912, dem Attentat von Dojcic in Agram 1913 gegen Sterlecz und dem missglueckten Attentat Schaefers am 20. Mai im Aramer Theater. Es verbreitet sich hierauf ueber den Zusammenhang des Attentats auf den Thronfolger und dessen Gemahlin, ueber die Art, wie sich die Jungen schon in der Schule an dem Gedanken der Narodna Dobrana vergifteten und wie sich die Attentaeter mit Hilfe von Pribicewic und Dacic die Werkzeuge zu dem Attentat verschafften, wobei insbesondere die Rolle des Majors Tankofte dargelegt wird, der die Mordwassen lieferte, wie auch die Rolle eines gewissen Ciganovic, eines gewesenen Komitatschi und jetzigen Beamten der serbischen Eisenbahndirektion Belgrad, der schon 1909 als Zoegling der Bandenschule der damaligen Narodna Odbrana austauchte. Ferner wird die Art dargelegt, wie Bomben und Waffen unbemerkt nach Bosnien eingeschmuggelt wurden, die keinen Zweifel darueber laesst, dass dies ein wohl voerberiteter und fuer die geheimnisvollen Zwecke der Narodna oft begangener Schleichweg war.

Eine Beilage enthaelt einen Auszug aus den Akten des Kreisgerichts in Serajewo ueber die Untersuchung des Attentats gegen den Erzherzog Franz Ferdinand und dessen Gemahlin. Danach sind Princip, Cabrinovic, Grabez, Crupilovic und Papovic gestaendig, in Gemeinschaft mit dem fluechtigen Mehmedbasic ein Komplott zur Erwordung des

161

Erzherzogs gebildet und ihm zu diesen Zweck aufgelauert zu haben. Cabrinovic ist gestaendig, die Bombe geworfen und Gabrilo Princip das Attentat mit der Browningpistole ausgefuehrt zu haben. Beide Taeter gaben zu, bei der Veruebung der Tat die Absicht des Mordes gehabt zu haben. Die weiteren Teile der Anlage enthalten weitere Angaben der Beschuldigten vor dem Untersuchungsrichter ueber Entstehung des Komplotts, Herkunft der Bomben, welche fabrikmaessig hergestellt wurden, fuer millitaerische Zwecke bestimmt waren und ihrer Originalpackung nach aus dem serbischen Waffenlager aus Kragujevac stammten. Endlich gibt die Beilage Auskunft ueber den Transport der drei Attentaeter und der Waffen von Serbien nach Bosnien. Aus dem weiteren Zeugenprotokoll ergibt sich, dass ein Angehoeriger der Monarchie einige Tage vor dem Attentat dem oesterreichisch–ungarischen Konsulat in Belgrad Meldung von der Vermutung erstatten wollte, dass ein Plan zur Veruebung des Attentats gegen den Erzherzog waehrend dessen Anwesenheit in Bosnien bestehe. Dieser Mann soll nun durch Belgrader Polizeiorgane, welche ihn unmittelbar vor Betreten des Konsulats aus nichtigen Gruenden verhafteten, an der Erstattung der Meldung verhindert worden sein. Weiter gehe aus dem Zeugenprotokoll hervor, dass die betreffenden Polizeiorgane von dem geplanten Attentat Kenntnis gehabt haetten. Da diese Angaben noch nicht nachgeprueft sind, kann ueber deren Stichhaltigkeit vorlaeufig noch kein Urteil gefaellt werden. In der Beilage zum Memoire heisst es: Vor dem Empfangssaal des serbischen Kriegsministeriums befinden sich an der Wand vier allegorische Bilder, von denen drei Darstellungen serbischer Kriegserfolge sind, waehrend das vierte die Verwirklichung der monarchiefeindlichen Tendenzen Serbiens versinnbildlicht. Ueber einer Landschaft, die teils Gebirge (Bosnien), teils Ebene (Suedungarn) darstellt, geht die Zora, die Morgenroete der serbischen Hoffnungen, auf. Im Vordergrunde steht eine bewaffnete Frauengestalt, auf deren Schilde die Namen aller "noch zu befreienden Provinzen": Bosnien, Herzegowina, Wojwodina, Gyrmien, Dalmatien usw. stehen.

APPENDIX V. Extract from the Dispatch from His Majesty's Ambassador at Vienna respecting the Rupture of Diplomatic Relations with the Austro–Hungarian Government.

(Cd. 7596)

Sir M. de Bunsen to Sir Edward Grey.

Why We Are At War

London, September 1, 1914.

Sir,

The rapidity of the march of events during the days which led up to the outbreak of the European war made it difficult, at the time, to do more than record their progress by telegraph. I propose now to add a few comments.

The delivery at Belgrade on the 23rd July of the Austrian note to Servia was preceded by a period of absolute silence at the Ballplatz. Except Herr von Tchinsky, who must have been aware of the tenour, if not of the actual words of the note, none of my colleagues were allowed to see through the veil. On the 22nd and 23rd July, M. Dumaine, French Ambassador, had long interviews with Baron Macchio, one of the Under–Secretaries of State for Foreign Affairs, by whom he was left under the impression that the words of warning he had been instructed to speak to the Austro–Hungarian Government had not been unavailing, and that the note which was being drawn up would be found to contain nothing with which a self–respecting State need hesitate to comply. At the second of these interviews he was not even informed that the note was at that very moment being presented at Belgrade, or that it would be published in Vienna on the following morning. Count Forgach, the other Under–Secretary of State, had indeed been good enough to confide to me on the same day the true character of the note, and the fact of its presentation about the time we were speaking.

So little had the Russian Ambassador been made aware of what was preparing that he actually left Vienna on a fortnight's leave of absence about the 20th July. He had only been absent a few days when events compelled him to return. It might have been supposed that Duc Avarna, Ambassador of the allied Italian Kingdom, which was bound to be so closely affected by fresh complications in the Balkans, would have been taken fully into the confidence of Count Berchtold during this critical time. In point of fact his Excellency was left completely in the dark. As for myself, no indication was given me by Count Berchtold of the impending storm, and it was from a private source that I received on the 15th July the forecast of what was about to happen which I telegraphed to you the following day. It is true that during all this time the "Neue Freie Presse" and other leading Viennese newspapers were using language which pointed unmistakably to war with Servia. The official "Fremdenblatt", however, was more cautious, and till the note was published, the prevailing opinion among my colleagues was that Austria would shrink from courses calculated to involve her in grave European complications.

On the 24th July the note was published in the newspapers. By common consent it was at once styled an ultimatum. Its integral acceptance by Servia was neither expected nor desired, and when, on the following afternoon, it was at first rumoured in Vienna that it had been unconditionally accepted, there was a moment of keen disappointment. The mistake was quickly corrected, and as soon as it was known later in the evening that the Servian reply had been rejected and that Baron Giesl had broken off relations at Belgrade, Vienna burst into a frenzy of delight, vast crowds parading the streets and singing patriotic songs till the small hours of the morning.

The demonstrations were perfectly orderly, consisting for the most part of organised processions through the principal streets ending up at the Ministry of War. One or two attempts to make hostile manifestations against the Russian Embassy were frustrated by the strong guard of police which held the approaches to the principal embassies during those days. The demeanour of the people at Vienna, and, as I was informed, in many other principal cities of the Monarchy, showed plainly the popularity of the idea of war with Servia, and there can be no doubt that the small body of Austrian and Hungarian statesmen by whom this momentous step was adopted gauged rightly the sense, and it may even be said the determination, of the people, except presumably in portions of the provinces inhabited by the Slav races. There had been much disappointment in many quarters at the avoidance of war with Servia during the annexation crisis in 1908 and again in connection with the recent Balkan war. Count Berchtold's peace policy had met with little sympathy in the Delegation. Now the flood–gates were opened, and the entire people and press clamoured impatiently for immediate and condign punishment of the hated Servian race. The country certainly believed that it had before it only the alternative of subduing Servia or of submitting sooner or later to mutilation at her hands. But a peaceful solution should first have been attempted. Few seemed to reflect that the forcible intervention of a Great Power in the Balkans must inevitably call other Great Powers into the field. So just was the cause of Austria held to be, that it seemed to her people inconceivable that any country should place itself in her path, or that questions of mere policy or prestige should be regarded anywhere as superseding the necessity which had arisen to exact summary vengeance for the crime of Serajevo. The conviction had been expressed to me by the German Ambassador on the 24th July that Russia would stand aside. This feeling, which was also held at the Ballplatz, influenced no doubt the course of events, and it is deplorable that no effort should have been made to secure by means of diplomatic negotiations the acquiescence of Russia and Europe as a whole in some peaceful compromise of the Servian question by which Austrian fears of Servian aggression and intrigue might have been removed for the future. Instead of adopting this course the Austro–Hungarian Government resolved upon war. The inevitable consequence ensued. Russia replied to a partial Austrian mobilisation and declaration of war against Servia by a partial Russian mobilisation against Austria. Austria met this move by completing her own mobilisation, and Russia again responded with results which have passed into history. The fate of the proposals put forward by His Majesty's Government for the preservation of peace is recorded in the White Paper on the European Crisis[191]. On the 28th July I saw Count Berchtold and urged as strongly as I could that the scheme of mediation mentioned in your speech in the House of Commons on the previous day should be accepted as offering an honourable and peaceful settlement of the question at issue. His Excellency himself read to me a telegraphic report of the speech, but added that matters had gone too far; Austria was that day declaring war on Servia, and she could never accept the conference which you had suggested should take place between the less interested Powers on the basis of the Servian reply. This was a matter which must be settled directly between the two parties immediately concerned. I said His Majesty's Government would hear with regret that hostilities could not be arrested, as you feared they would lead to European complications. I disclaimed any British lack of sympathy with Austria in the matter of her legitimate grievances against Servia, and pointed out that, whereas Austria seemed to be making these the starting point of her policy, His Majesty's Government were bound to look at the question primarily from the point of view of the maintenance of the peace of Europe. In this way the two countries might easily drift apart.

His Excellency said that he too was keeping the European aspect of the question in sight. He thought, however, that Russia would have no right to intervene after receiving his assurance that Austria sought no territorial aggrandisement. His Excellency remarked to me in the course of his conversation that, though he had been glad to co–operate towards bringing about the settlement which had resulted from the ambassadorial conferences in London during the Balkan crisis, he had never had much belief in the permanency of that settlement, which was necessarily of a highly artificial character, inasmuch as the interests which it sought to harmonise were in themselves profoundly divergent. His Excellency maintained a most friendly demeanour throughout the interview, but left no doubt in my mind as to the determination of the Austro–Hungarian Government to proceed with the invasion of Servia.

Why We Are At War

The German Government claim to have persevered to the end in the endeavour to support at Vienna your successive proposals in the interest of peace. Herr von Tchirsky abstained from inviting my co-operation or that of the French and Russian Ambassadors in carrying out his instructions to that effect, and I had no means of knowing what response he was receiving from the Austro-Hungarian Government. I was, however, kept fully informed by M. Schebeko, the Russian Ambassador, of his own direct negotiations with Count Berchtold. M. Schebeko endeavoured on the 28th July to persuade the Austro-Hungarian Government to furnish Count Szapary with full powers to continue at St. Petersburgh the hopeful conversations which had there been taking place between the latter and M. Sazonof. Count Berchtold refused at the time, but two days later (30th July), though in the meantime Russia had partially mobilised against Austria, he received M. Schebeko again, in a perfectly friendly manner, and gave his consent to the continuance of the conversations at St. Petersburgh. From now onwards the tension between Russia and Germany was much greater than between Russia and Austria. As between the latter an arrangement seemed almost in sight, and on the 1st August I was informed by M. Schebeko that Count Szapary had at last conceded the main point at issue by announcing to M. Sazonof that Austria would consent to submit to mediation the points in the note to Servia which seemed incompatible with the maintenance of Servian independence. M. Sazonof, M. Schebeko added, had accepted this proposal on condition that Austria would refrain from the actual invasion of Servia. Austria, in fact, had finally yielded, and that she herself had at this point good hopes of a peaceful issue is shown by the communication made to you on the 1st August by Count Mensdorff, to the effect that Austria had neither "banged the door" on compromise nor cut off the conversations.[192] M. Schebeko to the end was working hard for peace. He was holding the most conciliatory language to Count Berchtold, and he informed me that the latter, as well as Count Forgach, had responded in the same spirit. Certainly it was too much for Russia to expect that Austria would hold back her armies, but this matter could probably have been settled by negotiation, and M. Schebeko repeatedly told me he was prepared to accept any reasonable compromise.

Unfortunately these conversations at St. Petersburgh and Vienna were cut short by the transfer of the dispute to the more dangerous ground of a direct conflict between Germany and Russia. Germany intervened on the 31st July by means of her double ultimatums to St. Petersburgh and Paris. The ultimatums were of a kind to which only one answer is possible, and Germany declared war on Russia on the 1st August, and on France on the 3rd August. A few days' delay might in all probability have saved Europe from one of the greatest calamities in history.

Russia still abstained from attacking Austria, and M. Schebeko had been instructed to remain at his post till war should actually be declared against her by the Austro–Hungarian Government. This only happened on the 6th August when Count Berchtold informed the foreign missions at Vienna that "the Austro–Hungarian Ambassador at St. Petersburgh had been instructed to notify the Russian Government that, in view of the menacing attitude of Russia in the Austro–Servian conflict and the fact that Russia had commenced hostilities against Germany, Austria–Hungary considered herself also at war with Russia."

M. Schebeko left quietly in a special train provided by the Austro–Hungarian Government on the 7th September. He had urgently requested to be conveyed to the Roumanian frontier, so that he might be able to proceed to his own country, but was taken instead to the Swiss frontier, and ten days later I found him at Berne.

M. Dumaine, French Ambassador, stayed on till the 12th August. On the previous day he had been instructed to demand his passport on the ground that Austrian troops were being employed against France. This point was not fully cleared up when I left Vienna. On the 9th August, M. Dumaine had received from Count Berchtold the categorical declaration that no Austrian troops were being moved to Alsace. The next day this statement was supplemented by a further one, in writing, giving Count Berchtold's assurance that not only had no Austrian troops been moved actually to the French frontier, but that none were moving from Austria in a westerly direction into Germany in such a way that they might replace German troops employed at the front. These two statements were made by Count Berchtold in reply to precise questions put to him by M. Dumaine, under instructions from his Government. The French Ambassador's departure was not attended by any hostile demonstration, but his Excellency before leaving had been justly offended by a harangue made by the Chief Burgomaster of Vienna to the crowd assembled before the steps of the town hall, in which he assured the people that Paris was in the throes of a revolution, and that the President of the Republic had been assassinated.

The British declaration of war on Germany was made known in Vienna by special editions of the newspapers about midday on the 5th August. An abstract of your speeches in the House of Commons, and also of the German Chancellor's speech in the Reichstag of the 4th April, appeared the same day, as well as the text of the German ultimatum to

Belgium. Otherwise few details of the great events of these days transpired. The "Neue Freie Presse" was violently insulting towards England. The "Fremdenblatt" was not offensive, but little or nothing was said in the columns of any Vienna paper to explain that the violation of Belgian neutrality had left His Majesty's Government no alternative but to take part in the war.

The declaration of Italian neutrality was bitterly felt in Vienna, but scarcely mentioned in the newspapers.

On the 5th August I had the honour to receive your instruction of the previous day preparing me for the immediate outbreak of war with Germany, but adding that, Austria being understood to be not yet at that date at war with Russia and France, you did not desire me to ask for my passport or to make any particular communication to the Austro–Hungarian Government. You stated at the same time that His Majesty's Government of course expected Austria not to commit any act of war against us without the notice required by diplomatic usage.

On Thursday morning, the 13th August, I had the honour to receive your telegram of the 12th, stating that you had been compelled to inform Count Mensdorff, at the request of the French Government, that a complete rupture had occurred between France and Austria, on the ground that Austria had declared war on Russia who was already fighting on the side of France, and that Austria had sent troops to the German frontier under conditions that were a direct menace to France. The rupture having been brought about with France in this way, I was to ask for my passport, and your telegram stated, in conclusion, that you had informed Count Mensdorff that a state of war would exist between the two countries from midnight of the 12th August.

After seeing Mr. Penfield, the United States Ambassador, who accepted immediately in the most friendly spirit my request that his Excellency would take charge provisionally of British interests in Austria–Hungary during the unfortunate interruption of relations, I proceeded, with Mr. Theo Russell, Counsellor of His Majesty's Embassy, to the Ballplatz. Count Berchtold received me at midday. I delivered my message, for which his Excellency did not seem to be unprepared, although he told me that a long telegram from Count Mensdorff had just come in but had not yet been brought to him. His Excellency received my communication with the courtesy which never leaves him. He deplored the unhappy complications which were drawing such good friends as Austria and England into war. In point of fact, he added, Austria did not consider herself then at war with France, though diplomatic relations with that country had been broken off. I explained in a few words how circumstances had forced this unwelcome conflict upon us. We both avoided useless argument...

[Footnote 191: "Miscellaneous, No. 6 (1914)."]

[Footnote 192: See No. 137, "Miscellaneous, No. 6 (1914)."]

APPENDIX VI. EXTRACTS FROM

THE RUSSIAN ORANGE BOOK

Recueil de Documents Diplomatiques:

Negociations ayant precede la guerre

10/23 Juillet—24 Juillet/6 Aout 1914

PREFATORY NOTE TO APPENDIX VI

This important collection of documents, which has only reached us since the publication of our first edition, confirms the conclusion, which we had deduced from other evidence in our fifth chapter (*supra*, pp. 66–107), that Germany consistently placed obstacles in the way of any proposals for a peaceful settlement, and this in spite of the willingness of all the other Powers, including Austria–Hungary and Russia, to continue discussion of the Servian question. That the crisis took Russia by surprise seems evident from the fact that her ambassadors accredited to France, Berlin, and Vienna were not at their posts when friction began with Russia. (*Infra*, Nos. 4, 7, 8.)

The Russian evidence shows that, on July 29, Germany threatened to mobilize if Russia did not desist from military preparations. This threat was viewed by M. Sazonof as an additional reason for taking all precautions; 'since we cannot accede to Germany's desire, the only course open to us is to accelerate our own preparations and to assume that war is probably inevitable.' (*Infra*, No. 58.) The reader will also notice the curious fact that on

July 30 the decree mobilizing the German army and navy was published, only to be immediately withdrawn; and that the German Government explained that the publication had been premature and accidental. (*Infra*, Nos. 61, 62.) We know from the British White Book (*Correspondence*, No. 99, Sir F. Bertie to Sir E. Grey, July 30) that, on July 30, Germany showed signs of weakening in her attitude to Russia.

It will be noted that war between Austria–Hungary and Russia was not officially declared until August 6, five days after Germany had declared war on Russia. (*Infra*, No. 79.)

In Nos. 36 and 46 will be found some curious details of the methods employed by Austria–Hungary and Germany to delay the publication of the Servian reply to Austria–Hungary.

MINISTERE DES AFFAIRES ETRANGERES.

RECUEIL

DE DOCUMENTS DIPLOMATIQUES.

Negociations ayant precede la guerre.

10/23 Juillet—24 Juillet/6 Aout 1914.

Petrograde, Imprimerie de l'Etat. 1914.

No. 1.

Le Charge d'affaires en Serbie au Ministre des Affaires Etrangeres.

(*Telegramme*).

Belgrade, le 10/23 Juillet 1914.

Le Ministre d'Autriche vient de transmettre, a 6 heures du soir, an Ministre des Finances Patchou, qui remplace Pachitch, une note ultimative de son Gouvernement fixant un delai de 48 heures pour l'acceptation des demandes y contenues. Giesl a ajoute verbalement que pour le cas ou la note ne serait pas acceptee integralement dans un delai de 48 heures, il avait l'ordre de quitter Belgrade avec le personnel de la Legation. Pachitch et les autres Ministres qui se trouvent en tournee electorale ont ete rappeles et sont attendus a Belgrade demain Vendredi a 10 heures du matin. Patchou qui m'a communique le contenu de la note, sollicite l'aide de la Russie et declare qu'aucun Gouvernement Serbe ne pourra accepter les demandes de l'Autriche.

(Signe) Strandtman.

No. 2.

Le Charge d'affaires en Serbie au Ministre des Affaires Etrangeres.

(Telegramme).

Belgrade, le 10/23 Juillet 1914.

Texte de la note qui a ete transmise aujourd'hui par le Ministre d'Autriche–Hongrie an gouvernement Serbe:...

(*For this note, see German White Book, pp. 18–22* (supra *in Appendix I.*))

Un memoire concernant les resultats de l'instruction de Sarajevo a l'egard des fonctionnaires mentionnes aux points 7 et 8 est annexe a cette note'.[193]

(Signe) Strandtman.

[Footnote 193: This memorandum is in the German White Book, pp. 22–3 (*supra*, Appendix I), and not reproduced in the Russian Orange Book.]

No. 3.

Note Verbale transmise personnellement par l'Ambassadeur d'Autriche–Hongrie a St.–Petersbourg au Ministre des Affaires Etrangeres le 11/24 Juillet 1914 a 10 heures du matin.

Le Gouvernement Imperial et Royal s'est trouve dans la necessite de remettre le Jeudi 10/23 du mois courant, par l'entremise du Ministre Imperial et Royal a Belgrade, la note suivante an Gouvernement Royal de Serbie:

(Suit le texte de la note).

Voir document No. 2.

No. 4.

Le Ministre des Affaires Etrangeres au Charge d'affaires en Autriche–Hongrie.

(Telegramme).

St.–Petersbourg, le 11/24 Juillet 1914.

Veuillez transmettre au Ministre des Affaires Etrangeres d'Autriche–Hongrie ce qui suit....

(This communication is printed in the British White Book (*Correspondence*, No. 13); see p. 177 *supra* for the text in English.)

Communique a Londres, Rome, Paris, Belgrade.

(Signe) Sazonow.

No. 5.

Le Ministre des Affaires Etrangeres aux Representants de Sa Majeste l'Empereur en Angleterre, en Allemagne, en Italie et en France.

(Telegramme).

St.–Petersbourg, le 11/24 Juillet 1914.

Why We Are At War

Me refere a mon telegramme a Koudachew d'aujourd'hui; nous esperons que le Gouvernement aupres duquel. Vous etes accredite partagera notre point de vue et prescrira d'urgence a son Representant a Vienne de se prononcer dans le meme sens.

Communique a Belgrade.

(Signe) Sazonow.

No. 6.

Telegramme de Son Altesse Royale le Prince Regent de Serbie a Sa Majeste l'Empereur.

Belgrade, le 11/24 Juillet 1914.

Le Gouvernement Austro–Hongrois a remis hier soir au Gouvernement serbe une note concernant l'attentat de Sarajevo. Consciente de ses devoirs internationaux, la Serbie des les premiers jours de l'horrible crime a declare qu'elle le condamnait et qu'elle etait prete a ouvrir une enquete sur son territoire si la complicite de certains de ses sujets etait prouvee au cours du proces instruit par les autorites Austro–hongroises. Cependant les demandes contenues dans la note Austro–hongroise sont inutilement humiliantes pour la Serbie et incompatibles avec sa dignite comme Etat independant. Ainsi on nous demande sur un ton peremptoire une declaration du gouvernement dans l'officiel et un ordre du souverain a l'armee, ou nous reprimerions l'esprit hostile contre l'Autriche en nous faisant a nous memes des reproches d'une faiblesse criminelle envers nos menees perfides.—On nous impose ensuite l'admission des fonctionnaires austro–hongrois en Serbie pour participer avec les notres a l'instruction et pour surveiller l'execution des autres conditions indiquees dans la note. Nous avons recu un delai de 48 heures pour accepter le tout, faute de quoi la Legation d'Autriche–Hongrie quittera Belgrade. Nous sommes prets a accepter les conditions austro–hongroises qui sont compatibles avec la situation d'un Etat independant, ainsi que celles dont l'acception nous sera conseillee par Votre Majeste; toutes les personnes dont la participation a l'attentat sera demontree seront severement punis par nous. Certaines parmi ces demandes ne pourraient etre executees sans des changements de notre legislation, ce qui exige du temps. On nous a donne un delai trop court. Nous pouvons etre attaques apres l'expiration du delai par l'armee austro–hongroise qui se concentre sur notre frontiere. Il nous est impossible de nous defendre et nous supplions Votre Majeste de nous donner Son aide le plus tot possible. La bienveillance precieuse de Votre Majeste qui s'est manifestee tant de fois a notre egard nous fait esperer fermement que cette fois encore notre appel sera entendu par Son genereux coeur slave.

En ces moments difficiles l'interprete les sentiments du peuple serbe qui supplie Votre Majeste de vouloir bien s'interesser au sort du Royaume de Serbie.

(Signe) Alexandre.

No. 7.

Le Charge d'Affaires en Allemagne au Ministre des Affaires Etrangeres.

(Telegramme).

Berlin, le 11/24 Juillet 1914.

Tous les journaux du matin, meme ceux, rares, qui reconnaissent l'impossibilite pour la Serbie d'accepter les conditions posees, accueillent avec une grande sympathie le ton energique adopte par l'Autriche. L'officieux "Local–Anzeiger" est particulierement agressif; il qualifie de superflus les recours eventuels de la Serbie a St. Petersbourg, a Paris, a Athenes et a Bucarest, et termine en disant que le peuple allemand respirera librement quand il aura appris que la situation dans la peninsule Balcanique va enfin s'eclaircir.

(Signe) Bronewsky.

No. 8.

Le Charge d'Affaires en France an Ministre des Affaires Etrangeres.

(Telegramme). Paris, le 11/24 Juillet 1914.

La copie de la note officiellement remise a Belgrade a ete communiquee par l'Ambassadeur d'Autriche an Gouvernement Francais. Plus tard l'Ambassadeur d'Allemagne a visite le Ministre et lui a lu une communication reproduisant les arguments autrichiens et indiquant qu'en cas de refus de la part de la Serbie, l'Autriche serait obligee de recourir a une pression et, en cas de besoin, a des mesures militaires; la communication se terminait par la remarque qu'a l'avis de l'Allemagne cette question devrait etre resolue directement entre l'Autriche et la Serbie et qu'il etait de l'interet des Puissances de circonscrire l'affaire en l'abandonnant aux Parties interessees. Le Gerant du Departement Politique, qui assistait a l'entretien, demanda a l'Ambassadeur s'il fallait considerer l'action autrichienne comme un ultimatum—en d'autres termes, si, dans le cas ou la Serbie ne se soumettrait pas entierement aux demandes autrichiennes, les hostilites etaient inevitables? L'ambassadeur evita une reponse directe en alleguant l'absence d'instructions.

(Signe) Sevastopoulo.

No. 9.

Le Charge d'Affaires en Serbie au Ministre des Affaires Etrangeres.

(Telegramme). Belgrade, le 11/24 Juillet 1914.

Pachitch est rentre a Belgrade. Il a l'intention de donner dans le delai fixe, c'est a dire demain Samedi a 6 heures du soir, une reponse a l'Autriche indiquant les points acceptables et inacceptables. On adressera aujourd'hui meme aux Puissances la priere de defendre l'independance de la Serbie. Ensuite, ajouta Pachitch, si la guerre est inevitable—nous ferons la guerre.

(Signe) Strandtman.

No. 10.

Communique du Gouvernement Imperial.

St.–Petersbourg, le 12/25 Juillet 1914.

Les derniers evenements et l'envoi par l'Autriche–Hongrie d'un ultimatum a la Serbie preoccupent le Gouvernement Imperial an plus haut degre. Le Gouvernement suit attentivement l'evolution du conflit serbo–autrichien qui ne peut pas laisser la Russie

175

indifferente.

No. 11.

Le Charge d'Affaires en Autriche–Hongrie au Ministre des Affaires Etrangeres.

(Telegramme). Vienne, le 12/25 Juillet 1914.

Le comte Berchtold se trouve a Ischl. Vu l'impossibilite d'y arriver a temps, je lui ai telegraphie notre proposition de prolonger le delai de l'ultimatum et l'ai repetee verbalement au Baron Macchio. Ce dernier m'a promis de la communiquer a temps au Ministre des Affaires Etrangeres, mais a ajoute qu'il pouvait predire avec assurance un refus categorique.

(Signe) Koudachew.

No. 12.

Le Charge d'Affaires en Autriche–Hongrie an Ministre des Affaires Etrangeres.

(Telegramme). Vienne, le 12/25 Juillet 1914.

Suite a mon telegramme d'aujourd'hui. Viens de recevoir de Macchio la reponse negative du Gouvernement Austro–Hongrois a notre proposition de prolonger le delai de la note.

(Signe) Koudachew.

No. 13.

Le Charge d'Affaires en Serbie an Ministre des Affaires Etrangeres.

(Telegramme). Belgrade, le 12/25 Juillet 1914.

Recu avec retard le 14—27 Juillet 1914.

Je transmets la reponse que le President du Conseil des Ministres Serbe a remis an ministre Austro–Hongrois a Belgrade aujourd'hui avant l'expiration du delai de l'ultimatum....

(The text of the reply will be found in the British White Book (*Correspondence*, No. 39) and also in the German White Book, pp. 23–32 (supra, Appendix I.).)

No. 14.

Le Charge d'affaires en Allemagne au Ministre des affaires Etrangeres.

(Telegramme). Berlin, le 12/25 Juillet 1914.

Ai recu Votre telegramme du 11/24 Juillet. Ai communique son contenu an Ministre des Affaires Etrangeres. Il me dit que le Gouvernement Anglais l'a egalement prie de conseiller a Vienne la prolongation du delai de l'ultimatum; il a communique cette demarche telegraphiquement a Vienne, il va en faire autant pour notre demarche, mais il craint qu'a la suite de l'absence de Berchtold parti pour Ischl, et vu le manque de temps, ses telegrammes ne restent sans resultats; il a, en outre, des doutes sur l'opportunite pour l'Autriche de ceder an dernier moment et il se demande si cela ne pouvait pas augmenter l'assurance de la Serbie. J'ai repondu qu'une grande Puissance comme l'Autriche pourrait ceder sans porter atteinte a son prestige et ai fait valoir tous les arguments conformes, cependant je n'ai pu obtenir des promesses plus precises. Meme lorsque je laissais entendre qu'il fallait agir a Vienne pour eviter la possibilite de consequences redoutables, le Ministre des Affaires Etrangeres repondait chaque fois negativement.

(Signe) Bronewsky.

No. 15.

Le Charge d'affaires en France an Ministre des Affaires Etrangeres.

(*Telegramme*). Paris, le 12/25 Juillet 1914.

Ai recu le telegramme du 11/24 Juillet concernant la prolongation du delai de l'ultimatum autrichien et ai fait la communication prescrite. Le Representant de France a Vienne a ete muni d'instructions conformes.

(Signe) Sevastopoulo.

No. 16.

L'Ambassadeur en Angleterre an Ministre des Affaires Etrangeres.

(*Telegramme*). Londres, le 12/25 Juillet 1914.

Recu telegramme du 11 Juillet. Grey a prescrit a l'Ambassadeur d'Angleterre a Vienne d'appuyer notre demarche concernant la prolongation du delai de l'ultimatum. Il m'a dit en meme temps que l'Ambassadeur d'Autriche etait venu le voir et avait explique qu'on ne devrait pas attribuer a la note autrichienne le caractere d'un ultimatum; il faudrait la considerer comme une demarche qui, en cas d'absence de reponse ou en cas de reponse insuffisante au terme fixe, aurait comme suite la rupture des relations diplomatiques et le depart immediat de Belgrade du Ministre d'Autriche–Hongrie, sans entrainer cependant le commencement immediat des hostilites.—Grey a ajoute qu'a la suite de cette explication il a indique a l'Ambassadeur d'Angleterre a Vienne que dans le cas ou il serait trop tard pour soulever la question de la prolongation du delai de l'ultimatum, celle de l'arret des hostilites pourrait peut–etre servir de base a la discussion.

(Signe) Benckendorff.

No. 17.

Le Ministre des Affaires Etrangeres a l'Ambassadeur a Londres.

(Telegramme). St.–Petersbourg, le 12/25 Juillet 1914.

Dans le cas d'une nouvelle aggravation de la situation, pouvant provoquer de la part des Grandes Puissances des actions conformes, nous comptons que l'Angleterre ne tardera pas de se ranger nettement du cote de la Russie et de la France, en vue de maintenir l'equilibre europeen, en faveur duquel elle est intervenue constamment dans le passe et qui serait sans aucun doute compromis dans le cas du triomphe de l'Autriche.

(Signe) Sazonow.

No. 18.

Note verbale remise par l'Ambassadeur d'Allemagne au Ministre des Affaires Etrangeres le 12/25 Juillet 1914.

Il nous revient de source autoritative que la nouvelle repandue par quelques journaux d'apres laquelle la demarche du Gouvernement d'Autriche–Hongrie a Belgrade aurait ete faite a l'instigation de l'Allemagne est absolument fausse. Le Gouvernement Allemand n'a pas eu connaissance du texte de la note Autrichienne avant qu'elle ait ete remise et n'a exerce aucune influence sur son contenu. C'est a tort qu'on attribue a l'Allemagne une attitude comminatoire.

L'Allemagne appuie naturellement comme allie de l'Autriche les revendications a son avis legitimes du Cabinet de Vienne contre la Serbie.

Avant tout elle desire comme elle l'a deja declare des le commencement du differend Austro–Serbe que ce conflit reste localise.

No. 19.

Le Charge d'affaires en France an Ministre des affaires Etrangeres.

(Telegramme) *Paris, le 12/25 Juillet 1914.*

Me refere a mon telegramme du 11/24 Juillet.

Aujourd'hui un journal du matin a publie, sous une forme pas entierement exacte, les declarations d'hier de l'Ambassadeur d'Allemagne, en les faisant suivre de commentaires qui attribuent a cette demarche le caractere d'une menace. L'Ambassadeur d'Allemagne, tres impressionne par ces divulgations, a visite aujourd'hui le Gerant du Departement Politique pour lui dire que ses paroles n'avaient nullement eu le caractere de menace qu'on leur attribue. Il a declare que l'Autriche avait presente sa note a la Serbie sans entente precise avec Berlin, mais que cependant l'Allemagne approuvait le point de vue de l'Autriche et que certainement 'la fleche une fois partie' (ce sont la ses propres paroles), l'Allemagne ne pouvait se laisser guider que par ses devoirs d'alliee.

(Signe) Sevastopoulo.

No. 20.

L'ambassadeur en Angleterre au Ministre des Affaires Etrangeres.

(Telegramme). Londres, le 12/25 Juillet 1914.

Grey m'a dit que l'Ambassadeur d'Allemagne lui a declare que le Gouvernement Allemand n'avait pas ete informe du texte de la note autrichienne, mais qu'il soutenait entierement la demarche autrichienne. L'Ambassadeur a demande en meme temps si l'Angleterre pouvait consentir a agir a St. Petersbourg dans un esprit de conciliation. Grey a repondu que cela etait completement impossible. Le Ministre a ajoute que tant que les complications n'existaient qu'entre l'Autriche et la Serbie, les interets Anglais n'etaient engages qu'indirectement, mais qu'il devait prevoir que la mobilisation autrichienne aurait comme suite la mobilisation de la Russie et que des ce moment on se trouverait en presence d'une situation a laquelle seraient interessees toutes les Puissances. L'Angleterre se reservait pour ce cas une complete liberte d'action.

(Signe) Benckendorff.

No. 21.

Le Charge d'affaires en Serbie an Ministre des Affaires Etrangeres.

(Telegramme). Belgrade, le 12/25 Juillet 1914.

Malgre le caractere extremement conciliant de la reponse serbe a l'ultimatum, le Ministre d'Autriche vient d'informer, a 6–1/2 du soir, le Gouvernement Serbe par note, que n'ayant pas recu an delai fixe une reponse satisfaisante il quitte Belgrade avec tout le personnel de la Legation. La Scoupchtina est convoquee a Nich pour le 14/27 Juillet. Le Gouvernement Serbe et le Corps Diplomatique partent ce soir pour la meme ville.

(Signe) Strandtman.

No. 22.

L'Ambassadeur en Angleterre an Ministre des Affaires Etrangeres.

(Telegramme). Londres, le 12/25 Juillet 1914.

Grey a dit a l'Ambassadeur d'Allemagne qu'a son avis la mobilisation autrichienne devait entrainer la mobilisation de la Russie, qu'alors surgirait le danger aigu d'une guerre generale et qu'il ne voyait qu'un seul moyen pour une solution pacifique: qu'en presence des mobilisations autrichienne et russe, l'Allemagne, la France, l'Italie et l'Angleterre s'abstiennent d'une mobilisation immediate et proposent tout d'abord leurs bons offices. Grey m'a dit que ce plan necessitait avant tout l'agrement de l'Allemagne et l'engagement de cette Puissance de ne pas mobiliser. En consequence il a adresse tout d'abord a Berlin une question a ce sujet.

(Signe) Benckendorff.

No. 23.

Le Ministre des Affaires Etrangeres a l'Ambassadeur en Italie.

(Telegramme). St. Petersbourg, le 13/26 Juillet 1914.

L'Italie pourrait jouer un role de tout premier ordre en faveur du maintien de la paix, en exercant l'influence necessaire sur l'Autriche et en adoptant une attitude nettement defavorable au conflit, car ce dernier ne saurait etre localise. Il est desirable que vous exprimiez la conviction qu'il est impossible pour la Russie de ne pas venir en aide a la Serbie.

(Signe) Sazonow.

No. 24.

Le Gerant du Consulat a Prague au Ministre des Affaires Etrangeres.

(Telegramme). Prague, le 13/26 Juillet 1914.

Why We Are At War

La mobilisation a ete decretee.

(Signe) Kazansky.

No. 25.

Le Ministre des Affaires Etrangeres a l'Ambassadeur en Autriche–Hongrie.

(Telegramme). St. Petersbourg, le 13/26 Juillet 1914.

J'ai eu aujourd'hui un long entretien sur un ton amical avec l'Ambassadeur d'Autriche–Hongrie. Apres avoir examine avec lui les 10 demandes adressees a la Serbie, j'ai fait observer qu'a part la forme peu habile sous laquelle elles sont presentees, quelques–unes parmi elles sont absolument inexecutables, meme dans le cas ou le gouvernement Serbe declarerait les vouloir accepter. Ainsi, par exemple, les points 1 et 2 ne pourraient etre executes sans un remaniement des lois serbes sur la presse et sur les associations, pour lequel le consentement de la Scoupchtina pourrait etre difficilement obtenu; quant a l'execution des points 4 et 5, elle pourrait produire des consequences fort dangereuses et meme faire naitre le danger d'actes de terrorisme diriges contre les membres de la Maison Royale et contre Pachitch, ce qui ne saurait entrer dans les vues de l'Autriche. En ce qui regarde les autres points, il me semble, qu'avec certains changements dans les details, il ne serait pas difficile de trouver un terrain d'entente si les accusations y contenues etaient confirmees par des preuves suffisantes.

Dans l'interet de la conservation de la paix qui, aux dires de Szapary, est precieuse a l'Autriche au meme degre qu'a toutes les Puissances, il serait necessaire de mettre au plus tot possible une fin a la situation tendue du moment. Dans ce but il me semblerait tres desirable que l'Ambassadeur d'Autriche–Hongrie fut autorise d'entrer avec moi dans un echange de vues prive aux fins d'un remaniement en commun de quelques articles de la note autrichienne du 10/23 Juillet. Ce procede permettrait peut–etre de trouver une formule qui fut acceptable pour la Serbie, tout en donnant satisfaction a l'Autriche quant au fond de ses demandes. Veuillez avoir une explication prudente et amicale dans le sens de ce telegramme avec le Ministre des Affaires Etrangeres. Communique aux Ambassadeurs en Allemagne, en France, en Angleterre et en Italie.

(Signe) Sazonow.

No. 26.

Le Ministre des Affaires Etrangeres a l'Ambassadeur en Allemagne.

(Telegramme). St. Petersbourg, le 13/26 Juillet.

Veuillez communiquer le contenu de mon telegramme a Vienne d'aujourd'hui au Ministre des Affaires Etrangeres Allemand et lui exprimer l'espoir, que de son cote il trouvera possible de conseiller a Vienne d'aller au-devant de notre proposition.

(Signe) Sazonow.

No. 27.

Le Charge d'Affaires en France au Ministre des Affaires Etrangeres.

(Telegramme). Paris, le 13/26 Juillet 1914.

Le Directeur du Departement Politique m'informe, que lors de la communication qu'il a faite a l'Ambassadeur d'Autriche du contenu de la reponse serbe a l'ultimatum, l'Ambassadeur n'a pas cache son etonnement de ce qu'elle n'ait pas donne satisfaction a Giesl. L'attitude conciliante de la Serbie doit, selon l'avis du Directeur du Departement Politique, produire la meilleure impression en Europe.

(Signe) Sevastopoulo.

No. 28.

Le Charge d'Affaires en France an Ministre des Affaires Etrangeres.

(*Telegramme*). Paris, le 13/26 Juillet 1914.

Aujourd'hui l'Ambassadeur d'Allemagne a de nouveau rendu visite au Gerant du Ministere des Affaires Etrangeres et lui a fait les declarations suivantes:

"L'Autriche a declare a la Russie qu'elle ne recherche pas des acquisitions territoriales et qu'elle ne menace pas l'integrite de la Serbie. Son but unique est d'assurer sa propre tranquillite. Par consequent il depend de la Russie d'eviter la guerre. L'Allemagne se sent solidaire avec la France dans le desir ardent de conserver la paix et espere fermement que la France usera de son influence a Petersbourg dans un sens moderateur". Le Ministre fit observer que l'Allemagne pourrait de son cote entreprendre des demarches analogues a Vienne, surtout en presence de l'esprit de conciliation dont a fait preuve la Serbie. L'Ambassadeur repondit que cela n'etait pas possible, vu la resolution prise de ne pas s'immiscer dans le conflit austro–serbe. Alors le Ministre demanda, si les quatre Puissances—l'Angleterre, l'Allemagne, l'Italie et la France—ne pouvaient pas entreprendre des demarches a St. Petersbourg et a Vienne, puisque l'affaire se reduisait en somme a un conflit entre la Russie et l'Autriche. L'Ambassadeur allegua l'absence d'instructions. Finalement le Ministre refusa d'adherer a la proposition allemande.

(Signe) Sevastopoulo.

No. 29.

Le Charge d'Affaires en France au Ministre des Affaires Etrangeres.

(*Telegramme*). Paris, le 13/28 Juillet 1914.

Le Directeur du Departement Politique a declare qu'a son avis personnel, les demarches successives allemandes a Paris ont pour but d'intimider la France et d'amener son intervention a St. Petersbourg.

(Signe) Sevastopoulo.

No. 30.

Le Charge d'Affaires en Allemagne au Ministre des Affaires Etrangeres.

(*Telegramme*). Berlin, le 13/26 Juillet 1914.

Apres la reception a Berlin de la nouvelle de la mobilisation de l'armee autrichienne contre la Serbie une grande foule, composee, aux dires des journaux, en partie d'elements autrichiens, se livra a une serie de bruyantes manifestations en faveur de l'Autriche. A une heure avancee de la soiree les manifestants se masserent a plusieurs reprises devant le palais de l'Ambassade Imperiale en poussant des cris hostiles a la Russie; la police etait presque absente et ne prenait aucune mesure.

(Signe) Bronewsky.

No. 31.

L'Ambassadeur en Angleterre au Ministre des Affaires Etrangeres.

(Telegramme).

Londres, le 14/27 Juillet 1914.

Ai recu votre telegramme du 13–26 Juillet. Prie me telegraphier si, a Votre avis, Vos pourparlers directs avec le cabinet de Vienne s'accordent avec le projet de Grey concernant la mediation des 4 Gouvernements. Ayant appris de l'Ambassadeur d'Angleterre a St. Petersbourg que Vous etiez dispose a accepter cette combinaison, Grey a decide de la transformer en une proposition officielle qu'il a faite hier soir a Berlin, a Paris et a Rome.

(Signe) Benckendorff.

No. 32.

Le Ministre des Affaires Etrangeres aux Ambassadeurs en France et en Angleterre.

(Telegramme).

St. Petersbourg, le 14/27 Juillet 1914.

(Printed in the British White Book (*Correspondence*, No. 53.).)

No. 33.

Le Ministre des Affaires Etrangeres aux Ambassadeurs en France, en Angleterre, en Allemagne, en Autriche–Hongrie et en Italie.

(Telegramme).

St. Petersbourg, le 14/27 Juillet 1914.

Ai pris connaissance de la reponse transmise par le Gouvernement Serbe au Baron Giesl. Elle depasse toutes nos previsions par sa moderation et son desir de donner la plus complete satisfaction a l'Autriche. Nous ne voyons pas quelles pourraient etre encore les demandes de l'Autriche, a moins que le Cabinet de Vienne ne cherche un pretexte pour une guerre avec la Serbie.

(Signe) Sazonow.

No. 34.

Le Charge d'Affaires en France au Ministre des Affaires Etrangeres.

(Telegramme).

Paris, le 14/27 Juillet 1914.

L'Ambassadeur d'Allemagne a confere aujourd'hui de nouveau longuement sur la situation avec le Directeur du Departement Politique. L'Ambassadeur a beaucoup insiste sur l'exclusion de toute possibilite d'une mediation ou d'une conference.

(Signe) Sevastopoulo.

No. 35.

L'Ambassadeur en France au Ministre des Affaires Etrangeres.

(Telegramme). Paris, le 14/27 Juillet 1914.

Ai confere avec le Gerant du Ministere des Affaires Etrangeres, en presence de Berthelot, immediatement apres mon retour a Paris. Tous les deux m'out confirme les details concernant les demarches de l'Ambassadeur d'Allemagne que Sevastopoulo Vous a communiques dans ses telegrammes. Ce matin le Baron de Schoen a confirme par ecrit sa declaration d'hier, savoir: 1) l'Autriche a declare a la Russie qu'elle ne recherche pas d'acquisitions et n'attente pas a l'integrite de la Serbie. Son unique but est d'assurer sa propre tranquillite. 2) Par consequent il depend de la Russie d'eviter la guerre. 3) L'Allemagne et la France, completement solidaires dans l'ardent desir de ne pas rompre la paix, doivent agir sur la Russie dans un sens moderateur. Le Baron de Schoen a specialement souligne l'expression de la solidarite entre l'Allemagne et la France. D'apres la conviction du Ministre de la Justice, les demarches susdites de l'Allemagne out pour but evident de desunir la Russie et la France, d'entrainer le Gouvernement Francais dans la voie des representations a St. Petersbourg et de compromettre ainsi notre allie a nos yeux; enfin, en cas de guerre, d'en rejeter la responsabilite non sur l'Allemagne, qui emploie soi–disant tous ses efforts pour le maintien de la paix, mais sur la Russie et la France.

(Signe) Iswolsky.

No. 36.

L'Ambassadeur en France au Ministre des Affaires Etrangeres.

(Telegramme). Paris, le 14/27 Juillet 1914.

Il ressort de vos telegrammes du 13/26 Juillet que vous ne connaissiez pas encore la reponse du Gouvernement Serbe. Le telegramme par lequel cette nouvelle m'a ete communiquee de Belgrade a ete egalement en route pendant 20 heures. Le telegramme du Ministre des Affaires Etrangeres Francais expedie avant–hier, au triple tarif, a onze heures du matin, et contenant l'ordre d'appuyer notre demarche, n'est parvenu a sa destination qu'a 6 heures. Il n'y a aucun doute que ce telegramme n'ait ete retenu intentionnellement par le telegraphe autrichien.

(Signe) Iswolsky.

No. 37.

L'Ambassadeur en France au Ministre des Affaires Etrangeres.

(Telegramme). Paris, le 14/27 Juillet 1914.

D'ordre de son Gouvernement, l'Ambassadeur d'Autriche a communique au Gerant du Ministere des Affaires Etrangeres que la reponse de la Serbie a ete jugee insuffisante a Vienne et que demain, mardi, l'Autriche procederait a des 'actions energiques' don't le but serait de forcer la Serbie de lui donner les garanties necessaires. Le Ministre ayant demande en quoi consisteraient ces actions, l'Ambassadeur repondit qu'il n'avait pas de renseignements exacts a ce sujet, mais qu'il pouvait s'agir d'un passage da la frontiere serbe, d'un ultimatum et meme d'une declaration de guerre.

(Signe) Iswolsky.

No. 38.

Le Charge d'Affaires en Allemagne au Ministre des Affaires Etrangeres.

(Telegramme). Berlin, le 14/27 Juillet 1914.

J'ai prie le Ministre des Affaires Etrangeres d'appuyer a Vienne votre proposition tendant a autoriser Szapary d'elaborer, par la voie d'un echange de vues prive avec Vous, une redaction des demandes austro–hongroises acceptable pour les deux parties. Jagow a repondu qu'il etait an courant de cette proposition et qu'il partageait l'avis de Pourtales que, puisque Szapary avait commence cette conversation, il pourrait aussi bien la continuer. Il telegraphiera dans ce sens a l'Ambassadeur d'Allemagne a Vienne. Je l'ai prie de conseiller d'une facon plus pressante a Vienne de s'engager dans cette voie de conciliation; Jagow a repondu qu'il ne pouvait pas conseiller a l'Autriche de ceder.

(Signe) Bronewsky.

No. 39.

Le Charge d'Affaires en Allemagne au Ministre des Affaires Etrangeres.

(Telegramme). Berlin, le 14/27 Juillet 1914.

Aujourd'hui, avant ma visite au Ministre des Affaires Etrangeres, ce dernier avait recu celle de l'Ambassadeur de France qui avait tente de lui faire accepter la proposition anglaise relative a une action en faveur de la paix, action qui serait exercee simultanement a St.–Petersbourg et a Vienne par l'Angleterre, l'Allemagne, l'Italie et la France. Cambon a propose que ces Puissances donnent a Vienne un conseil dans les termes suivants: "S'abstenir de tout acte qui pourrait aggraver la situation de l'heure actuelle". En adoptant cette formule voilee on eviterait de mentionner la necessite de s'abstenir d'une invasion de la Serbie. Jagow a oppose a cette proposition un refus categorique, et cela malgre les instances de l'Ambassadeur qui a fait valoir, comme un bon cote de la proposition, le groupement mixte des Puissances grace auquel on evitait l'opposition de l'Alliance a l'Entente, ce dont s'etait si souvent plaint Jagow lui–meme.

(Signe) Bronewsky.

No. 40.

Telegramme de Sa Majeste Imperiale l'Empereur a Son Altesse Royale le Prince Alexandre de Serbie en date du 14/27 Juillet 1914.

Votre Altesse Royale en s'adressant a Moi dans un moment particulierement difficile ne s'est pas trompee sur les sentiments qui M'animent a Son egard et sur Ma sympathie cordiale pour le peuple serbe.

Ma plus serieuse attention est attiree par la situation actuelle et Mon Gouvernement s'applique de toutes ses forces a aplanir les presentes difficultes. Je ne doute point que Votre Altesse et le Gouvernement Royal ne veuillent faciliter cette tache en ne negligeant rien pour arriver a une solution qui permette de prevenir les horreurs d'une nouvelle guerre tout en sauvegardant la dignite de la Serbie.

Tant qu'il y a le moindre espoir d'eviter une effusion de sang, tous nos efforts doivent tendre vers ce but. Si, malgre Notre plus sincere desir, Nous ne reussissons pas, Votre Altesse peut etre assuree qu'en aucun cas la Russie ne se desinteressera du sort de la Serbie.

(Signe) Nicolas.

No. 41.

L'Ambassadeur en Autriche–Hongrie au Ministre des Affaires Etrangeres.

(*Telegramme*). Vienne, le 14/17 juillet 1914.[194]

Le Ministre des Affaires Etrangeres est absent. Pendant un entretien prolonge, que j'ai eu aujourd'hui avec Macchio, j'ai, en termes tout a fait amicaux, attire son attention sur l'impression defavorable qu'a produite en Russie la presentation par l'Autriche a la Serbie de demandes absolument inacceptables pour chaque etat independant, bien que petit. J'ai ajoute que ce procede, qui pourrait amener des complications les moins desirables, a provoque en Russie une profonde surprise et une reprobation generale. Il faut supposer que l'Autriche, sous l'influence des assurances du Representant Allemand a Vienne, lequel pendant toute cette crise a joue un role d'instigateur, a compte sur la probabilite de la localisation de son conflit avec la Serbie et sur la possibilite de porter a cette derniere impunement un coup grave. La declaration du Gouvernement Imperial concernant l'impossibilite pour la Russie de rester indifferente en presence d'un tel procede a provoque ici une grande impression.

(Signe) Schebeko.

[Footnote 194: Evidently the date July 17 is a misprint for July 27.]

No. 42.

L'Ambassadeur en Angleterre au Ministre des Affaires Etrangeres.

(*Telegramme*). Londres, le 14/17 Juillet 1914.[195]

Grey vient de repondre a l'Ambassadeur d'Allemagne, qui etait venu le questionner sur la possibilite d'une action a St.-Petersbourg, que cette action devrait se produire a Vienne et que le cabinet de Berlin serait le mieux qualifie pour l'exercer. Grey a fait observer en meme temps que la reponse serbe a la note autrichienne depassait par sa moderation et son esprit de conciliation tout ce a quoi on pouvait s'attendre. Grey a ajoute qu'il en concluait que la Russie avait conseille a Belgrade de donner une reponse moderee et qu'il pensait que la reponse serbe pouvait servir de base a une solution pacifique et acceptable de la question.

Dans ces conditions, a continue Grey, si l'Autriche malgre cette reponse commencait les hostilites, elle prouverait son intention d'aneantir la Serbie. La question placee sur ce terrain produirait une situation qui pourrait amener une guerre dans laquelle seraient impliquees toutes les Puissances.

Grey a enfin declare que le Gouvernement Anglais etait bien sincerement dispose a collaborer avec le gouvernement Allemand tant qu'il s'agirait de la conservation de la paix; mais que pour le cas contraire l'Angleterre se reservait une pleine liberte d'action.

(Signe) Benckendorff.

[Footnote 195: Evidently the date July 17 is a misprint for July 27.]

No. 43.

Le Ministre des Affaires Etrangeres a l'Ambassadeur en Angleterre.

(*Telegramme*). St.–Petersbourg, le 15/28 Juillet 1914.

(Printed in the British White Book (*Correspondence*, No. 54.).)

No. 44.

Le Consul general a Fiume au Ministre des Affaires Etrangeres.

(Telegramme). Fiume, le 15/28 Juillet 1914.

L'etat de siege a ete proclame en Slavonie, en Croatie et a Fiume et en meme temps les reservistes de toutes les categories ont ete mobilises.

(Signe) Salviati.

No. 45.

L'Ambassadeur en Autriche–Hongrie au Ministre des Affaires Etrangeres.

(Telegramme). Vienne, le 15/28 Juillet 1914.

(Printed in the British White Book (*Correspondence*, No. 93 (I)).)

No. 46.

Le Charge d'affaires en Allemagne au Ministre des Affaires Etrangeres.

(Telegramme). Berlin, le 15/28 Juillet 1914.

Le Bureau Wolff n'a pas publie le texte de la note responsive serbe qui lui avait ete communique. Jusqu'a ce moment cette note n'a paru in extenso dans aucun des journaux locaux, qui selon toute evidence ne veulent pas lui donner place dans leurs colonnes, se rendant compte de l'effet calmant que cette publication produirait sur les lecteurs allemands.

(Signe) Bronewsky.

No. 47.

L'Ambassadeur en Autriche–Hongrie au Ministre des Affaires Etrangeres.

(Telegramme). Vienne, le 15/28 Juillet, 1914.

Le decret sur la mobilisation generale a ete signe.

(Signe) Schebeko.

No. 48.

Le Ministre des Affaires Etrangeres a l'Ambassadeur a Londres.[196]

(Telegramme). St.–Petersbourg, le 15/28 Juillet, 1914.

En presence des hostilites entre l'Autriche–Hongrie et la Serbie il est necessaire que l'Angleterre entreprenne d'urgence une action mediatrice et que l'action militaire de l'Autriche contre la Serbie soit immediatement suspendue. Autrement la mediation ne servira que de pretexte pour tirer en longueur la solution de la question et donnera entre temps a l'Autriche la possibilite d'ecraser completement la Serbie et d'occuper une situation dominante dans les Balcans.

Communique a Paris, Berlin, Vienne et Rome.

(Signe) Sazonow.

[Footnote 196: An English (abbreviated) version of this telegram is given in the British White Book (*Correspondence*, No. 70 (2)).]

No. 49.

Le Ministre des Affaires Etrangeres au Charge d'Affaires en Allemagne.

(Telegramme). St.–Petersbourg, le 16/29 Juillet, 1914.

(Printed in the British White Book (*Correspondence*, No. 93 (2)).)

No. 50.

Le Ministre des Affaires Etrangeres aux Ambassadeurs en Angleterre et en France.

(Telegramme). St.–Petersbourg, le 16/29 Juillet 1914.

(Printed in the British White Book (*Correspondence*, No. 93 (3)).)

No. 51.

Le Charge d'Affaires en Allemagne au Ministre des Affaires Etrangeres.

(Telegramme). Berlin, le 16/29 Juillet 1914.

Sur ma question s'il avait une reponse de Vienne relativement a Votre proposition de pourparlers prives a St.–Petersbourg, le Secretaire d'Etat a repondu negativement.

Il declare qu'il lui est fort difficile d'agir sur Vienne, surtout ouvertement. Parlant a Cambon, il a meme ajoute qu'en cas d'une pression trop evidente l'Autriche se haterait de mettre l'Allemagne en presence d'un fait accompli.

Le Secretaire d'Etat dit qu'il a recu aujourd'hui un telegramme de Pourtales d'ou il constate que plus que les premiers jours Vous etes dispose a trouver un compromis acceptable pour tous. J'ai replique que probablement Vous avez ete des le commencement en faveur d'un compromis, bien entendu a la condition qu'il soit acceptable non seulement pour l'Autriche, mais egalement pour nous. Il m'a dit ensuite qu'il paraissait que nous avions commence a mobiliser sur la frontiere autrichienne et qu'il craignait que ceci rendrait plus difficile pour l'Autriche la possibilite de s'entendre avec nous, d'autant plus que l'Autriche ne mobilisait que contre la Serbie et ne faisait pas de preparatifs sur notre frontiere. J'ai repondu que, d'apres les renseignements dont je disposais, l'Autriche mobilisait egalement sur notre frontiere et que par consequent nous devions prendre des mesures analogues. J'ai ajoute que les mesures que nous avons peut–etre prises de notre cote n'etaient nullement dirigees contre l'Allemagne.

(Signe) Bronewsky.

No. 52.

Le Charge d'affaires en Serbie au Ministre des Affaires Etrangeres.

(Telegramme). Nich, le 16/29 Juillet 1914.

Aujourd'hui le Ministre de Bulgarie, an nom de son Gouvernement, a declare a Pachiteh que la Bulgarie observerait la neutralite.

(Signe) Strandtman.

No. 53.

L'Ambassadeur en France au Ministre des Affaires Etrangeres.

Why We Are At War

(Telegramme). Paris, le 16/29 Juillet 1914.

A l'occasion de l'arrivee du President de la Republique Francais le Ministre des Affaires Etrangeres avait prepare un court expose de la situation politique actuelle, a pen pres dans les termes suivants: L'Autriche, craignant la decomposition interieure, s'est emparee du pretexte de l'assassinat de l'Archiduc pour essayer d'obtenir des garanties qui pourront revetir la forme de l'occupation des communications militaires serbes ou meme du territoire serbe. L'Allemagne soutient l'Autriche. Le maintien de la paix depend de la seule Russie, parce qu'il s'agit d'une affaire qui doit etre "localisee" entre l'Autriche et la Serbie, c'est a dire de la punition de la politique precedente de la Serbie et des garanties pour l'avenir. De ceci l'Allemagne conclue qu'il faut exercer une action moderatrice a Petersbourg. Ce sophisme a ete refute a Paris comme a Londres. A Paris, le Baron de Schoen a en vain tache d'entrainer la France a une action solidaire avec l'Allemagne sur la Russie en faveur du maintien de la paix. Les memes tentatives out ete faites a Londres. Dans les deux capitales il a ete repondu que l'action devrait etre exercee a Vienne, car les demandes excessives de l'Autriche, son refus de discuter les rares reserves de la Serbie, et la declaration de guerre menacent de provoquer la guerre generale. La France et l'Angleterre ne peuvent exercer une action moderatrice sur la Russie, laquelle jusqu'ici a fait preuve de la plus grande moderation, surtout en conseillant a la Serbie d'accepter ce qui etait possible de la note autrichienne. Aujourd'hui l'Allemagne parait renoncer a l'idee d'une action sur la Russie seule et incline vers une action mediatrice a Petersbourg et a Vienne, mais en meme temps l'Allemagne comme l'Autriche tachent de faire trainer l'affaire. L'Allemagne s'oppose a la Conference sans indiquer aucune autre maniere d'agir pratique. L'Autriche mene des pourparlers manifestement dilatoires a Petersbourg. En meme temps elle prend des mesures actives, et si ces mesures sont tolerees, ses pretentions augmenteront proportionnellement. Il est tres desirable que la Russie prete tout son appui an projet de mediation que presentera Sir E. Grey. Dans le cas contraire l'Autriche, sous pretexte de "garantie", pourra, en fait, changer le status territorial de l'Europe orientale.

(Signe) Iswolsky.

No. 54.

L'Ambassadeur en Angleterre au Ministre des Affaires Etrangeres.

Why We Are At War

(Telegramme). Londres, le 10/29 Juillet 1914.

Ai communique le contenu de Vos telegrammes du 15/28 Juillet a Grey. Il a declare aujourd'hui a l'Ambassadeur d'Allemagne que les pourparlers directs entre la Russie et l'Autriche avaient echoue, et que les correspondants des journaux mandaient de St.–Petersbourg que la Russie mobilisait contre l'Autriche a la suite de la mobilisation de cette derniere. Grey dit qu'en principe le Gouvernement Allemand s'est declare en faveur de la mediation, mais qu'il rencontre des difficultes quant a la forme. Grey a insiste pour que le Gouvernement Allemand indiquat la forme laquelle a l'avis de l'Allemagne pourrait permettre aux 4 Puissances d'exercer leur mediation pour eviter la guerre; vu le consentement de la France, de l'Italie et de l'Angleterre la mediation pourrait avoir lieu seulement dans le cas ou l'Allemagne consentirait a se ranger du cote de la paix.

(Signe) Benckendorff.

No. 55.

L'Ambassadeur en France au Ministre des Affaires Etrangeres.

(Telegramme). Paris, le 16/29 Juillet 1914.

Viviani vient de me confirmer l'entiere resolution du Gouvernement Francais d'agir d'accord avec nous. Cette resolution est soutenue par les cercles les plus etendus et par les partis, y compris les radicaux–socialistes, qui viennent de lui presenter une declaration exprimant la confiance absolue et les dispositions patriotiques du groupe. Des son arrivee a Paris, Viviani a telegraphie d'urgence a Londres que vu la cessation des pourparlers directs entre Petersbourg et Vienne il etait necessaire que le Cabinet de Londres renouvelat le plus tot possible sous telle ou autre forme sa proposition concernant la mediation des Puissances. Avant moi Viviani a recu aujourd'hui l'Ambassadeur d'Allemagne qui lui a renouvele l'assurance des tendances pacifiques de l'Allemagne. Viviani ayant fait observer que si l'Allemagne desirait la paix elle devrait se hater d'adherer a la proposition de mediation anglaise, le Baron Schoen a repondu que les mots "conference" ou "arbitrage" effrayaient l'Autriche. Viviani a replique qu'il ne s'agissait pas de mots et qu'il serait facile de trouver une autre forme de mediation. D'apres l'avis du Baron de Schoen, pour le succes des negociations entre les Puissances il serait necessaire de savoir ce que l'Autriche compterait demander a la Serbie. Viviani a repondu que le Cabinet de Berlin pourrait bien facilement s'en enquerir aupres de l'Autriche, mais qu'en attendant la note responsive serbe pourrait servir de base a la discussion; il a ajoute que la France desirait sincerement la paix, mais qu'elle etait en meme temps resolue d'agir en pleine harmonie avec ses allies et amis, et que lui, le Baron de Schoen, avait pu se convaincre que cette resolution rencontrait la plus vive approbation du pays.

(Signe) Iswolsky.

No. 56.

Telegramme de son Altesse Royale le Prince Alexandre de Serbie a sa Majeste l'Empereur.

Profondement touche par le telegramme que Votre Majeste a bien voulu M'adresser hier, Je M'empresse de La remercier de tout mon coeur. Je prie Votre Majeste d'etre persuadee que la cordiale sympathie, dont Votre Majeste est animee envers Mon pays, nous est particulierement precieuse et remplit notre ame de l'espoir que l'avenir de la Serbie est assure etant devenu l'objet de la Haute sollicitude de Votre Majeste. Ces moments penibles ne peuvent que raffermir les liens de l'attachement profond qui unissent la Serbie a la sainte Russie slave, et les sentiments de reconnaissance eternelle pour l'aide et la protection de Votre Majeste seront conserves pieusement dans l'ame de tous les Serbes.

(Signe) Alexandre,

No. 57.

Le Charge d'Affaires en Serbie au Ministre des Affaires Etrangeres.

(Telegramme). Nich, le 16/29 Juillet 1914.

J'ai communique a Pachitch le texte du telegramme responsif de Sa Majeste l'Empereur an Prince Alexandre. Pachitch apres l'avoir lu, se signa et dit: "Seigneur! Le Tzar est grand et clement"! Ensuite il m'embrassa, ne pouvant contenir l'emotion qui l'avait gagne. L'heritier est attendu a Nich dans la nuit.

(Signe) Strandtman.

No. 58.

Le Ministre des Affaires Etrangeres a l'Ambassadeur en France.

(Telegramme). St. Petersbourg, le 10/29 Juillet 1914.

Aujourd'hui l'Ambassadeur d'Allemagne m'a communique la resolution prise par son gouvernement de mobiliser, si la Russie ne cessait pas ses preparatifs militaires. Or, nous n'avons commence ces derniers qu'a la suite de la mobilisation a laquelle avait deja procede l'Autriche et vu l'absence evidente chez cette derniere du desir d'accepter un mode quelconque d'une solution pacifique de son conflit avec la Serbie.

Puisque nous ne pouvons pas acceder au desir de l'Allemagne, il ne nous reste que d'accelerer nos propres armements et de compter avec l'inevitabilite probable de la guerre.—Veuillez en avertir le Gouvernement Francais et lui exprimer en meme temps notre sincere reconnaissance pour la declaration que l'Ambassadeur de France m'a faite en son nom en disant que nous pouvons compter entierement sur l'appui de notre alliee de France. Dans les circonstances actuelles cette declaration nous est particulierement precieuse. Communique aux Ambassadeurs en Angleterre, Autriche–Hongrie, Italie, Allemagne.

(Signe) Sazonow.

No. 59.

Le Charge d'Affaires en Serbie au Ministre des Affaires Etrangeres.

(Telegramme). Nich, le 17/30 Juillet 1914.

Le Prince–Regent a publie hier un manifeste signe par tous les Ministres a l'occasion de la declaration de la guerre par l'Autriche a la Serbie. Le manifeste se termine par les paroles suivantes: "Defendez de toutes vos forces vos foyers et la Serbie". Lors de l'ouverture solennelle de la Scouptchina, le Regent lut en son nom le discours du trone, an debut duquel il indiqua que le lieu de la convocation demontrait l'importance des evenements actuels. Suit l'expose des faits des derniers jours—l'ultimatum autrichien, la reponse serbe, les efforts du gouvernement Royal de faire tout ce qui etait compatible avec la dignite de l'Etat pour eviter la guerre et enfin l'agression armee du voisin plus puissant contre la Serbie, aux cotes de laquelle se tient le Montenegro. En passant a l'examen de l'attitude des Puissances en presence du conflit, le Prince insista tout d'abord sur les sentiments dont est animee la Russie et sur la Toute Gracieuse Communication de sa Majeste l'Empereur disant que la Russie en aucun cas n'abandonnera la Serbie. A chaque mention du nom de Sa Majeste Imperiale et de la Russie un "jivio" formidable et febrile secouait la salle des seances. Les marques de sympathie de la part de la France et de l'Angleterre furent aussi relevees separement et provoquerent des "jivio" d'approbation de la part des deputes. Le discours du trone se termine par la declaration d'ouverture de la Scouptchina et par l'expression du voeu que toutes les mesures soient prises pour faciliter la tache du Gouvernement.

(Signe) Strandtman.

No. 60.

Le Ministre des Affaires Etrangeres aux Ambassadeurs en Allemagne, en Autriche–Hongrie, en France, en Angleterre, et en Italie.

(Telegramme). St. Petersbourg, le 17/30 Juillet 1914.

L'Ambassadeur d'Allemagne qui vient de me quitter m'a demande si nous ne pouvions pas nous contenter de la promesse que l'Autriche pourrait donner—de ne pas porter atteinte a l'integrite du Royaume de Serbie—et indiquer a quelles conditions nous pourrions encore consentir a suspendre nos armements; je lui ai dicte, pour etre transmise d'urgence a Berlin, la declaration suivante: "Si l'Autriche, reconnaissant que la question austro–serbe a assume le caractere d'une question europeenne, se declare prete a eliminer de son ultimatum les points qui portent atteinte aux droits souverains de la Serbie, la Russie s'engage a cesser ses preparatifs militaires."

Veuillez telegraphier d'urgence quelle sera l'attitude du Gouvernement Allemand en presence de cette nouvelle preuve de notre desir de faire le possible pour la solution pacifique de la question, car nous ne pouvons pas admettre que de semblables pourparlers ne servent qu'a faire gagner du temps a l'Allemagne et a l'Autriche pour leurs preparatifs militaires.

(Signe) Sazonow.

No. 61.

L'Ambassadeur en Allemagne au Ministre des Affaires Etrangeres.

(Telegramme). Berlin, le 17/30 Juillet 1914.

J'apprends que le decret de mobilisation de l'armee et de la flotte allemandes vient d'etre promulgue.

(Signe) Swerbeew.

No. 62.

L'Ambassadeur en Allemagne au Ministre des Affaires Etrangeres.

(Telegramme). Berlin, le 17/30 Juillet 1914.

Le Ministre des Affaires Etrangeres vient de me telephoner pour me communiquer que la nouvelle lancee tout a l'heure de la mobilisation de l'armee et de la flotte allemandes est fausse; que les feuillets des journaux etaient imprimes d'avance en prevision de toutes eventualites, et mis en vente a l'heure de l'apres—midi, mais que maintenant ils sont confisques,

(Signe) Swerbeew.

No. 63.

L'Ambassadeur en Allemagne au Ministre des Affaires Etrangeres.

(Telegramme). Berlin, le 17/30 Juillet 1914.

Ai recu Votre telegramme du 16—29 Juillet et ai transmis le texte de Votre proposition au Ministre des Affaires Etrangeres que je viens de voir; il m'a dit qu'il avait recu un telegramme identique de l'Ambassadeur d'Allemagne a St.—Petersbourg et m'a declare ensuite qu'il trouvait notre proposition inacceptable pour l'Autriche.

(Signe) Swerbeew.

No. 64.

L'Ambassadeur en Angleterre au Ministre des Affaires Etrangeres.

(Telegramme). Londres, le 17/30 Juillet 1914.

Ai communique le contenu de Vos telegrammes du 16 et 17 Juillet a Grey lequel considere la situation comme tres serieuse, mais desire continuer les pourparlers. J'ai fait observer a Grey que depuis que Vous lui aviez fait la proposition d'accepter tout ce qu'il proposerait en faveur du maintien de la paix, pourvu que l'Autriche ne put profiter de ces atermoiements pour ecraser la Serbie, la situation dans laquelle Vous vous trouviez s'etait apparemment modifiee. A cette epoque nos rapports avec l'Allemagne n'etaient pas compromis. Apres la declaration de l'Ambassadeur d'Allemagne a St.–Petersbourg concernant la mobilisation allemande, ces rapports avaient change et sa demande avait recu de Votre part la seule reponse que pouvait donner une grande Puissance. Lorsque l'Ambassadeur d'Allemagne etait revenu aupres de Vous et s'etait enquis de Vos conditions, Vous les aviez formulees dans des circonstances tout-a-fait speciales. J'ai en meme temps de nouveau insiste aupres de Grey sur la necessite de prendre en consideration la situation nouvelle creee par la faute de l'Allemagne a la suite de l'action de l'Ambassadeur d'Allemagne. Grey a repondu qu'il le comprenait et qu'il tiendrait compte de ces arguments.

(Signe) Benckendorff.

No. 65.

L'Ambassadeur en Angleterre au Ministre des Affaires Etrangeres.

(Telegramme). Londres, le 17/30 Juillet 1914.

L'Ambassadeur d'Allemagne a demande a Grey pour quelle raison l'Angleterre prenait des mesures militaires sur terre et sur mer. Grey a repondu que ces mesures n'avaient pas un caractere agressif, mais que la situation etait telle que chaque Puissance devait se preparer.

(Signe) Benckendorff.

No. 66.

L'Ambassadeur en Autriche–Hongrie au Ministre des Affaires Etrangeres.

(Telegramme). Vienne, le 18/31 Juillet 1914.

Malgre la mobilisation generale je continue a echanger des vues avec le Comte Berchtold et ses collaborateurs. Tous insistent sur l'absence chez l'Autriche d'intentions agressives quelconques contre la Russie et de visees de conquete a l'egard de la Serbie, mais tous insistent egalement sur la necessite pour l'Autriche de poursuivre jusqu'an bout l'action commencee et de donner a la Serbie une lecon serieuse qui pourrait constituer une certaine garantie pour l'avenir.

(Signe) Schebeko.

No. 67.

Le Ministre des Affaires Etrangeres aux Ambassadeurs en Allemagne, Autriche–Hongrie, en France, en Angleterre et en Italie.[197]

(Telegramme). St. Petersbourg, le 18/31 Juillet 1914.

Me refere a mon telegramme du 17/30 Juillet. D'ordre de son gouvernement, l'Ambassadeur d'Angleterre m'a transmis le desir du Cabinet de Londres d'introduire quelques modifications dans la formule que j'ai proposee hier a l'Ambassadeur d'Allemagne. J'ai repondu que j'acceptais la proposition anglaise. Ci–dessous je vous transmets la formule modifiee en consequence.

'Si l'Autriche consent a arreter la marche de ses armees sur le territoire Serbe et si, reconnaissant que le conflit austro–serbe a assume le caractere d'une question d'interet europeen, elle admet que les Grandes Puissances examinent la satisfaction que la Serbie pourrait accorder au gouvernement d'Autriche–Hongrie sans laisser porter atteinte a ses droits d'Etat souverain et a son independance,—la Russie s'engage a conserver son attitude expectante.'

(Signe) Sazonow.

[Footnote 197: The second paragraph is printed in the British White Book (*Correspondence* No. 132).]

No. 68.

L'Ambassadeur en Allemagne au Ministre des Affaires Etrangeres.

(Telegramme). Berlin, le 18/31 Juillet 1914.

Le Ministre des Affaires Etrangeres vient de me dire que nos pourparlers, qui etaient deja difficiles a la suite de la mobilisation contre l'Autriche, le deviennent encore davantage en presence des graves mesures militaires que nous prenons contre l'Allemagne; des nouvelles y relatives sont, d'apres lui, recues ici de tous les cotes et devront provoquer inevitablement des mesures analogues de la part de l'Allemagne. A cela j'ai repondu que, d'apres des renseignements surs dont je disposais et qui etaient confirmes par tous nos compatriotes arrivant a Berlin, la prise contre nous des mesures susdites se poursuivait egalement en Allemagne avec grande activite. Malgre cela, le Ministre des Affaires Etrangeres affirme qu'ici on n'a fait que rappeler les officiers de leurs conges et les troupes des champs de manoeuvres.

(Signe) Swerbeew.

No. 69.

Le Ministre des Affaires Etrangeres a l'Ambassadeur en Angleterre.

(Telegramme). St.–Petersbourg, le 18/31 Juillet 1914.

J'ai prie l'Ambassadeur d'Angleterre de transmettre a Grey l'expression de ma plus sincere reconnaissance pour le ton amical et ferme dont il a use pendant les pourparlers avec l'Allemagne et l'Autriche, grace a quoi l'espoir de trouver une issue pacifique de la situation actuelle n'est pas encore perdu.

Je l'ai aussi prie de dire au Ministre Anglais que je pensais que ce n'etait qu'a Londres que les pourparlers auraient encore quelques chances d'un succes quelconque, en facilitant a l'Autriche la necessite d'un compromis.

Communique a l'Ambassadeur en France.

(Signe) Sazonow.

No. 70.

Telegramme secret aux Representants de Sa Majeste l'Empereur a l'etranger.

(*Telegramme*). Le 19 Juillet/1 Aout 1914.

A minuit l'Ambassadeur d'Allemagne m'a declare, d'ordre de son Gouvernement, que si dans les 12 heures, c'est−a−dire a midi, Samedi, nous ne commencions pas la demobilisation, non seulement a l'egard de l'Allemagne, mais aussi a l'egard de l'Autriche, le Gouvernement Allemand serait force de donner l'ordre de mobilisation. A ma question si c'etait la guerre, l'Ambassadeur a repondu par la negative, mais en ajoutant que nous etions fort pres d'elle.

(Signe) Sazonow.

No. 71.

L'Ambassadeur en Angleterre au Ministre des Affaires Etrangeres.

(Telegramme). Londres, 19 Juillet/1 Aout 1914.

Grey m'a dit qu'il a telegraphie a Berlin qu'a son avis la derniere formule acceptee par le Gouvernement Russe constitue la base de negociations qui presente le plus de chances pour une solution pacifique du conflict. Il a exprime en meme temps l'espoir qu'aucune grande Puissance ne commencerait les hostilites avant l'examen de cette formule.

(Signe) Benckendorff.

No. 72.

L'Ambassadeur eu Angleterre au Ministre des Affaires Etrangeres.

(*Telegramme*). Londres, le 19 Juillet/1 Aout 1914.

Le Gouvernement de la Grande−Bretagne a pose aux Gouvernements Francais et Allemand la question s'ils respecteraient la neutralite de la Belgique.

La France a repondu dans l'affirmative, tandis que le Gouvernement Allemand a declare ne pouvoir repondre a cette question categoriquement.

(Signe) Benckendorff.

No. 73.

L'Ambassadeur en France au Ministre des Affaires Etrangeres.

(Telegramme). Paris, le 19 Juillet/1 Aout 1914.

L'Ambassadeur d'Autriche a visite hier Viviani et lui a declare que l'Autriche non seulement n'avait pas le dessein de porter atteinte a l'integrite territoriale de la Serbie, mais etait prete a discuter avec les autres Puissances le fond de son conflit avec la Serbie. Le Gouvernement Francais est tres preoccupe par les preparatifs militaires extraordinaires de l'Allemagne sur la frontiere francaise, car il est convaincu que sous le voile du "Kriegszustand" se produit une veritable mobilisation.

(Signe) Iswolsky.

No. 74.

L'Ambassadeur en France au Ministre des Affaires Etrangeres.

(Telegramme). Paris, le 19 Juillet/1 Aout 1914.

A la reception ici du telegramme de l'Ambassadeur de France a St.–Petersbourg contenant la communication que Vous a faite l'Ambassadeur Allemand concernant la resolution de l'Allemagne de decreter aujourd'hui la mobilisation generale, le President de la Republique a signe le decret de mobilisation. Dans les rues on procede a l'affichage des listes d'appel des reservistes. L'Ambassadeur d'Allemagne vient de rendre visite a Viviani, mais ne lui a fait aucune nouvelle communication, en alleguant l'impossibilite de dechiffrer les telegrammes qu'il a recus. Viviani l'a informe de la signature du decret de mobilisation en reponse a la mobilisation allemande et lui a fait part de son etonnement de ce que l'Allemagne eut pris une telle mesure a un moment ou se poursuivait encore un echange de vues amical entre la Russie, l'Autriche et les Puissances; il a ajoute que la mobilisation ne prejugeait pas necessairement la guerre et que l'Ambassadeur d'Allemagne pourrait rester a Paris comme l'Ambassadeur de Russie est reste a Vienne et celui d'Autriche a St.–Petersbourg.

(Signe) Iswolsky.

No. 75.

L'Ambassadeur en France au Ministre des Affaires Etrangeres.

(Telegramme). Paris, le 19 Juillet/1 Aout 1914.

Je tiens du President que pendant les dernieres journees l'Ambassadeur d'Autriche a assure avec force le President du Conseil des Ministres et lui meme, que l'Autriche nous aurait declare etre prete a respecter non seulement l'integrite territoriale de la Serbie, mais aussi ses droits souverains, mais que nous aurions intentionnellement fait le silence sur cette declaration. J'ai oppose un dementi categorique a cela.

(Signe) Iswolsky.

No. 76.

Note remise par l'Ambassadeur d'Allemagne a St.–Petersbourg le 19 Juillet 1914 a 7 h. 10 du soir.

Le Gouvernement Imperial s'est efforce des les debuts de la crise de la mener a une solution pacifique. Se rendant a un desir qui lui en avait ete exprime par Sa Majeste l'Empereur de Russie, Sa Majeste l'Empereur d'Allemagne d'accord avec l'Angleterre s'etait applique a accomplir un role mediateur aupres des Cabinets de Vienne et de St.–Petersbourg, lorsque la Russie, sans en attendre le resultat, proceda a la mobilisation de la totalite de ses forces de terre et de mer. A la suite de cette mesure menacante motivee par aucun presage militaire de la part de l'Allemagne, l'Empire Allemand s'est trouve vis–a–vis d'un danger grave et imminent. Si le Gouvernement Imperial eut manque de parer a ce peril, il aurait compromis la securite et l'existence meme de l'Allemagne. Par consequent le Gouvernement Allemand se vit force de s'adresser au Gouvernement de Sa Majeste l'Empereur de Toutes les Russies en insistant sur la cessation desdits actes militaires. La Russie ayant refuse de faire droit a (n'ayant pas cru devoir repondre a[198]) cette demande et ayant manifeste par ce refus (cette attitude [198]) que son action etait dirigee contre I'Allemagne, j'ai l'honneur, d'ordre de mon Gouvernement, de faire savoir a Votre Excellence ce qui suit:

Sa Majeste l'Empereur Mon Auguste Souverain au nom de l'Empire, relevant le defi se considere en etat de guerre avec la Russie.

St.–Petersbourg, le 19 Juillet/1 Aout 1914.

(Signe) F. Pourtales.

[Footnote 198: Les mots places entre parentheses se trouvent dans l'original. Il faut supposer que deux variantes avaient ete preparees d'avance et que par erreur elles out ete inserees toutes les deux dans la note.]

No. 77.

Communique du Ministre des Affaires Etrangeres concernant les evenements des derniers jours.

Le 20 Juillet/2 Aout 1914.

Un expose defigurant les evenements des derniers jours ayant paru dans la presse etrangere, le Ministere des Affaires Etrangeres croit de son devoir de publier l'apercu suivant des pourparlers diplomatiques pendant le temps susvise.

Le 10/23 Juillet a.c. le Ministre d'Autriche–Hongrie a Belgrade presenta an Ministre President Serbe une note ou le Gouvernement Serbe etait accuse d'avoir favorise le mouvement panserbe qui avait abouti a l'assassinat de l'heritier du trone austro–hongrois. En consequence l'Autriche–Hongrie demandait au Gouvernement Serbe non seulement de condamner sous une forme solennelle la susdite propagande, mais aussi de prendre, sous le controle de l'Autriche–Hongrie, une serie de mesures tendant a la decouverte du complot, a la punition des sujets serbes y ayant participe et a la prevention dans l'avenir de tout attentat sur le sol du Royaume. Un delai de 48 heures fut fixe au Gouvernement Serbe pour la reponse a la susdite note.

Le Gouvernement Imperial, auquel l'Ambassadeur d'Autriche–Hongrie a St.–Petersbourg avait communique le texte de la note 17 heures apres sa remise a Belgrade, ayant pris connaissance des demandes y contenues, dut s'apercevoir que quelques–unes parmi elles etaient inexecutables quant an fond, tandis que d'autres etaient presentees sous une forme incompatible avec la dignite d'un Etat independant. Trouvant inadmissibles la diminution de la dignite de la Serbie contenue dans ces demandes, ainsi que la tendance de l'Autriche–Hongrie d'assurer sa preponderance dans les Balcans demontree par ces memes exigences, le Gouvernement Russe fit observer dans la forme la plus amicale a l'Autriche–Hongrie qu'il serait desirable de soumettre a un nouvel examen les points contenus dans la note austro–hongroise. Le Gouvernement Austro–Hongrois ne crut possible de consentir a une discussion de la note. L'action moderatrice des autres Puissances a Vienne ne fut non plus couronnee de succes.

Malgre que la Serbie eut reprouve le crime et se fut montree prete a donner satisfaction a l'Autriche dans une mesure qui depassa les previsions non seulement de la Russie, mais aussi des autres Puissances, le Ministre d'Autriche–Hongrie a Belgrade jugea la reponse serbe insuffisante et quitta cette ville.

Reconnaissant le caractere exagere des demandes presentees par l'Autriche, la Russie avait declare encore auparavant qu'il lui serait impossible de rester indifferente, sans se refuser toutefois a employer tous ses efforts pour trouver une issue pacifique qui fut acceptable pour l'Autriche et menageat son amour–propre de grande puissance. En meme temps la Russie etablit fermement qu'elle admettait une solution pacifique de la question seulement dans une mesure qui n'impliquerait pas la diminution de la dignite de la Serbie comme Etat independant. Malheureusement tous les efforts deployes par le Gouvernement Imperial dans cette direction resterent sans effet. Le Gouvernement Austro—Hongrois, apres s'etre derobe a toute intervention conciliatrice des Puissances dans son conflit avec la Serbie, proceda a la mobilisation, declara officiellement la guerre a la Serbie, et le jour suivant Belgrade fut bombardee. Le manifeste qui a accompagne la declaration de guerre accuse ouvertement la Serbie d'avoir prepare et execute le crime de Seraiewo. Une pareille accusation d'un crime de droit commun lancee contre tout un peuple et tout un Etat attira a la Serbie par son inanite evidente les larges sympathies des cercles de la societe europeenne.

A la suite de cette maniere d'agir du Gouvernement Austro—Hongrois, malgre la declaration de la Russie qu'elle ne pourrait rester indifferente au sort de la Serbie, le Gouvernement Imperial jugea necessaire d'ordonner la mobilisation des circonscriptions militaires de Kiew, d'Odessa, de Moscou et de Kazan. Une telle decision s'imposait parce que depuis la date de la remise de la note austro—hongroise au Gouvernement Serbe et les premieres demarches de la Russie cinq jours s'etaient ecoules, et cependant le Cabinet de Vienne n'avait fait aucun pas pour aller au—devant de nos efforts pacifiques; au contraire, la mobilisation de la moitie de l'armee austro—hongroise avait ete decretee.

Le Gouvernement Allemand fut mis au courant des mesures prises par la Russie; il lui fut en meme temps explique qu'elles n'etaient que la consequence des armements autrichiens et nullement dirigees contre l'Allemagne. En meme temps, le Gouvernement Imperial declara que la Russie etait prete a continuer les pourparlers en vue d'une solution pacifique du conflit, soit par la voie de negociations directes avec le Cabinet de Vienne, soit en suivant la proposition de la Grande—Bretagne, par la voie d'une Conference des quatre Grandes Puissances non interessees directement, voire l'Angleterre, la France, l'Allemagne et l'Italie.

Cependant cette tentative de la Russie echoua egalement. L'Autriche—Hongrie declina un echange de vues ulterieur avec nous, et le Cabinet de Vienne se deroba a la participation a la Conference des Puissances projetee.

Neanmoins, la Russie ne discontinua pas ses efforts en faveur de la paix. Repondant a la question de l'Ambassadeur d'Allemagne, a quelles conditions nous consentirions encore a suspendre nos armements, le Ministre des Affaires Etrangeres declara que ces conditions seraient la reconnaissance par l'Autriche—Hongrie que la question Austro—Serbe avait revetu le caractere d'une question europeenne, et la declaration de cette meme Puissance qu'elle consentait a ne pas insister sur des demandes incompatibles avec les droits souverains de la Serbie.

La proposition de la Russie fut jugee par l'Allemagne inacceptable pour l'Autriche–Hongrie. Simultanement on recut a St.–Petersbourg la nouvelle de la proclamation de la mobilisation generale par l'Autriche–Hongrie.

En meme temps les hostilites continuaient sur le territoire Serbe et Belgrade fut bombardee derechef.

L'insucces de nos propositions pacifiques nous obligea d'elargir les mesures de precaution militaires.

Le Cabinet de Berlin nous ayant adresse une question a ce sujet, il lui fut repondu que la Russie etait forcee de commencer ses armements pour se premunir contre toutes eventualites.

Tout en prenant cette mesure de precaution, la Russie n'en discontinuait pas moins de rechercher de toutes ses forces une issue de cette situation et declara etre prete a accepter tout moyen de solution du conflit qui comporterait l'observation des conditions posees par nous.

Malgre cette communication conciliante, le Gouvernement Allemand, le 18/31 Juillet, adressa au Gouvernement Russe la demande d'avoir a suspendre ses mesures militaires a midi du 19 Juillet/ 1 Aout, en menacant, dans le cas contraire, de proceder a une mobilisation generale.

Le lendemain, 19 Juillet/1 Aout, l'Ambassadeur d'Allemagne transmit au Ministre des Affaires Etrangeres, an nom de son Gouvernement, la declaration de guerre.

No. 78.

Le Ministre des Affaires Etrangeres aux Representants de S. M. l'Empereur a l'etranger.

(*Telegramme*). St.–Petersbourg, le 20 Juillet/2 Aout 1914.

Why We Are At War

Il est absolument clair que l'Allemagne s'efforce des a present de rejeter sur nous la responsabilite de la rupture. Notre mobilisation a ete provoquee par l'enorme responsabilite que nous aurions assumee, si nous n'avions pas pris toutes les mesures de precaution a un moment ou l'Autriche, se bornant a des pourparlers d'un caractere dilatoire, bombardait Belgrade et procedait a une mobilisation generale.

Sa Majeste l'Empereur s'etait engage vis–a–vis de l'Empereur d'Allemagne par sa parole a n'entreprendre aucun acte agressif tant que dureraient les pourparlers avec l'Autriche. Apres une telle garantie et apres toutes les preuves de l'amour de la Russie pour la paix, l'Allemagne ne pouvait ni avait le droit de douter de notre declaration que nous accepterions avec joie toute issue pacifique compatible avec la dignite et l'independance de la Serbie. Une autre issue, tout en etant completement incompatible avec notre propre dignite, aurait certainement ebranle l'equilibre Europeen assurant l'hegemonie de l'Allemagne. Ce caractere Europeen, voire mondial, du conflit est infiniment plus important que le pretexte qui l'a cree. Par sa decision de nous declarer la guerre a un moment ou se poursuivaient les negociations entre les Puissances, l'Allemagne a assume une lourde responsabilite.

(Signe) Sazonow.

No. 79.

Note remise par l'Ambassadeur d'Autriche–Hongrie a St.–Petersbourg au Ministre des Affaires Etrangeres le 24 Juillet a 6 h. du soir.

D'ordre de son Gouvernement le soussigne Ambassadeur d'Autriche–Hongrie a l'honneur de notifier a Son Excellence Monsieur le Ministre des Affaires Etrangeres de Russie ce qui suit:

"Vu l'attitude menacante prise par la Russie dans le conflit entre la Monarchie Austro–Hongroise et la Serbie et en presence du fait qu'en suite de ce conflit la Russie, d'apres une communication du Cabinet de Berlin, a cru devoir ouvrir les hostilites contre l'Allemagne et que celle–ci se trouve par consequent en etat de guerre avec ladite Puissance, l'Autriche–Hongrie se considere egalement en etat de guerre avec la Russie a partir du present moment.

"(Signe) Szapary. St.–Petersbourg. 6 Aout/24 Juillet 1914."

CPSIA information can be obtained at www.ICGtesting.com
Printed in the USA
BVOW04s1021060814

361905BV00021B/538/P